INDUSTRIAL NETWORKS AND PROXIMITY

Industrial Networks and Proximity

Edited by

MILFORD B. GREEN
The University of Western Ontario

ROB B. McNAUGHTON
University of Otago

Ashgate

Aldershot • Burlington USA • Singapore • Sydney

Published by
Ashgate Publishing Limited
Gower House
Croft Road
Aldershot
Hampshire GU11 3HR
England

Ashgate Publishing Company
131 Main Street
Burlington
Vermont 05401
USA

Ashgate website: http://www.ashgate.com

British Library Cataloguing in Publication Data
Industrial networks and proximity
    1. Business networks 2. Business networks - Case studies
    3. Industrial location 4. Industrial organization
    I. Green, Milford B. II. McNaughton, Rod B.
    338.8'7

Library of Congress Control Number: 00-132592

ISBN 0 7546 1176 0

Printed and bound by Athenaeum Press, Ltd.,
Gateshead, Tyne & Wear.

Contents

List of Figures

List of Tables

List of Contributors

Akoorie, Michèle E.M., Department of Marketing and International Management, University of Waikato, Hamilton, New Zealand. Mema@mngt.waikato.ac.nz

Boekema, Frans W.M., Department of Human Geography, University of Nijmegen, PO Box 9108, NL-6500 HK Nijmegen, The Netherlands. F.boekema@bw.kun.nl

Bruce, David, Rural and Small Town Programme, Mount Allison University, 76 York St., Sackville, New Brunswick, Canada E4L 1E9. Dwbruce@mta.ca

Burmeister, Antje, National Institute for Transport and Safety Research (INRETS), Centre for Research on Socio-economics of Transportation and Regional Planning (TRACES), 20 rue Elisée Reclus, 59650 Villeneuve d'Ascq, France. Antje.burmeister@inrets.fr

Cecil, Ben P., Department of Geography, University of Western Ontario, London, Ontario, Canada N6A 5C2. bencecil@hotmail.com

Gilly, Jean-Pierre, LEREP, Université des Sciences Sociales de Toulouse, 21 allées de Brienne, 3100 Toulouse, France. Gilly@univ-tlse1.fr

Green, Milford B., Department of Geography, University of Western Ontario, London, Ontario, Canada N6A 5C2. mbgreen@julian.uwo.ca

Lee, Boyoung, Department of Geography Education, Kyungpook National University, Taegu, South Korea. blee@bh.kyungpook.ac.kr

Liu, Lin, Department of Geography, University of Cincinnati, Cincinnati, Ohio, USA 45221-0131. lin.liu.uc.edu

MacPherson, Alan D., Department of Geography, University at Buffalo, State University of New York, Wilkeson Quad, Buffalo, New York, USA 14261-0023. Geoadm@acsu.buffalo.edu

McNaughton, Rod B., Department of Marketing, University of Otago, PO Box 56, Dunedin, New Zealand. Rmcnaughton@commerce.otago.ac.nz

Meeus, Marius T.H., Faculty of Technology Management, Eindhoven University of Technology, PO Box 513, Building DG 1.16, 5600 MB Eindhoven, The Netherlands. M.t.h.meeus@tm.tue.nl

Oerlemans, Leon A.G., Faculty of Technology Management, Eindhoven University of Technology, PO Box 513, Building TEMA 0.06, 5600 MB Eindhoven, The Netherlands. L.a.g.oerlemans@tm.tue.nl

Sabourin, Paul, Department of Geography, University of Minnesota, Minneapolis, Minnesota, USA. sabourin@tcinternet.net.

Stafford, Howard A., Department of Geography, University of Cincinnati, Cincinnati, Ohio USA 45221-0131. Howard.stafford@uc.edu

Torre, André, SADIF, INA PG, 16 rue Claude Bernard, 75231 Paris Cedex 05 France. andre.torre@wanadoo.fr

Wehrell, Roger, Department of Commerce, Mount Allison University, 76 York St., Sackville, New Brunswick, Canada, E4L 1E9. Rwehrell@mta.ca

Preface

No firm is an island. Over the last decade observers of industrial organization have paid increasing attention to what lies beyond the firm. Outside the ownership boundaries of the firm they have found a complex web of relationships that offer opportunities, control resources, and constrain the behavior of participants. The position a firm attains in a network, as well as the structure of the network and nature of the other participants, influences the way in which the firm is organized, and ultimately its performance. Firms can grow and be successful not only through their internal activities, but by leveraging their relationships to harness the abilities and resources of their partners.

A fundamental influence on the network structure of inter-firm relationships is the proximity of participants. At the heart of this line of reasoning is the proposition that firms that are located close to each other are more likely to know about each other, and to be able to co-operate for mutual advantage. *Industrial Networks and Proximity* investigates this proposition in detail. The chapters in this volume concern the theory, measurement, or empirical characterization of the role of proximity in industrial organization and economic exchange.

At least four major lines of theory development posit a role for proximity in network formation and performance: agglomeration, milieu, industrial districts, and Porterian clusters. A number of other important but narrower perspectives, for example, transaction cost analysis and social capital theory, also imply a role for proximity in the formation of relationships between firms. This literature cuts across several social sciences and management disciplines. Further, the issue is one that is important to firms and the government agencies that seek to assist them around the world. *Industrial Networks and Proximity* reflects this diversity of disciplinary interest, and its global importance. Chapters are included that represent the work of Economists, Geographers, Marketers, Sociologists, and Transportation specialists, from the United States, Canada, the United Kingdom, France, and New Zealand.

While each author has a different emphasis, the general argument is that proximity facilitates interaction. There is a direct effect in terms of higher familiarity and lower search, communication and logistics costs. There may also be an indirect effect, in which a locally shared history and culture facilitate the development of social capital in local business communities. The positive aspect of these effects help firms to leverage their competencies, reduce production and transaction costs, and contribute to endogenous growth and internationalization. The downside is that dense local networks can inhibit innovation, create barriers to entry, and reinforce poor management practices. Links with firms in other regions and countries are important for importing ideas and resources, and gaining intelligence about new market opportunities. Recent technological advances, especially in communications, and global mobility of managers play a role in offsetting the overall importance of proximity, and in limiting its potential downside.

Industrial Networks and Proximity begins with chapters that consider issues of proximity in terms of theory, and then progresses to chapters that empirically illustrate the issues. Both theory and empiricism have a role to play in furthering the understanding of the creation, and performance maintenance of industrial networks. What follows is a brief synopsis of the contents of each chapter:

The first chapter by Gilly and Torre stresses several major topics in the theoretical definition of proximity relations. It is organized around the main tenets of the French school of proximity, which is concerned with the integration of 'space' into economic analysis, revealing links between industrial and spatial economics. The four main points addressed in the chapter are: the definition of the notions of geographical and organizational proximities, the central role played by formal and informal interactions, the role played by coordination problems, and a comparison with similar works by various economists who belong to parallel or closely related schools of thought. This chapter suggests significant links between industrial and spatial economics, and provides insight into the research agenda of this group of French researchers.

Chapter two by Oerlemans, Meeus and Boekema discusses innovation and technological development and their meaning for economic development. They argue that innovation and technological development are important factors explaining economic growth and development. Time and again, production, diffusion and implementation of knowledge have proven to be crucial processes in this context. Firms often rely on their environments with regard to both production, and knowledge. This idea is contained in various theoretical approaches, such as transaction costs analysis and the economic network approach. Theoretical approaches in which the spatial aspect does form an important element are often characterized by insufficient attention to technology and innovation.

The authors examine the relationships between innovation and the environment in two distinct periods. The first is the spatial science literature before 1980. The second is developments after 1980 when insights from other scientific disciplines such as organizational behavior and sociology were recognized. A number of theoretical perspectives are discussed, such as the theories of 'new industrial spaces', 'industrial districts', the 'innovative environment' approach, 'regional innovations systems', and 'learning regions'.

Burmeister's chapter contributes to the conceptualization of 'accessibility'. It deals, in particular, with the theoretical and methodological analysis of the role of accessibility in the efficiency and the dynamics of production systems. Transportation and communication systems are, of course, crucial to the efficiency of production systems and, more generally, to regional development. Because of this, accessibility is often considered as a determinant of regional development. The chapter argues that accessibility, as a merely spatial concept, does not deal adequately with the spatial and organizational dynamics of production systems.

The first part of the chapter presents a survey of the literature on accessibility as a concept in transportation economics and geography. The limits of accessibility as a merely spatial (or space-time) concept for understanding the efficient organization of the circulation of goods, information and knowledge in contemporary production systems is discussed. Finally, Burmeister examines the possibility of integrating the organizational dimension into accessibility and into comprehensive indicators.

McNaughton examines the concept of 'social capital'. Social capital refers to the social structure that facilitates co-ordination and co-operation that in turn are important to the feasibility and productivity of economic activity. Social capital is an important agent in economic activity because it mitigates contracting (or transaction) costs by fostering high levels of trust.

This chapter reviews the literature on social capital, and compares the concept with the network literature. It concludes that social capital offers a powerful language for understanding many of the issues involving in the networks of relationships between firms, and their economic consequences. The financial capital concepts of appreciation and depreciation, value, portfolios and the like provide an unexpectedly clear insight into the way in which social networks can assist or hinder economic activity.

Social capital exists as the goodwill between individuals and firms. It is idiosyncratic and not easily transferred. Therefore, individual ownership can not appropriate its benefits. The result is that individual entrepreneurs and firms have little incentive to invest in social capital, as it is essentially a public good. This forms the basis of an argument in support of publicly funded network brokering programs, as there is a public interest in the potential welfare returns (e.g., increased employment and returns on investment) of increased social capital in business communities.

Proximity is an important element in the appreciation of social capital since it fosters frequent high quality interaction, and can provide a basis for friendly association based on common experiences, history and/or culture. Relatively small local groups of firms should experience low transaction costs due to trust and informal constraints. However, transaction costs within networks increase sharply as members are added.

The social capital literature also suggests some general problems that may accompany network strategies. The first is that strong ties between members of a network can be used to exclude outsiders. In some cases this might constitute a barrier to start-up firms by preventing access to an important resource controlled by the network. A second problem is that membership in a network brings demands for conformity that may limit creativity and stifle the entrepreneurial spirit. Third, network membership may reinforce poor management practices if they are also used by other members (more generally, social capital does not necessarily increase human capital). Lastly, networks may limit the extent to which firms have the resources or inclination to search further afield to acquire resources. Thus, they may fail to identify important new suppliers and customers, or to import new technologies.

Chapter five deals with a more specific type of networking both in terms of economic activity (manufacturing) and geographic scale (Cincinnati, Ohio). Lee and Stafford look at networking and the creation of industrial districts. Part of the success of manufacturing in some places is attributed to networking between firms. Supplier and market relationships, subcontracting, vertical specialization, and the frequent movements of workers from one firm to another all are purported to enhance the flow and quality of information to the firms embedded in the specific industrial culture. Networking is a key component of explanations of the reasons for, and advantages of, industrial clustering.

This chapter develops methodologies to identify industrial districts using variables in addition to product specialization and spatial proximity as the designators. Additional factors include markets, materials and producer services linkages, shared labor forces, collaborations, and information contacts. Networking can be inferred by the degree to which these factors operate locally, regionally, or out of the metropolitan area. 'Networking' is a defining attribute rather than an imputed factor. Questionnaire and interview information on a moderately large metropolitan region with a long and diverse history of manufacturing activity (Cincinnati, Ohio, USA) provide some benchmarks for 'normal' local interactions and networking among plants.

Bruce and Wehrell examine micro business networks for the case of peer lending and micro credit circles in a rural setting. The microenterprise literature identifies among other things the importance of peer lending circles and micro credit networks as important vehicles for helping emerging micro businesses become established or help them make important decisions about the future direction that their businesses might take. Participants in such networks identify the networking, sharing of ideas, peer group support, and business skill development as important or more important than the small amounts of business capital they receive.

This chapter focuses on the utility of peer lending circles as a means of stimulating and supporting small business development, and creating a link to broader community and regional development. It also focuses on their relative success in providing business development opportunities for members of groups that are traditionally outsiders in the business world.

This chapter also explores several dimensions of 'network' relationships including, relationships among participants, relationships between participants and their network coordinator, relationships between businesses inside the networks and those outside the network, and relationships between the network and the supplier or guarantor of credit.

The authors draw on their knowledge of peer lending circles in rural Atlantic Canada: Red Ochre Micro Business Lending Service, located on the Great Northern Peninsula of western Newfoundland; Microéntreprise Restigouche Microentreprise in northern New Brunswick; and Calmeadow Nova Scotia in Shelburne County, Nova Scotia. These examples offer different models or approaches to the provision of microcredit, including differences in economic context, clientele, financial partnerships, range of services, and degree of success in meeting organization objectives. The common link among the different approaches is the community-based nature of the programs. Locally based lending circles create of clusters of emerging entrepreneurs in small rural communities, encouraging co-operation and shared learning and development in a business environment.

Chapter seven by Akoorie also deals with a rural based networking phenomenon in New Zealand. New Zealand is an important example because it is often cited as a guiding light in deregulation and liberalization. Surprisingly, given the increasing interest internationally in the importance of industrial districts, networks and cluster activity, very little attention has been paid to these areas in the New Zealand environment.

The purpose of this chapter is to apply the existing theoretical frameworks on clusters/industrial districts to a resource dependent industry; thoroughbred breeding. The principal reason for the spatial location of these resource-dependent industries is a function of three specific features: actor location, historical accident and specific resource requirement. Using longitudinal case study techniques, this chapter provides an in-depth study of thoroughbred breeding.

The chapter concludes that the dynamics of this resource dependent industry is significant. While localization might explain the initial development of a cluster, the continuation of that cluster is the result of its ability to both regenerate internally over time (in response to changing environmental conditions) and to create spin-off clusters in new locations.

In a chapter that is both theoretically and empirically based, Cecil and Green examine strategic alliance networks in the United States information technology sectors. The chapter develops an eclectic theory of alliance formation, drawing heavily on transaction cost analysis and resources dependency theory. These theories, along with the notion of core competencies from strategic management provide a rational for first level of alliance activity, which is characterized by production and cost-based co-operative behavior.

A second tier of alliance networks is also identified which involve more complex motives in which co-operation creates a new set of transaction costs and resource dependencies based on the sharing of information and knowledge, rather than physical resources and costs. Taken together, these two levels of alliance activity suggest multiple, often inter-connected motives for alliance formation forming the basis for an eclectic model of alliance activity.

This eclectic model is used to frame an empirical study of the relationships between firms in the IT sectors, which are renowned for the level of alliance formation, and highly networked industrial structure. The data describe 3,382 alliances involving at least one US partner formed between 1985 and 1994. The notion of multiple eclectic motives is demonstrated by the inability to identify a single parsimonious statistical model of the motives for alliance activity, rather a number of statistical models adequately characterize the data, suggesting that a series of inter-connected motivations underlie alliance activity.

The next chapter by MacPherson focuses on the role of locational factors in the propensity of industrial firms to buy specialized inputs from vendors of scientific and technical services. Two hypotheses are tested. First, other things being equal, firms that exploit external sources of scientific and technical expertise perform better than those that do not use external sources. Second, a firm's propensity to exploit external expertise varies directly with the level of local service supply.

Overall, the goal is to show that local supply-side conditions (availability of S&T services) can significantly affect the business performance of industrial firms in the manufacturing sector. Data come from a sample of over 1000 New York State industrial firms across four sectors (scientific instruments, metal fabricating, office furniture, and electrical industrial products).

The final chapter by Sabourin investigates whether, in the producer service sector with a highly centralised locational pattern, firms located in the central business district are characterized by more intensive transaction patterns than the same sector firms located outside of the city centre.

Using the advertising industry as an example of a producer service sector that is highly centralised at both the inter- and intraurban scales, and which also exhibits a high degree of vertical disintegration, this chapter documents the widespread vertical disintegration of production.

Data collected through a mail survey of advertising agencies in the Twin Cities (Minneapolis, St. Paul), one of the leading centres of advertising production in the United States, this chapter also documents noticeable spatial variations in the patterns of input usage and outsourcing by advertising agencies in different parts of the metropolitan area. Advertising agencies located in the core of the advertising agglomeration in downtown Minneapolis both use and outsource a larger number of inputs than is the case for agencies in other locations; these downtown agencies also make use of a larger number of vendors, and have higher levels of expenditures on vendors than is the case for agencies in the remainder of the metropolitan area.

Meanwhile, advertising agencies located outside of downtown Minneapolis do not typically compensate for the relatively higher distance-related transactions costs they face by substituting internal for external provision of specialised inputs. Instead, they are more likely to be restricted to the production of types of advertising not requiring more specialised inputs.

In sum, each of these ten chapters brings something unique to *Industrial Networks and Proximity*, and highlights a different aspect or context of the proximity issue. The range is from a summary of the research agenda of the French school of proximity, to a study of how local conditions influence the extent to which external sources of expertise are used; from economics to geography; and from populous industrial regions in Europe to sparsely populated rural areas of Canada. Clearly, "proximity" has profound, complex and diverse influences on industrial organization and economic exchange. It is also a potentially unifying theme, underlying streams of research in a number of disciplines. Our hope is that this volume stimulates research that acknowledges these conclusions by adopting proximity as a central theme, and drawing on a diversity of approaches to develop a holistic understanding of the concept and its influences.

Milford B. Green

London, Canada

Rod B. McNaughton

Dunedin, New Zealand

1 Proximity Relations: Elements for an Analytical Framework

JEAN-PIERRE GILLY and ANDRÉ TORRE

Introduction

The objective of this paper is to emphasize some main topics concerning the theoretical definition of proximity relations. It focuses on the integration of the spatial variable within a framework of economic analysis in order to reveal the links between industrial and spatial economics. This area of research developed quite late in France compared with other countries, but now involves a growing number of researchers, and is an important part of French economic thought.

This paper describes the analysis of enterprise and space in French regional thought, especially the work of an informal group of about thirty industrial economists. This group focuses on 'Proximity Dynamics', the spatial dimension of enterprise and organization, and carries out collective work aimed at uncovering coherence and consistency in the new economic space approaches. Their point of departure is that space matters in industrial economic analysis. Consequently, the objective of these 'Proximity Economists' is to clarify the role of space as an endogenous variable in economic theory.

This article characterizes the theoretical choices of this research group, which are grounded in the interaction between theoretical discussions and empirical research. There are several common research themes adopted by this group: relations between actors, the institutional dimension, the innovation process, infrastructure, and the territorial problem of the firm. In fact, all of these deal with the causes and effects, positive or negative, of proximity. There are four analytical themes in our research domain. This paper is organized around these domains: geographical proximity versus organizational proximity, the central role of various forms of interaction, economic co-ordination, and theoretical confrontation with other analytical approaches dealing with the same spatial phenomenon.

Geographical Proximity Versus Organizational Proximity

Our research does not blindly defend the virtues of proximity. We are aware of the advantages and the dynamism that proximity relations can bring about, but also note that they can be a factor in mistrust or a brake on economic activity. The proximity approach also deals with the consistency of the proximity notion, and we approach the notion as an emerging concept, grounded in the disciplines of the participants in the proximity dynamics research group.

An Open Question

Our discussion of the proximity notion emerged because of its recent utilization in the economics literature, and especially in work dealing with the spatial dimension of economic activity, such as the literature on industrial districts, or technopoles. Moreover, this growing interest in proximity relations concerns research on:

- the innovation processes and the relations between science and industry (Jaffe et al, 1993, Audretsch and Feldman, 1996);
- the producers-users relations as well as the national systems of innovation (Lundvall, 1992, Nelson, 1993);
- the question of the area specificities in the frame of the transaction costs economy (Joskow, 1985);
- the recent researches within the frame of geographical economy (Fujita and Thisse, 1997).

For us, the proximity concept has both an academic dimension and importance in terms of societal questions like 'proximity employment', and 'proximity banks'. The debate is sharply grounded on the existence of continuous proximity links between actors. This position contradicts the classical hypothesis that globalization implies a vacuum of local relations. Our empirical inquiries contradict the thesis that the growing importance of distant communication leads to decentralized relations (telecommuting as an example), and the disappearance of a local economic dimension. In fact, we have empirical evidence of the opposite, that local associations of various types continue to be important. As already pointed out by others (e.g., Bellet and Alii, 1993), proximity matters, whether it is considered as a cause or an effect of human activities (Gilly and Torre, 1998).

The Two Proximity Notions

The proximity notion emerges in both economic and social contexts. This notion deals both with the geographic separation of the individual or collective agents endowed with various resources, and with their close position in an economic problem resolution process. Thus, our spatial-industrial problem has two dimensions, one geographic and one organizational.

The organizational proximity is based on two types of logics:

- according to the adherence logic, the actors close in organizational terms belong to the same space of relations (firms, networks,...), that is, they are in interactions of various nature (see after);
- according to the similarity logic, the actors close in organizational terms are quite alike, that is, they have the same reference space and share the same knowledges. In this case, the institutional dimension matters.

Concerning the first logic, adherence depends on the effectiveness of co-ordination, while in the second case, similarity depends on the closeness of the world representations and functioning modes. These two logics can both be involved. For example, when an adherence relation based on horizontal intra-industrial relations implies the emergence of interdependencies between organizations, characterizing a similarity relation (or institutional proximity) between actors.

While organizational proximity deals with economic separation and relations in terms of the organization of production, geographical proximity deals with the separation in space of relations in terms of distance. Geographical proximity refers to the notion of geonomic space, in the sense of Perroux. That is, it deals with the localization of enterprises and involves the social dimension of economic mechanisms, sometimes called 'functional distance'. In other words, reference to physical and natural constraints in the definition of proximity are not sufficient. Geographic proximity also implies some aspects of the social construction. For example, the transport infrastructure, which can modify access time, or the financial means to utilize information technologies.

The articulation of these two main components of proximity (organizational and geographical) brings about and justifies the relevance of the 'Proximity Dynamics' group research. Our research object involves these two types of proximity, because space also matters in relations of an organizational nature.

Our empirical studies confirm this analytical position. For example, an industrial district combines the two types in its definition: the enterprises involved in the district are linked both in terms of adherence and similarity. However, these enterprises also have a functional distance between them. When an enterprise looks for specific external know-how, both the surrounding productive environment and the choice of enterprises having the required competencies matters.

Besides these two basic definitions, the proximity concept can be analyzed according to some additional dimensions. For example, the 'circulation dimension' of proximity depends on the characteristics of the market and of the production process (intermediary or final product). Information and people have to circulate implying transport costs and time but also quality, liability, and security. This dimension captures the link between the two types of proximity (organizational and geographical), including the spatial aspect of accessibility, and the organizational aspect of the operation of the flows and their interconnection. Moreover, another dimension, the 'relational dimension', interacts with the circulation dimension because transformation activities and activities concerning individual-individual interaction are distinguished. This last dimension takes into account the relations between individuals (social networks), considered as the basis of organizational relations.

The Central Role of Interaction

The definition of proximity refers to the existence of interactions between economic actors, and also between actors and objects. These interactions have a spatial as well as an organizational nature. This is the very ground of the proximity notion, which refutes exclusive reference to transport costs as in orthodox analyses. Accordingly, the relation established by Marshall, Young and Becattini between the division of labor and the localization of enterprise is at the heart of our recognition of both the social and economical dimensions.

Various forms of interactions can be distinguished. They can be formal or informal, market or non-market, and they can refer to agent-agent relations (in the adoption and diffusion of innovations for example), or agent-innovation relations (collective innovation activities), or innovation-innovation relations (technological complementarities). These interactions are sometimes distinguished by whether they are intentional (e.g., market exchange, contracts, co-operation, partnership) or unintentional (e.g., because of technological externalities). There is a frontier between these elements depending on the actors' actions (intentional interactions) and elements depending on technical or distance conditions (unintentional interactions). This distinction grounds proximity analysis in the actions of economic actors, while also including factors such as the existence of non-rival goods, environmental factors, or diversity.

Unintentional Interactions

We refer here to a very old tradition originated in the works of Marshall and Hoover having to do with the regional analysis of agglomeration economies. The notion of externalities behind this analysis is also addressed in recent economic literature. A set of interactions including both the spatial and industrial dimensions is highlighted by this notion. Moreover, this notion, added to the two types of proximity, highlights the process of development and agglomeration at the local level.

According to the debate on externality, two tightly linked dimensions can be identified. These two dimensions concern either market relations or non-market relations. Technological externalities, external to the firm but internal to the industry, are non-market interdependencies. Numerous studies can be found in the literature dealing with spatial and regional economic problems, and especially their inter-sectoral dimension. The path dependence property is a key factor in this literature. This property reveals that agglomeration and localization factors result from the external effects between firms, and can quickly have an irreversible dimension within a given territory. In these conditions, the success of the adoption of a specific trajectory (right or not) depends on an assay-error process rather than on the intrinsic superiority of the selected technological scheme. For example, when firms settle down within a production area in order to take advantage of local external effects, the path dependence constraint can prevent them from reaching their objective.

Paradoxically, according to recent research carried out by some economic geographers, financial externalities can be taken into account in the analysis of transport costs. In fact, they refer to market relations, and especially to price effects, which are more tangible than non-market externalities. This is interesting in the frame of our analysis because it reveals the polarization capacity of large enterprises or groups of enterprises at the local level. These enterprises have traditional relations like buying, selling, subcontracting, or else a relation between the production of the firm and consumption by employees.

Intentional Interactions

This aspect concerns the basis of agents' action, whether individual or collective. First, the frequency of the interactions is a dynamic factor contrasting with the static aspect of firms' localization motives. The evolution of the system, the attraction/repulsion processes between agents, organizations and activities depend on the density and the length of the interactions. The density of interactions implies the number of interactions, but also their duration, and their degree of transitivity. The density level changes through time. It is a proximity indicator concerning organizational proximity, spatial proximity, or both. The analogy with some of the technological innovation process analysis (especially in the work of Rosenberg) is quite noticeable. These analyses consider that the existence of tight interactions is a key to identifying the proximity links between actors. Consequently, we can say that geographical proximity is associated with tight interactions. However, as Granovetter demonstrated, there is a high value for unique information even in the case of low interaction. Consequently, if density is a proximity indicator, it also reveals the limits of proximity in the case of its exclusive utilization.

Concerning the intentional interaction schemes structured by agents' strategies, our approach focuses on those that imply some relationship with other partners, but not competition or threats. They can be relations of co-operation, confidence, technical exchange of information, partnership, etc. Some of them are only grounded on a relational basis (for example the confidence of ones neighbors), but some can also ensure the neutrality of a third partner in an economic activity. The relations on whom we focus have a productive or organizational dimension because the firms, their strategies, and their environment are concerned.

The interactive natures of proximity as well as the density of the interactions are involved in our analyses when we examine co-operative relations, partnership relations, and the exchange of technological know-how. These phenomena are based on an iterative process, which implies not only the limited rationality of actors but also the cognitive dimension and the specific characteristic of knowledge. The difference between information and knowledge (tacit and codified) introduced by Polanyi and Machlup, and then summarized by Nonaka (1994), is involved in the analysis of innovation and its relationship with a territory. This difference has two consequences.

First, it reveals that information refers to the capacity of emission, circulation and reception of messages flows, whereas knowledge refers to individual actions that begin a process of comprehension of the information received, and implying that learning takes place. In this frame, the difference between tacit and codified knowledge leads to a distinction between knowledge that can be communicated in a formal way, and knowledge which cannot because it is difficult to formalize. Tacit knowledge is involved in the exchange of information, but it cannot be exchanged in a market.

Second, it reveals the importance of learning processes, which can take various forms according to the literature (e.g., practicing, using, etc.). Because of their interactive character, these processes concern both the individual and groups of individuals, whether inside the firm (between departments) or outside (social networks). They are at the core of innovation processes, defined as processes of new knowledge creation or as processes of existing knowledge combined in a new way. In the frame of an adapted organizational and institutional context, geographical proximity implies cognitive interactions. Thus, the innovation process analysis is the result of complex and changing relations between organizational proximity (conceived of as the adoption of behavior norms, social rules) and geographical proximity.

Space and Time

All of these analytical positions are relevant for proximity analysis. They contradict the hypothesis that relations involving tacit knowledge imply a geographical proximity, while the relations based on codified knowledge can cope with distance. Such a suggestion is grounded on a limited conception of the relationship between proximity/distance, and ignores:

- the frequent cohabitation between tacit and codified knowledges within enterprises or networks;
- the time factor in the proximity effects (the various stages as appropriation, learning, decodification, recodification of the information);
- the successive steps of the process of acquisition and transfer of know-how which concern more the tacit knowledges or those which concern more the codified knowledges.

Proximity and Economic Co-ordination

These various elements (and particularly the enlarged conception of interaction including the spatial dimension) lead to a renewal of co-ordination problem analysis, involving proximity relations. Our approach is close to that of other authors who take into account the localization aspects, or at introduce space into orthodox economic analysis. However, our approach is different in the sense that it is not only based on the price co-ordination system. It also:

- in introducing off-prices co-ordination elements, but various external effects, in the relations of agents;
- in taking into account the collective action phenomena and particularly the groups behavior;
- in pointing out the often essential role of institutions.

The objective is to describe a situated agent, being both 'here' and 'somewhere else'. Here because of its localization within a geographic and an economic space, and somewhere else because the agent interacts with other economic entities. A relevant case of this approach to co-ordination is the construction of a specific and territorialized resource, that is a resource tightly linked to its organizational and institutional context. Neither available, nor reproducible somewhere else, this resource is the result of local co-ordination of actors and of the role played by 'external constraints' (either economic or legal). Such local co-ordination is based on the three dimensions discussed above. It can only emerge when there is a similarity between the actors, and when there is an agreement on a common system of collective representations often built partly by formal institutions.

Non Market Co-ordination

In our approach co-ordination between actors goes beyond the information given by the prices. This co-ordination can be appreciated at two levels:

- a set of other modalities of co-ordination exist beside the interaction based on the prices: co-operation relations, trust relations, technological interaction relations, ... This position is close to the game theory postulate concerning the 'direct' communication (as called by Kirman) rather than the communication based on the prices;
- the reference to the information notion appears too restrictive (see above). The various co-ordination forms depend, in the analysis we suggest, on the cognitive dimension. Therefore, there is an impact on our analysis on proximity relations implying directly the spatial

dimension (see the scheme of the interaction between the geographical proximity and the organizational proximity).

In this frame, the relations between actors, technological transfers, and the co-operation between actors are analyzed in their spatial dimension. This analysis appears especially relevant when there is a dilemma between spatial competition and proximity localization of the enterprises. This problem is one of key debate in the literature about space and industry. Is it more attractive for a firm to be localized far from other firms in the sector in order to take advantage of monopolistic power resulting from transports costs, or is it more attractive for a firm to be localized in geographic proximity to other firms in order to take advantage of the externalities generated by knowledge, information and technology transfers?

This question leads to the issue of enterprise nomadism and territorial implementation. To avoid the contradiction implied in this issue, the idea of 'productive meeting' between a firm and its territory is introduced. This implies a common process of learning and construction of specific territorialized resources (see above). This firm-territory dialectic occurs at the intersection of geographical proximity and organizational proximity. This leads to the emergence of an interaction dynamic, characterizing the firm and its territory. This point of view on the problem of complex relations between firm and territory stands in contrast to the orthodox position, which postulates the anteriority of productive questions on spatial questions. We instead postulate that the productive and spatial components are tightly associated.

Collective Action

The standard Walrassian model is also questioned in our analysis of collective action forms. In identifying spatial inequality, the difference between the individual level and the social order can be pointed out. All individuals or enterprises are in various positions concerning geographic proximity as it is revealed by the two following examples: the handicaps of the isolated subscriber of a network, or the handicaps of outlying areas. But these actors can take advantage of the spatial dimension in carrying out collective actions. These behaviors question the relation between the micro-and the macro-levels. At least, those relations involving agents that have not only individual logics (even if their environment influences them), but also group strategies. These approaches partly refer to the work of Hayek (and especially his notion of 'yellow brick road'), to the work of Schelling pointing out that the behaviors are often based on imitation, and to the work of Kirman (1996) on the mimetic evolutions.

These works suggest three main ways to analyze the emergence of local dynamics in local systems of production and also the emergence of collective action:

- the notion of situated networks of actors is used to analyze the local functioning of producers. The network functioning avoid the possible isolation, make easier the transmission of informations and learnings, and define in a collective way the common norms and rules concerning the products properties or the knowledges exchange;
- the trust relations and/or the co-operation relations are used to study the systems organized by not formalized norms, in which the emergence endogenous dynamics are not formalized by explicit common rules. The processes of local interactions are analyzed by the evolutionary game theory, the genetic algorithms or the neuronal network modelizations. These approaches demonstrate the importance of recurring actions between neighbors, as well as the quickness of opinions or behaviors diffusion within small groups weakly connected;
- the local systems endowed with explicit common rules (like OCA or POI[1]), changing through time. In this case, the local actors agree on a set of common rules excluding other agents of the system. The struggle for power within these systems, as well as the problem of rules interpretation can lead to the instability of the system.

The analysis of situated agents according to the diptych of organizational/geographical proximity leads to a conception of non-deterministic micro-macro relations. Collective action is embedded in historic economic structures and social institutions. However, individual or collective actors are always able, when there is a crisis, to collectively transform the existing macro-structures. This approach leads us to analyze intermediary socio-economic spaces where the structural forms (inherited from the past) and the collective action of situated agents (anticipating the future) are articulated and regulated in the resolution of a productive problem. The territory is then a specifically constructed intermediary space. It is the result of the interactions between local actors, and between local actors and non-local actors (e.g., firms, unions, syndicates, banks, the State). In this complex dynamic of interactions, the key actors are those who play a mediation/hybridization role between the local level and the global level, taking part in the adaptation process between geographical proximity and organizational proximity.

Such an approach was developed in the analysis of the spatial dynamic in industrial models, which accept that technical, organizational and social systems are coherent and adapted to their environment. In these models, the emergent phase involves a process of organizational and institutional learning implying geographical proximity. Their diffusion into new spaces needs a hybridization process that ensures compatibility with the existing practices within these spaces.

The Role of Institutions

A third argument takes into account space and proximity notions in the analysis of co-ordination, and the role of institutions in co-ordination. This is the domain of the governance of territories. We have already pointed out the influence of institutional processes, whether the institutions are formal or not. In this approach, the territory is defined as a process of recovering organizational and geographical proximity. If a territory exists because of its capacity to resolve a productive problem with localized collective action, then a common vision of local actors is necessary. This vision demonstrates the institutional dynamic and specifically territorial governance, variously defined as contractual co-ordination (Williamson, 1985), legal-political co-ordination (Kooiman, 1993), or as social co-ordination (Granovetter, 1973).

Our concept of governance implies productive and institutional mechanisms, both in the local dimension (geographical proximity versus organizational proximity) and in the local-global dimension (local institutional proximity versus global institutional proximity). Territorial governance constitutes a process of recovering and hybridizing institutional proximities. As a result, there is an 'alliage' (in the sense of Dumont) of various representation systems. This 'alliage' reveals and activates the productive potential of geographical and organizational proximity. In other words, the territory is built on the interstice of the two proximities leading to the emergence of localized productive regularities.

This notion of territorial governance is not only an endogenous process. It also involves the relations between formal and informal local institutions and global institutional forms. In this frame, there is neither determinism in terms of micro-economic behaviors issued by the macro-structures, nor the emergence of a spontaneous order issued by individual agents behaving in a structureless world. In fact, governance is characterized by local-global mediation that ensures diffusion (from the global to the local) when the economy is stable, or emergent principles (from the local to the global) in case of crisis. Lastly, we emphasize the important role of formal institutions, and especially territorial collectivities, which influence the behavior of agents, and the viability of territorial governance. Institutional density is a characteristic of territorial governance, in terms of interactions between institutions, contributing to the territorial dynamic in complement with organizational density.

We recommend analyzing the co-ordination modalities of actors on this basis. Our approach refers to the spatial variable and to the situated agent, depending on its productive and relational environment as well as on the spatial interactions and neighborhood. Space and time are then both questioned. Any analysis of co-ordination denying the unique role of market prices is confronted by the inheritance of the past as well as the limited capacity to predict the future. For example, technology exchanges within a localized network depend on the inherited past relations which specify interactions forms and the acceptance of some rules, as well as on the willingness to conceive a common future within a group in the frame of an identified territory.

The Proximities - Theoretical Confrontations

The research carried out by the proximity dynamics group is part of the renewal of French regional thought, and also a wider worldwide research movement. This has two specificities:

- first, we refer to the various works between the industrial economy and the spatial economy. These analysis lead to a collective book concerning the technological phenomena (Rallet and Torre, 1995);
- second, we refer to the domain of geographic economy, and then to the renewal of the traditional spatial approaches, especially on the indivisibilities and the increasing returns.

If our approach comes along these debates, it also appears important to confront our acception of industrial and spatial phenomena with other researches carried out in the human sciences domain.

The various research domains Our research domain concerns the interface between the space economy and the industrial economy (including the analysis of innovation processes). Various related theoretical domains have been examined. For example, game theory, the French 'conventions' approach, innovation theories, French regulation school analysis, and research on industrial districts. The key points for comparison are the:

- the analysis of the competitive conditions at the local level;
- the involvement of externalities in the analysis of proximity effects;
- the innovation and technological change dimensions;
- the relations between the firms localization and the spatial division of work;
- the competition between territories;
- the organization between local institutions and global institutional forms;
- the correspondence between territorial and industrial organization forms.

Our research focuses on these themes in order to analyze the link between the problem of localization on one side and the problems of production, competition, innovation, organization and institutions on the other side.

Moreover, there is the recent confrontation with economic geography. This analytical domain concerns the spatial dimension in economic analysis, focusing on agglomeration problems, proximity, increasing returns, externalities (financial or technological), and even social determiners. In comparison, our approach is not grounded in a paradigm that only considers price co-ordination. Lastly, we agree on the importance of historical reference, on the multi-disciplinary approach taken by some of economic geographers, and on the willingness to analyze productive or urban problems according to spatial condition constraints.

The confrontation Interdisciplinary confrontations are today crucial in debates over economic science because they bring about new questions and problems. The research domains concerned are mainly Legal Science, Sociology, Geography, and Mathematics:

- in the Legal Science domain, the main questions concern the property, the regulation, the public actions, the rules determination, the infrastructure management;
- Sociology is one of our main sources of confrontation, concerning especially the relations between individuals, the actors strategies, the

> analysis of groups, or the relations between the science and the technique;
> - the researches carried out in Geography concerning the conception of the space, the territorial representations or the physical networks;
> - the mathematical aspect concerns mainly the formalization of the connexity relations and the spatial interaction phenomena.

These various confrontations are either involved in economic analysis or take a trans-disciplinary form. They can both deepen previous analysis and suggest new questions. Some of these domains undoubtedly hold additional material for us, for example, with respect to questions about notions of space and time, or questions about the role of institutions in the definition of local policies (especially technology policy). Our ambition is to launch research programs on broader societal questions, for example employment issues, furthering application of the proximity notion.

Conclusions

The objective of this chapter was to describe the theoretical background of the proximity notion in the work of the French school of proximity dynamics. Four main results were pointed out. The first and main result is related to the definition of geographical and organizational proximity. It was demonstrated that organizational proximity is based on two main logics, which are similarity and adherence (economic actors being involved in an organizational proximity relation when they belong to the same relational framework or when they share the same common knowledge and capacities). It was also demonstrated that geographical proximity deals with the spatial separation between economic actors (in reference to physical factors but also to social constructions such as transport infrastructures or telecommunication technologies).

Second, we stressed the central role played by various interactions, both between actors and of a technical nature, based on spatial or organizational relations. These informal and formal interactions are differentiated, and include the voluntary character of the relation.

Third, we developed the role played by co-ordination problems in the analysis of proximity relations. Three main points are underlined. The non-market co-ordination between economic agents, the collective action processes (groups and networks behaviors), and the essential role played by local and non-local institutions in the spatial dimension of the economic process.

Fourth, we drew a comparison with similar research performed by various researchers belonging to parallel or closely related schools of thought. Most of these works are in the frame either of regional science or the (re)birth of economic geography. A long research agenda still remains in the domain of proximity analysis, concerning local public policy, employment, and the city. All of these themes have high research potential.

Note

1   Original Controlled Appellations and Protected Original Indications, including the local producers in order to protect the products quality of the territory.

Bibliography

Audretsch D. and Feldman M. (1996), 'R&D Spillovers and the Geography of Innovation and Production', *The American Economic Review*, vol. 86, no. 3, pp. 630-640.

Becattini G. (1990), 'The Marshallian Industrial District as a Socio-Economic Notion', In F. Pyke, G. Beccatini and W. Sengenberger (eds), *Industrial Districts and Inter-Firm Co-operation in Italy*, International Institute for Labour Studies, Geneva.

Bellet M., Colletis G. and Lung Y. (eds) (1993), 'Economie de proximités', special issue of the *Revue d'Economie Régionale et Urbaine*, no. 3.

Fujita M. and Thisse J. F. (1997), 'Economie géographique, Problèmes anciens et nouvelles perspectives', *Annales d'Economie et de Statistiques*, no. 45, pp. 37-87.

Gilly J.P. and Torre A. (eds.) (1998), 'Prossimità: Dinamica industriale e Territorio. Studi Francesi', Special Issue of *l'Industria*, no. 3.

Hayek F. A. (1979), *The Counter Revolution in Social Sciences*, Liberty Press, Indianapolis.

Granovetter M. (1973), 'The strength of weak ties', *American Journal of Sociology*, vol. 78.

Hoover E.M. (1948), *The location of economic activity*, McGraw Hill, New York.

Jaffe A., Trajtenberg M., Henderson R. (1993), 'Geographic Localization of Knowledge Spillovers as Evidenced by Patent Citations', *Quarterly Journal of Economics*, vol. 108, pp. 577-598.

Joskow P. (1985), 'Vertical integration and long-term contracts : the case of coal-burning electric generating', *Journal of Law, Economics and Organization*, vol. 1, no. 1, pp. 33- 78.

Kirman A. (1996), *Some observations on interaction in Economics*, GREQAM-EHESS, Université d'Aix-Marseille.

Kooiman J. (1993), 'Findings, speculations and recommendations',In J. Kooiman (ed), *Modern Governance, New Government. Society Interactions*, Sage, London.

Lundvall B. A. (1992), 'Relations entre utilisateurs et producteurs, systèmes nationaux d'innovation et internationalisation', In D. Foray D. and Ch. Freeman (eds), *Technologie et Richesse des Nations,* Economica, Paris.

Machlup F. (1972), *The production and distribution of knowledge in the United States*, Princeton University Press, Princeton.

Marshall A. (1890), *Principles of Economics*, The Royal Economic Society, MacMillan (1961), London.

Nelson R. (ed) (1993), *National Innovation Systems: A Comparative Analysis*, Oxford University Press, New York.

Nonaka I. (1994), 'A Dynamic Theory of Organizational Knowledge Creation', *Organization Science*, vol. 5, no. 1, pp. 14-37.

Perroux F. (1961), L'économie du XXéme Siécle, Presses Universitaires de France, Paris.

Polanyi M. (1966), *The Tacit Dimension*, Routledge and Kegan, London.

Rallet A. and Torre A. (eds) (1995), *Economie Industrielle et Economie Spatiale*, Economica, Paris.

Rosenberg N. (1972), *Inside the black box. Technology and economics*, Cambridge University Press.

Schelling T. (1978), *Micromotives and macrobehaviour*, Norton.

Williamson O. E. (1985), *The Economics of Institutions of Capitalism*, The Free Press, New York.

Young A. (1928), 'Increasing returns and economic progress', *Economic Journal*, vol. 38, pp. 527-542.

2 Innovation and Proximity: Theoretical Perspectives

LEON A.G. OERLEMANS, MARIUS T.H. MEEUS and
FRANS W.M. BOEKEMA

Introduction

In economics, the discussion on innovation and technological development and their significance for economic development has become increasingly important in recent years. The spatial (economic) sciences have also contributed to this discussion.

It is generally agreed that innovation and technological development are important factors in explaining economic growth and development. Time and again, production, diffusion, and implementation of knowledge have proven to be crucial aspects of economic growth and development. The importance of the exchange of knowledge compels researchers to further investigate the theoretical and empirical relation between a firm and its (spatial) environment. Firms often depend on their immediate surroundings with regards to production, diffusion and the implementation of knowledge. This idea is built into various theoretical approaches, such as for example Williamson's (1975) theory of transaction costs and the economic network approach as described by Håkansson (1992, 1993). However, Oerlemans (1996) evaluated several of these approaches and found that the spatial economic dimension was often neglected. Theoretical approaches that did build in the spatial aspect paid often insufficient attention to technology and innovation.

The spatial dimension of the relationship between a firm and its environment will be addressed in this chapter within the framework of a study of innovation. The central question is: What is the relationship between innovation and proximity?

This question will be elaborated as follows. In the second section of this chapter, some observations are presented concerning how general regional economic theories look at the relationship between organizations and their spatial environment. In the third section, in the light of the relationship between innovation and proximity, regional theory development up until 1980 is discussed. The fourth section deals with the most important of a number of new theoretical perspectives in the relationship between innovation and proximity, which emerged during the 1980s. Finally, in the last section of the chapter the theoretical perspectives discussed in the fourth section are evaluated.

The Relationship Between Organizations and Their Environment in General Regional Economic Theory

In our view, based on an action-structure interaction model, there are two approaches to explain the relationship between a firm and its spatial environment (cf. also: Vaessen, 1993, Chapter 2). In the first approach, the action of an organization is seen as a function of the spatial environment in which an organization is located. In other words, the characteristics of the spatial environment largely determine the origins, actions and performance of an organization. The influence of a firm on its environment is not seen as important: the prime element of this approach is the spatial context.

In the second approach, more or less the opposite is argued. The spatial environment in which a particular organization is located is seen as resulting from the actions and activities of a firm. The spatial environment is thought to be directly influenced by decisions and actions of entrepreneurs and firms. In this approach, organizations are conceived as 'area organizing institutions'. In other words, firms largely determine their (spatial) environment in this approach the prime element is the organization.

Exponents of the first approach, such as regional economic development theories, all emphasize the importance of the spatial environment, on the basis of the concept of agglomeration economies.[1] They suppose that agglomeration economies occur mainly in urban areas. It is assumed that the geographical concentration of economic activities is advantageous because lower transport and delivery costs can be achieved. In recent years, the concept of agglomeration economies has broadened. It now includes not only costs of material relations, but also takes into account various immaterial relations, such as the exchange of knowledge, the provision of services, and labor market relations.

To sum up, theories based on the first approach conclude that agglomeration economies in urban areas are more productive than in non-urban areas because spatial economic concentration of economic activities results in lower information, communication, and transaction costs. Moreover, urban areas offer firms more benefits than cost efficiency alone. Urban areas provide more easy access to information, a more differentiated and better-qualified supply of labor, as well as more opportunities to contract out. In other words: '...agglomeration economies are not only expressed in lower production costs but also in so-called differential advantages...' (Vaessen, 1993, 19-20). The effect of the presence of agglomeration economies is that urban economic activity is more dynamic, innovative, and as expected, more profitable. In short, the characteristics of the local production environment largely determine the functioning and results of an organization.

The second approach to the relationship between organization and environment emphasizes the features and behavior of enterprises and how this influences their spatial environment. This behaviorist approach to economics evolved in the second half of the 1960s on the basis of the work by Simon. In response to shortcomings in classical economic thinking, more attention was given to the economic processes of choice, the behavior of the entrepreneur and to his personal motives. In the spatial sciences, this induced an interest in the underlying (individual) factors that could explain location behavior as well as the spatial effect of a firms' behavior. Within this behaviorist view, two, to a certain extent overlapping, approaches are relevant in terms of the relationship between an organization and its spatial environment: the behavioral location theory and the 'geography of the enterprise' approach.

Proponents of behavioral location theory criticize a number of assumptions in classical location theory. The fully informed, profit-maximizing entrepreneur is in the behavioral location theory succeeded by a bounded rational 'satisficer'. This view means that the motives of manufacturers and consumers and the extent to which they acquire and are able to process information are important elements in choosing a location. The work of A. Pred (1967) was of great influence in developing this theory.

The 'geography of the enterprise' approach can also be seen as a spatial-economic approach which refutes several principles of classical and neo-classical location theory. Opponents particularly object to those aspects of classical location theory, which take the small 'single-plant family firm' as the object of study and the assumption that a company's choice of location is completely determined by the characteristics of the spatial environment. They refer to the impact of large, often multinational, enterprises on the modern Western industrial economy. They are also of the opinion that (large) enterprises in fact influence their (spatial) environment to a considerable extent. In other words: they reject the idea of mechanistic location behavior that is used in traditional theory.

Within the 'geography of the enterprise' approach, two perspectives have arisen (Vaessen, 1993, p. 26).[2] One perspective concentrates on the way in which firms adapt to their environment and in this view, the (spatial) environment is considered to be a precondition for organizations to act. The other perspective focuses mainly on the impact of the organizational structure and behavior of large companies on regional-economic developments. In this second view, the condition of the spatial and regional environment is directly related to decisions made (by managers) within enterprises.

If we take a critical look at the 'environmental approach' and the 'geography of the enterprise' approach', both theories have their inherent weaknesses. These are summarized in Table 2.1. In the 'environmental approach', the different regional conditions of production are seen as exogenous. This theory cannot explain the development of differentiated conditions of production and therefore, is not able to give a satisfactory

Table 2.1 Theoretical Problems of the Environmental Approach and of the 'Geography of the Enterprise'

Environmental approach	Geography of the enterprise
Differences between regions are exogenous	Great emphasis on large, multinational enterprises
Theories are one-dimensional. Only the cumulative discrepancy between center and periphery can be explained.	Approach usually concentrates on one single company or region.
The individual organization is treated as a 'black box.'	The business environment is narrowly conceptualized.
Uni-directional: behavior of actors is determined by the spatial environment ('action follows structure')	Uni-directional: behavior of actors determines the spatial environment ('structure follows action')

Source: Elaboration of: Vaessen (1993, pp. 23-24, pp. 31-34)

interpretation of spatial-economic dynamics. Moreover, McDermott and Taylor (1982) point out that some locational advantages (for instance, services and infrastructure) materialize *after* a concentration of economic activities has occurred. Vaessen (199, 23) states that the failure to provide a comprehensive explanation is because '...these theories conceive of regions as predefined spatial units, having dynamics in and of themselves and existing in isolation from the rest of the economy...'. In addition, this approach can be called uni-directional as it sees the behavior and performance of firms as being fully determined by the regional characteristics of the location in which they are located. This makes the theory inflexible and vulnerable. Another criticism is aimed at the total disregard of the individual organization. McDermott and Taylor (1982, p. 7) argue that spatial science '...has tended to disregard the individual organization and treats all decision-making units in much the same manner as black boxes, capable of a limited number of actions determined by particular environmental contexts...'. Little scope is given to explain the economic behavior of actors, as that behavior is seen as being completely determined by the spatial environment. It comes as no surprise that critics have coined terms like 'spatial determinism' or 'spatial fetishism' to typify the environmental approach.

Similarly, there are also a number of theoretical problems with the 'geography of the enterprise' approach. Firstly, it suffers from an one-sided emphasis on large multinational and multilocational enterprises, while ignoring small and medium-sized enterprises and their relevance to the functioning of spatial economies. As a result, one of the central issues of the spatial economy, *viz.*, the interaction between the origin and development of enterprises and the spatial environment becomes concealed.[3] Secondly, the region is usually treated as a closed system. Such an approach does not enable one to draw conclusions about, for example, the different economic achievements of comparable organizations under various spatial conditions. Thirdly, in this approach, a remarkably narrow conception of the notion 'environment' is employed. Only general socio-economic aspects of the environment (such as changing consumer demand) are examined for their influence on the actions and functioning of organizations (input), otherwise the environment is merely seen as the result of a firm's actions. In other words, this approach fails to take due note of the influence of spatially dissimilar circumstances of production on the behavior of firms.

In summary, we can say that, in the two approaches described above, the theoretical relationship between a firm and its spatial environment is, at the very least, problematic. Both approaches are characterized by one-sidedness.

In one, the emphasis is on the influence of the spatial environment while economic actors are reduced to 'puppets on a string.' In the other, the actions of (large) enterprises are central whereas the environment is a 'black box.' The current discussions and conclusions in the spatial sciences show a strong resemblance to those in the organizational sciences (see Oerlemans, 1996, 39ff).

The Relationship Between Innovation and Proximity in the Spatial Economic Sciences in the Period until 1980

To Vaessen's critical comments, we can add that the spatial aspects of technological development in general, and those of innovation in particular, receive only scant attention in the approaches mentioned above. Malecki (1991, p. 72) states, '...Technology is one of the principal factors behind regional dynamics, but is dealt with least satisfactorily by either conventional or Marxist approaches...'.

In neo-classical models of regional economic development, technological development is introduced via the Cobb-Douglas production function, which looks upon capital as a flexible and manipulable production factor. Capital can appear in various forms and embody new technologies. Since labor and capital are substitutable, and productivity is measured in terms of output per unit of labor, labor saving investments are generally preferred when the aim is to increase the amount of output. This neo-classical model of regional development is both a growth theory and a factor mobility theory, because, if the assumption is correct that production-functions are identical in all regions, labor will migrate from low-wage regions to high-wage regions. Conversely, capital will move in the opposite direction.[4] Eventually, these regional economic growth processes will lead to converging per capita regional incomes. In this sense, neo-classical models of regional-economic growth are in essence re-allocation models, which consequently contribute little to the explanation of spatial economic inequalities. Malecki's assessment of the role of technology in neo-classical theory hits the nail on the head (1991, p. 79): '...And, significantly, technical progress is accorded surprisingly little recognition of its importance...'.

Theories building on the concept of agglomeration economies do pay some attention to technological development. In a variant on Myrdal's principle of cumulative causation, Siebert (1969) argues that a higher regional turnover leads to higher investments in research and development ('demand pull' hypothesis). The resulting innovation and knowledge yields a number of initial advantages for the region in question. In turn, these advantages lead to higher regional turnover and R and D. Although knowledge has a certain geographical mobility; it tends, in Siebert's view, to polarize in certain geographical locations. This technological polarization is matched by a polarization of capital and labor resulting from the initial advantages of innovation mentioned before (higher profits and wages). These polarization effects are reinforced if economic advantages of scale present themselves in a region, i.e., internal advantages of scale and agglomeration economies. Siebert argues (op. cit., p. 40): '...The more mobile capital and labor, the stronger are the polarizing effects which technical knowledge induces...'. The result is that cumulative causation processes are reinforced by the spread of new technologies after their introduction in cities and urban regions. In other words, what this type of regional economic growth model addresses is the association between the size of a certain geographical area (often an urban area with the internal and external advantages of scale) and the diffusion of innovations. These innovations spread in accordance with the urban hierarchy (the 'trickle-down-effect'). In order to accentuate the subordinate role of technology in this kind of approach, Malecki (1991, p. 87) remarks, '...Agglomeration economies, rather than technology, become the driving forces behind regional growth in these models...'.

The Relationship between Innovation and Proximity 'Revisited'

Introduction

During the 1980s, discussion in the spatial sciences about the relationship between innovation and proximity was strongly influenced by insights from other scientific disciplines, such as industrial organization and sociology. The introduction of the concept 'transaction costs' or the use of such concepts as governance structures, embeddedness, clusters and networks illustrate this. In addition, the relationship between innovation and spatial economic development was given a far more prominent place on the agenda. In this context, a number of theoretical perspectives, such as the theory of the 'new industrial spaces,' the 'district' theory, the innovative milieu approach, and 'regional innovation systems' emerged.

Before going into these theoretical perspectives, we must first elaborate on the concept of innovation. More than any other economic activity, innovation depends on knowledge; knowledge in a variety of forms. In an iterative process in which invention, development, and introduction or implementation are important steps, attempts are made to realize new or improved products and processes through the (re)combination of heterogeneous resources.

At this point, it is important to compare traditional views on technological knowledge with what may be called the 'modern' view (Smith, 1995, p. 75). In many economic theories, especially those taking a neo-classical perspective, technological knowledge has a number of specific features that are often left implicit. The features of technological knowledge used in these theories are explained below:

- *generic knowledge*. This means that applicability and transferability characterize technological knowledge;
- *'codified' knowledge*. The applicability and transferability of technological knowledge implies that it is codified in economically usable forms;
- *freely available*: The costs of transferring or obtaining technological knowledge are negligible and identical for all enterprises;
- *context-independent*. The applicability and transferability ensures that all enterprises have the opportunity to harness technological knowledge for their production process. This is independent of the nature of the product produced, the production techniques employed, or the sector to which the enterprise belongs.

In view of these features, innovation is not really problematic. Neither the use of existing technology nor the introduction of new technology confronts an organization with severe problems. In this view, the environment of the organization can be seen as a source of exogenous technology inputs on which a firm can draw at will.

This view on technology and technological knowledge has its critics who consider it unrealistic (Rosenberg, 1994). Smith (1995, pp. 78-81) systematizes the characteristics of technological knowledge in what he calls a 'modern' view. He argues that enterprises innovate on the basis of a specific set of internal resources, called the 'knowledge base'. These 'knowledge bases' have the following characteristics:

- *resources are 'differentiated and multi-layered'*. A specific set of resources consists of various forms and levels of knowledge. The knowledge in question can be, for example, coded scientific knowledge or uncoded ('tacit') knowledge embodied in the experience and skills of employees or other actors;

- *resources are specific.* The technological resources an organization has at its disposal are in part specific to the enterprise. Firms possess knowledge about, and have experience with, the technologies, which affect their competitiveness. Although a firm can innovate, it is limited to the technologies it has at its disposal. To compensate for restrictions imposed by a limited knowledge base, a firm is compelled to acquire additional knowledge from outside the organization. It can been seen that innovation is inevitable interwoven with the environment and far from simple;

- *the development of resources is expensive and cumulative.* Improving resources (innovation) is an expensive process in which firms, through learning, adapting and investing in knowledge try to master specific technologies. Building up a stockpile of experience and skill underlines the cumulative character of the innovation process;

- *resources are 'internally systemic'.* Innovation is not only a technical process but is linked to other (economic) activities within the firm. This means that innovation also implies that technological and market possibilities must be explored; that innovations must be financed; and that employees must be trained to handle the new technologies;

- *resources are 'interactive and externally systemic'.* Innovation often requires the acquisition of extra knowledge and skills not available in the organization. This means structured interaction with other economic actors.

In summary, we can conclude that in this 'modern' view, technological development is far from simple. Innovation is an expensive, erratic, uncertain, complex learning process in which specific resources are improved and expanded through the acquisition of various kinds of knowledge. The environment is seen as a collection of institutions and resources with which the innovating actor interacts. This interaction takes place through the structured exchange of resources and through learning processes. To a greater or lesser extent, all these characteristics of resources and the underlying view of the innovation process are present in what will be discussed below, viz., the new insights into spatial economics with respect to the relationship between innovation and proximity.

'Industrial District' Approach

The concept 'industrial district' originates from the English economist Marshall. In his book 'Principles of Economics' which was published in 1890, two types of 'economies' are distinguished: *internal economies*, i.e., the efficiency of the production organization of an individual enterprise, and *external economies*, which refer to the cost benefits resulting from the distribution of work among enterprises. The 'external economies,' according to Marshall, can be achieved by the spatial concentration of small companies. If we add to this (see also Lambooy, Wever and Atzema, 1997, p. 114) qualitative elements like mutual trust among market parties, 'atmosphere', and 'skills and knowledge', we have the most important components of an industrial district.

Hence, industrial districts can be regarded as a special type of agglomeration. They are characterized by '...a local "thickening" of interindustrial relationships which is reasonably stable over time...' (Becattini, 1989, p. 132). Small specialized and innovative firms operating in national and international competitive markets populate the districts. This contrasts with the New Industrial Space (NIS) approach (discussed in the next section) which sees the characteristics of economic transactions and structures at the root of specific forms of economic coordination. Industrial district theory sees interorganizational relationships among enterprises in industrial districts to be based on cooperation, mutual dependence, and trust. The relations between enterprises stimulate innovation, while kinship ties among entrepreneurs often facilitate the spread of information among enterprises. In short, the building blocks of the industrial district are the *social* links and networks among firms and individual actors.

It should be pointed out that the social character of the 'industrial district' approach is based on work by the social psychologist Weick (1976) and sociologist Granovetter (1985). They regard networks as 'loosely coupled systems'[5]; institutions that coordinate the actions between organizations without restricting the autonomy of the individual organization more than is strictly necessary. Based on this social division of labor, a picture emerges of an economy consisting of a number of 'industrial districts' that, on the basis of their flexible production systems manage to operate in international competitive markets.

Although there are a number of examples in literature of successful 'districts' such as 'Third Italy' (Benneton), Central Portugal (wooden and metal furniture) and the Japanese Sakari district, these examples are the exception rather than the rule, as Zeitlin (1992) confirms in an overview article. The fact is that firms in these successful regions have managed to apply 'best practice' technology. In addition, the socio-cultural circumstances in these regions are such that they stimulate innovation. Moreover, as Malecki (1991, p. 223) points out, the emergence of this type of local production system as for example in the case of Emilia-Romagna, the heart of 'Third Italy', is often the result of specific local conditions, which originated in 16th-century silk industry. In other words, the industrial district approach puts too much emphasis on the significance of successful, small-scale localized production systems in specific sectors that have developed under special circumstances. It remains to be seen whether a theory based on such examples can be predictive for other regions (see also Hadjimichalis and Papamichos, 1991, pp. 145-149).

'New Industrial Spaces'

During the 1980s, an approach was developed that was to exert a powerful influence on the spatial sciences. Strongly inspired by neo-Marxist theories about unequal spatial development and Piore and Sabel's 'Second Industrial Divide,' authors like Scott, Storper, Harrison and Walker managed to create a theoretical framework that shed a new light on the economic dynamics of regions. Within this framework, the regulationist interpretation of capitalist development is interwoven with elements from Williamson's transaction-cost approach and labor economics.

At the core of the 'New Industrial Spaces' (NIS) theory lies the assumption that there is a reciprocal relationship between vertical disintegration and the spatial organization of production (Scott and Storper, 1992, p. 8). On the one hand, we are reminded of the emergence of a more disintegrated network-economy causing agglomeration of economic activities in certain regions (Silicon Valley, Third Italy). On the other hand, these territorial production systems facilitate a further disintegration of production and a further distribution of labor.

The effects of external economies of scale and scope are the main triggers in this process. New technologies, especially flexible production techniques, have enabled firms to abandon the Fordistic mass-production systems. These systems are being replaced by post-Fordistic production systems in which firms are more specialized. The external economies of scale resulting from this are further supported by improved (tele)communication between firms and the development and use of common production factors such as the local labor market and support institutions.

With regard to the relationship between (technological) innovation and space, it must be pointed out that in the NIS approach, technological innovation is often restricted to a particular area. Here, we refer to two geographic aspects of the innovation process. A specialized workforce as part of the knowledge base required for technological development characterizes highly innovative sectors. These specialized workers have a tendency to concentrate in certain geographical areas and display little geographical mobility. In addition, localized relations between firms in these sectors are the channels through which knowledge is spread.

Storper and Harrison (1991) developed a systematic framework of analysis that accommodates localized production systems. In this framework, they distinguished two dimensions: the level of internal economies of scale and scope of a *production-unit*, and the level of these economies of the entire *input-output system*.[6] The existence of external economies of scope depends on the

Table 2.2 Types of Input-output Systems

The system: External Economies of Scale and Scope (Social Division of Labor in Production)	Territorial dimension	Units: Internal Economies of Scale and Scope	
		Low	High
Low		Isolated Workshops	Process Producers
High	Territorial Dispersion	Dispersed Network Production mostly small units	Dispersed Network Production some large units
	Territorial Agglomeration	Agglomerated Network Production mostly small units	Agglomerated Network Production some large units

Source: Storper and Harrison, 1991

degree of fragmentation of the production process. Extensive fragmentation means that the input-output system consists of highly specialized production units, which encourages the emergence of external economies of scope.

A matrix was constructed on the basis of the distinction between high and low internal and external economies of scale and scope. In addition, two aspects of the spatial distribution of production units are included for further differentiation. This results in six types of production systems. This is shown in Table 2.2.

The question of which factors determine the spatial concentration of production units is answered as follows (Scott and Storper, 1992, p. 8):

> in general, it is evident that in industrial complexes marked by much inter-linkage at least some producers will have a tendency to converge around a territorial center of gravity, especially where linkages are small in scale, unstandardized with respect to substance, and rapidly changing in time and space, and hence incur high unit costs. In this manner, the external economies created by disintegration are transformed into and consumed in the form of agglomeration economies.

What this boils down to is that, in this approach, characteristics of transactions (scale, the extent of standardization, uncertainty) between production units are the cause of spatial agglomeration.

In Storper and Harrison's framework of analysis, the relationship between innovation and proximity is established in the following manner. External economies of scale and scope are caused by production flexibility. Although there are various ways to achieve this flexibility, they consider network production to be of crucial importance. It is precisely through adaptation of interorganizational relations that it is possible to introduce changes in the quality and the quantity of the output. This enhances the ability of the system to cushion external shocks and stimulate internal change such as innovation. Moreover, spatially concentrated networks play an important role in innovation. The knowledge necessary for innovation can be disseminated via these firm relations. Since there often is unstandardized and dynamic exchange in these relations, there is a strong tendency for innovative production units to move towards agglomeration.

What makes the theory of 'new industrial spaces' attractive is the fact that it constitutes a plausible attempt to link structural developments, such as internationalization, to changes at the local and regional level. In addition, we agree with Morgan (1997, p. 494), who calls this a successful marriage of two scientific disciplines, namely, the spatial and the innovation sciences.

In spite of the widespread acceptance of the NIS approach, it has also attracted criticism. Lagendijk (1997, p. 7), for example, points out that the approach uncritically combines a timeless principle of cumulative causation in explanation of spatial agglomeration with a fundamentally aspatial theory on structural economic development in explanation of the emergence of new forms of industrial organization.

The NIS approach is also criticized for the inadequate explanation of the behavior of economic actors and the neglect of the social dimensions of interorganizational relations. Firms are reduced to passive actors who do nothing but enter into transactions and mindlessly adopt new flexible production technologies. As a result, the NIS approach displays several forms of economic and technological determinism. Since there is such an emphasis on economic transactions ('traded interdependencies'), the social and institutional aspects of transactions and innovation are also lost sight of.

These shortcomings have been addressed in more recent NIS approach publications. For example, Storper (1995, 1997) now makes a distinction between 'traded' and 'untraded interdependencies'. The former consists of the input-output relations (localized or not) which together form a web of user-producer relations and which are extremely important for the exchange of information. The latter, according to Storper, included among others, (regional) labor skills, conventions, norms and values, and (semi)public institutions, all elements of the process of economic and organizational learning and coordination. In this line of argument, innovation and proximity are again linked. As Storper (1995) puts it:

> where these input-output relations or untraded interdependencies are localized, and this is quite frequent in cases of technological or organizational dynamism, than we can say that the region is the key, necessary element in the "supply architecture" for learning and innovation.

In our view, the 'untraded interdependencies' should be looked upon as a form of 'tacit knowledge.' Since this form of knowledge is often restricted to one area, sector, or even a single firm, the (core) region becomes more significant in the analysis of technological development and subsequent economic development.

The Innovative Milieu Approach

In order to develop a more accurate theoretical and empirical insight into the effect of technological innovation and the rise of high-tech industries on local and regional economic development, a group of European researchers (GREMI[7]) introduced the concept of 'milieux innovateurs': the innovative milieu. This approach is part of the renewed discussion concerning the economic dynamics in different regions. According to Aydalot and Keeble (1988, p. 7), these new dynamics are an effect of the rise of new technologies and new spatial concentrations of industrial activity in previously underdeveloped regions.

In this approach, the (innovating) firm is placed in its local or regional context. The main aim is to understand what external conditions contribute to the emergence of new (high tech) firms and why existing firms adopt particular innovations. Firms are seen as products of their environment. Access to technological know-how, the availability of local linkages and inputs, the proximity of markets, and the presence of qualified and skilled labor are seen, in this approach, as factors determining the innovativeness of an area. Such 'innovative' environments are the breeding grounds of innovation and innovative firms. It is therefore not surprising that the central hypothesis of the innovative environment approach is as follows: '...it is often the local environment which is, in effect, the entrepreneur or innovator, rather than the firm...' (Aydalot and Keeble, 1988, p. 9). However, as a consequence, the difference between the actor and the environment is blurred in this hypothesis. After all, it remains unclear under what conditions the environment becomes the 'innovator'.

Furthermore, it is assumed that there are spatial differences in the costs of innovation. If one or more of the above-mentioned factors are missing or insufficiently available, the innovative firms will be faced with higher costs and perhaps lower returns. On balance, innovative firms must invest more time and money into acquiring the necessary resources.

Although the above may have given the impression that the innovative capabilities of firms are exclusively determined by the environment in which the firms operates, several authors also take the characteristics of the *innovating firm* into account. In this context the nature of production, the strategy used, intensity of research and development, or the nature of the innovation process may be considered (Aydalot and Keeble, 1988, pp. 12-14; Maillat, 1991; pp. 110-113; Saxenian, 1994, pp. 7-9). Maillat's contribution is particularly important because he sees direct links between the innovation process and the local production environment. He does not see the innovative environment as a kind of department store where the innovative firm merely 'shops' for the necessary resources. In his view, the production environment must be seen as a spatial complex of economic and technical interdependencies, which encourages synergetic processes.

Maillat argues that the importance of the local environment for the innovation process is dependent on the type of innovation, on the one hand, and on the innovation strategies of the firms, on the other. The local production environment is of little importance for incremental innovators. According to Maillat, the resources necessary for incremental innovation can, in many cases, be found within the firm itself. Radical innovators, however, are more likely to develop relations with the local production environment especially if internal resources are insufficient to realize their innovative goals. In addition, Maillat sees links between the spatial environment and innovation strategies. He distinguishes two types of strategies: 'exploitation of a technological trajectory' and 'technology creation.' In the first case, innovation is seen as a process that builds on an existing technology. Companies which innovate using such a strategy see the production environment as '...an external datum whence the firm derive[s] its inputs...' (Maillat, 1991, p. 111). In the second case, innovation is seen as a process that is entirely original and could for example involve designing a new production method from scratch without an existing template to work from. For firms with this innovation strategy, the local environment is an essential part of the innovation process. Maillat (1991, p. 111) states:

indeed, the creation of technologies presupposes that the environment becomes an essential component of innovation, that these various resources be used and combined to generate a new form of localized production organization. The enterprise is then no longer isolated in a territory which represents to it only an external component, it helps to create its environment by setting up a network of partnership-style relations, both with other firms [....] and with public or private training and research centers, technology transfer centers and local authorities.

Although the distinctions used by Maillat do better justice to the various dimensions of the innovation process, they do present some problems. Particularly, in our view, the idea of radical innovations which strongly resembles the concept of 'technology creation'. If a firm generates radical innovations, this usually involves the creation and application of (entirely) new knowledge. This means that the two concepts have approximately the same content and that the distinction is, therefore, not of much value.

Regional Innovation Systems

The central idea behind the concept of (regional) innovation systems (RIS) is that the innovative performance of an (regional) economy does not exclusively depend on the individual innovative performance of companies and research institutions, but is also related to the way in which these organizations interact with each other and with the public sector as regards production and distribution of knowledge. Innovative firms function in a shared, institutional context. In this sense, they depend on and contribute to a joint knowledge infrastructure. This infrastructure is viewed as a system that creates and distributes knowledge, and applies it to achieve innovation, and thus generating economic value (Gregersen and Johnson, 1997, p. 482).

Within the RIS approach, various systems are identified. Innovation systems are defined, on the one hand, for particular sectors or specific technologies or, on the other hand, on the basis of (geographical) proximity.[8] Within (geographical) innovation systems, the concept of 'interactive learning' plays an important role. Learning is conceived as a process in which all types of knowledge are (re)combined in various ways to form something new. The concept of interactivity refers to the fact that learning is dependent on communication between people or organizations in possession of different types of knowledge.

If innovations are considered to be the result of cumulative learning processes (Lundvall, 1992a, p. 8), the performance of territorial innovation systems depends on the relations between a diversity of sources of knowledge and proximity. To formulate it simply: '...A larger territorial space may contain more diversity, but this will not lead to innovation if there is not enough proximity to support communication...' (Gregersen and Johnson, 1997, p. 482). In this context, proximity does not merely refer to physical distance, measured in kilometers, but also to time. However, there are also other dimensions of proximity. Lundvall (1992b) describes economic, organizational, and cultural proximity.[9] His central idea is that interactive learning and, as a consequence, innovation will be restricted if economic and organizational distances are too great. In short, in the RIS approach (geographical) proximity facilitates the innovation process.

Within the National Systems of Innovation approach, Lundvall (1992b) also developed a line of thought that is of importance in the discussion about the relation between innovation and proximity. Lundvall studies the relationship between the character of technological change and spatial interactions. Three types of technical change are identified: stationary technology, incremental innovation, and radical innovation. Each is associated with specific patterns of spatial interaction between users (customers, industrial buyers) and producers.

In the case of stationary technology, the technical opportunities as well as the needs of users are fairly constant. Norms, standards, methods and terminologies have been established giving a near complete description of the technology involved. In other words, this type of knowledge is highly codified. Such a high degree of codification means that communication between users and producers is not restricted by distance. In these cases, industries become virtually footloose with respect to technological innovation.

For incremental innovation, codes and channels of communication must be flexible in order to include technological opportunities and changing users needs. Recurring changes in product specifications, functions and the quality of artefacts obstruct standardization. Consequently, codification of knowledge is more difficult. This means that messages will be relatively complex and information will not be easily transferred. In this case the physical proximity of advanced users plays an important role, as they are vital in adapting an artefact to local conditions. Such firms and industries, often a part of national industrial complexes or clusters, are not footloose. Comparative advantages are often based on spatial proximity.

In the case of radical innovation, codes developed to communicate a constant or a gradually shifting technology are inadequate. Producers who follow a given technological trajectory will have difficulties in evaluating the potentials of the new paradigm. Users will have difficulties in decoding messages from producers, who are developing new products according to the new paradigm. The lack of standard criteria to select the best paradigm means that 'subjective' elements, such as mutual trust and even personal friendship, will be decisive factors in the user-producer relationships. These subjective elements are not easily transferred across regional borders and in these cases geographically clustered user-producer interaction networks are extremely important.

To sum up, more radical processes of innovation involve a less codified and more tacit communication of knowledge, which means that spatial proximity of user and producer becomes important. In this way, Lundvall assumes a positive relationship between the degree of knowledge tacitness and the importance of spatial proximity.

Although the innovation systems approach may initially seem applicable to various geographical levels, authors are divided on the question of whether the approach yields useful explanations for (small) regional economies. This is particularly related to the importance attached to institutions in this approach. The argument is as follows. By definition, innovative activities almost always involve a considerable degree of uncertainty. Institutions, which are characterized by stability, are brought into action by actors in order to operate and survive in this uncertain world. In this context, institutions are defined as '...the humanly devised constraints that structure human action. They are made up of formal constraints (e.g., rules, laws, constitutions), informal constraints (e.g., norms of behavior, conventions, and self-imposed codes of conduct)...' (North, 1994, p. 360).

The question is now whether these institutions operate on the local or the regional level. Gregersen and Johnson (1997, p. 483), for example, let the national level prevail over the regional or local level. They point out that institutional changes that are important for the process of technological innovation often involve government interference. This usually concerns e.g. intellectual property law, standards or contract law. In addition, an important part of the knowledge infrastructure is regulated and funded at the national level. Finally, they argue that the performance of innovation systems depends on effective communication and interaction between people possessing various types of knowledge and skills. This communication and interaction are more effective if they take place in a shared culture. In their opinion, this cultural homogeneity can especially be achieved at a national rather than a regional level.

The proponents of 'Regional Innovation Systems' are of the opinion that the region is the most relevant factor. In this context, Lagendijk (1997, p. 18) quotes Howells, who argues that, in regional innovation systems, the way in which the national institutional environment (for instance, education and legislation) affects the local or regional level is of importance. This, in turn, depends on the so-called "local institutional capacity". In Howells' view, the regional innovation system is an efficient level for localized learning, implicit ('tacit') knowledge playing an important role.

Evaluation

It can be concluded from the above that in the 'modern' theoretical approaches, proximity is a relevant factor in innovation processes. However, there are clear

Table 2.3 Innovation and Proximity: A Summary of Theoretical Perspectives

Subject	Industrial District	New Industrial Spaces
Conception of behavior of actors	Actors behave as independent flexible organizations	Actors behave as passive mechanisms for economic exchange and adopters of flexible production technologies
Conception of spatial environment	Environment consists of other actors with whom to establish social links	Environment consists of localized or spread production systems coordinating exchange
Relation between behavior and spatial environment	Voluntarism: cooperation, mutual dependence and trust are important behavioral features of actors	Economic and technological determinism
Relation between innovation and proximity	Through social links and networks of actors, information, knowledge, standards, etc., are communicated and distributed	Localized knowledge (labor) is an immobile resource; Exchange relations with other actors are resources for innovation
Proximity mechanism	Districts are a way in which a production organization can compete internationally (think global, act local)	Vertical disintegration and characteristics of transactions between organizations generate spatial concentration
New developments	Study of more different types of districts	More emphasis on importance of 'untraded interdependencies' and conventions

Table 2.3 Continued

Subject	Innovative Milieux	Regional Innovation System
Conception of behavior of actors	Actors behave as Schumpeterian entrepreneurs	Actors behave as learning entities
Conception of spatial environment	Environment consists of resources which facilitate the economic process	Environment is a macro- and meso-economic system of institutions
Relation between behavior and spatial environment	Mix of spatial determinism and voluntarism	Interactive: actors are dependent on, contribute to, and make use of the spatial environment
Relation between innovation and proximity	Depending on nature of innovations and technology strategies of actors, the environment is a supply of resources or a supporting production system	Institutions, proximity and diversity of resources stimulate or restrict interactive communication, learning, and innovation in regions
Proximity mechanism	Innovative milieus are an effect of capacities of certain regions to better organize collective learning processes and to realize lower information costs	Spatial proximity stimulates interactive learning as a result of the characteristics of technological change. The meso-institutional system supports the emergence and the application of new forms of production
New Developments	Strong emphasis on institutional factors	More applications at regional and sectoral level

Source: Elaboration of Lagendijk, 1997, p. 23

differences in emphasis in how this takes place. The most important characteristics of the various approaches are summarized in Table 2.3.

The four theoretical perspectives discussed above have several aspects in common in the sense that they emphasize different theoretical aspects of spatial economic development. The most important theoretical perspectives developed before 1980 were concerned with the description and explanation of general patterns of unequal spatial development. After 1980, perspectives have gradually shifted. Currently, more attention is being paid to the economic performance of specific regions in an economy that has become increasingly internationalized. Here, economic performance is explained on the basis of the specific characteristics of *regional* production, innovation, and coordination systems.

A second shift in emphasis is the greater importance attached to the web of the regional economy. Although in different ways, each of the four approaches discussed (industrial district approach, new industrial spaces approach, innovative milieu approach and the regional innovation system approach) pay a great deal of attention to patterns of economic or social relations (networks, interorganizational relations), which either stimulate or restrict economic processes in general and innovation in particular.

The importance of several types of knowledge for the economic functioning of regional economies is strongly emphasized in all four approaches. Knowledge is no longer seen as generic, codified, free of charge or context-independent. This is the third shift in emphasis, which we want to point out. A new broader approach to the role of knowledge is more appropriate to modern views of technological knowledge. Recognition of the role of 'tacit knowledge' and a better understanding of the interactive character of knowledge development are especially striking advances

The emphasis on interorganizational relations and the knowledge base of firms also has consequences for the way the relationship between innovation and proximity is conceptualized. All the four theoretical perspectives stress that localized networks of economic actors are important facilitators of innovation. Therefore, proximity between actors in networks is viewed as an important stimulus for innovation. Although the four perspectives all state the importance of interorganizational modes of coordination, they stress different aspects of these networks. In the NIS approach, the emphasis is on the results of vertical disintegration and the characteristics of localized economic transactions between actors in networks, whereas in 'industrial district theory' the social bonds between actors in local networks are the channels through which communication, beneficial to innovation, takes place. In the 'innovative milieu' approach and in the 'regional innovation system' approach, proximity stimulates (collective or interactive) learning processes and communication in regions and between firms.

Although the four theoretical perspectives have invigorated thinking in the study of spatial economic development, a number of reservations must be kept in mind. First, the 'new' theoretical perspectives fail to advance alternative approaches to the actor-structure problem. In the second section, it was concluded that one of the most important theoretical problems of the older 'environmental' and 'geography of the enterprise' approaches was caused by a reductionist conceptualization of the relationship between a firm and its spatial environment: both perspectives were strongly deterministic. The four 'new' approaches do not solve this problem either. Thus, in the 'New Industrial Spaces' approach the actors are reduced to passive mechanisms for economic exchange exclusively reacting to developments in their environment, basically making them 'black boxes' again. In the 'Innovative Milieu' approach, actor and structure are conflated, thus limiting its explanatory powers considerably.

Second, although innovation and knowledge are important aspects in the 'new' theoretical perspectives, in our view, their multiform nature is hardly acknowledged. In most cases, sectoral differences in technological dynamics, different technologies, and types of innovation processes and innovations and so on, are not included in the theoretical models, although empirical research has shown that these are relevant distinctions.

Third, we agree with Lagendijk (1997, p. 20) that the spatial economic sciences are characterized by a '...weak tradition in advancing its own conceptual and theoretical foundation...'. Until now, the work of the theoreticians, often subject to theoretical fashions, has failed to accumulate into a body of theory. Moreover, in our view, there is a lack of interdisciplinary awareness and consequently the benefits of using the theoretical results of other scientific disciplines are lost. Organization sciences, in particular the 'resource dependency' theory (Pfeffer and Salancik, 1978) and the 'social exchange theory' (Turner, 1974; Cook and Whitmeyer, 1992), offer useful elements which spatial scientists could use to improve their theoretical models and hypotheses considerably.[10]

So, which of these four theoretical perspectives on innovation and proximity should be advanced? In our view, the Regional Innovation System (RIS) approach is the most promising, especially because of the stimulating way the innovation-proximity issue (i.e. the actor-structure problem) is dealt with. There are several reasons for this view. Firstly, in the RIS approach, an actor is not reduced to a black box; actors are seen as learning entities. Because of heterogeneity and bounded rationality, different actors act differently in the same situation, i.e. know and learn different things, which leads to different innovations. That is to say, innovating actors, to a certain extent, have freedom of choice. Secondly, the regional innovation system is not described as a homogeneous structure. It is populated by a large variety of heterogeneous actors and institutions possessing different types of knowledge. Thirdly, interaction between the innovating actor and the regional innovation system (structure) is described as a two way process. On the one hand, learning is dependent on the communication between people and organizations that posses various types of knowledge and how this knowledge is tailored to meet the demands of the innovation process. This process is described by the concept of interactive learning. The way actors interact with the regional innovation system, and how spatial proximity affects this, is largely dependent on the way innovation processes are organized. On the other hand, the regional innovation system also influences the behavior of actors. For example, institutions, one of the elements of the innovation system, constrain or enable action by regional firms.

However, researchers should be aware of the fact that the relationships between action and structure are not the same or of equal importance to all firms. It is very well possible that a regional innovation system cannot provide all the required resources for innovation. If this is the case, innovating firms have to acquire resources from actors located further away, mitigating the overall importance of proximity for innovative activity. Even if all resources are available in the regional innovation system, bounded rationality prevents innovating actors from utilizing these resources to the full extent. Subsequently, the structural effects of individual behavior on the regional system of innovation are limited, especially if the regional production structure is made up of a large number of small and medium sized firms. Finally, the behavior of actors is only partially determined by the characteristics of the regional environment. If, for example, many regional firms compete on international markets, international socio-economic forces probably will have more influence on the behavior of firms than regional economic ones. To conclude, the Regional Innovation System approach has great theoretical potential. However, there is still a large gap between the theoretical ambition and empirical evidence, which can be related to the policy-driven nature of most RIS literature. A lot of theoretical and empirical work still has to be done. In the next paragraph, some perspectives for future research are sketched.

In general, RIS literature tends to be biased towards successful regions and strong network relations, particularly user-producer relations. Moreover, it is predominantly oriented at the resource and knowledge base perspective. In fact, RSI literature stresses the supply side of an economy, in general, and the institutions that deliver resources crucial to learning and interaction, in particular. Yet this supply architecture for innovations does not tell the whole story (Storper, 1997, p. 107). The heterogeneity of actors, inputs and outputs in modern economies implies that various kinds of innovation systems are needed to stimulate innovative *behavior*. This idea contrasts strongly with the theoretical base of the RIS approach, especially with regard to the structure-action nexus.

So, is a resource-based perspective comprehensive enough to describe and explain the processes and patterns of interaction within regional systems of innovation? Moreover, are simple distinctions, such as tacit versus codified knowledge and incremental versus radical innovations, adequate to explain spatial patterns of interaction? In our view, they are not. Future research should, therefore, focus on a more detailed definition of types of resources, and investigate their predictive value for the performance of innovation systems more thoroughly. In addition, the resource/knowledge-based perspective could be expanded to include an activity-based perspective. After all, not only the presence and the number of resources inside and outside the firm are of importance, but also the way they are utilized in the innovation process. A recent paper by Meeus, Oerlemans and Hage (1999) shows that this is a promising and productive line of research (see also Audretsch, 1998).

Furthermore, research within the RSI approach could be broadened to include a wider set of actors, going beyond user-producer relations. A regional system of innovation is composed of a large variety of heterogeneous actors. Explaining the different theoretical mechanisms behind the interactions between these actors and the innovating firm is a challenge for future research. The importance of proximity for these various actor sets remains an important aspect for study. As our own research shows (Oerlemans, Meeus and Boekema, 1999) this is not an easy task. For example, in contrast to assumptions found in RIS literature, it was found that firms with incremental innovations were more regionally embedded than firms with radical innovations. It can be seen that such a finding is greatly affected by the definition of a particular region. Consequently, this raises new questions on the relationship between spatial proximity and various types of external knowledge bases (see e.g. Caniëls and Verspagen, 1999).

By raising these research issues, we do not advocate abandoning the other theoretical perspectives discussed in this chapter. On the contrary, we wish to put forward a case for selecting useful theoretical findings from former perspectives and incorporating them within the framework of the RIS approach. In this way, the theoretical discussion on innovation and proximity can move forward in a truly cumulative manner.

Notes

1   Agglomerate advantages (or disadvantages) can be considered as a special form of external economies of scale. **External** economies of scale refer to the phenomenon that companies can profit from the division of labor between companies. If these economies occur in a geographically confined area, we call them agglomerate economies. See also: Ter Hart and Lambooy (1989, pp. 39-45) or Saxenian (1994, p. 173).

2   He calls these trends 'adaptation corporate geography' and 'regional development corporate geography,' respectively.

3   After all, large multinationals once started out as small or medium-sized enterprises.

4   Low returns on capital mean high wages, while high returns on capital can be achieved in regions with low wages.

5   Networks as 'loosely coupled systems' are here compared to the organization or enterprise that is seen as a 'strongly coupled system.'

6   Storper and Harrison (1991, p. 408) define an input-output system as 'a collection of activities which lead up to the production of a specific marketable output'. This also includes a situation in which the activities of the units in a system are involved in more than one input-output system.

7   GREMI is the acronym of Groupe de Recherche Européen sur les Milieux Innovateurs.

8   Various geographical levels are taken into account: local, regional, national, continental, and global innovation systems.

9   B-Å Lundvall (1992b, pp. 55-56) distinguishes four dimensions of space or proximity: 1) Economic space: this concerns the way in which various economic activities are positioned in the production system (input-output table); 2) Organizational space concerns the level of horizontal or vertical integration; 3) Geographical space: concerns the distance between activities at various spatial locations; 4) Cultural space: concerns, amongst other things, the context, such as norms and values, within which communication takes place.

10   In an in-depth discussion of exchange theories, J. H. Turner comes to similar conclusions as regards the development of theories. He argues that the Emerson-Cook program 'Exchange Theory and Network Analysis' contains a direct relation between 'resource dependency,' exchange theory, and network analysis.

References

Audretsch, D.B. (1998), 'Agglomeration and the Location of Innovative Activity', *Oxford Review of Economic Policy*, vol. 14, no. 2.

Aydalot, Ph. and Keeble, D. (1988), 'High Technology Industry and Innovative Environments in Europe: An Overview', In Ph. Aydalot and D. Keeble (eds), *High Technology Industry and Innovative Environments: The European Experience*, Routledge, London/New York, pp. 1-21.

Becanttini, G. (1989), 'Sectors and/or Districts: Some Remarks on the Conceptual Foundations of Industrial Economics', In E. Goodman, J. Bamford, P. Saynor (eds), *Small Firms and Industrial Districts in Italy,* Routledge, London, pp. 123-135.

Caniëls, M.C.J. and B. Verspagen (1999), 'Spatial Distance in a Technology Gap Model'. *ECIS Working Paper* 99/4, Faculty of Technology Management, Eindhoven University of Technology, Eindhoven.

Cook, K.S. and Whitmeyer, J.M. (1992), 'Two Approaches to Social Structure: Exchange Theory and Network Analysis', *Annual Review of Sociology*, vol. 18, pp. 109-127.

Florida, R. (1995), 'Toward the Learning Region', *Futures*, vol. 27, pp. 527-536.

Granovetter, M. (1985), 'Economic Action and Social Structure: The Problem of Embeddedness', *American Journal of Sociology*, vol. 91, no. 3, pp. 481-510.

Gregersen, B. and Johnson, B. (1997), 'Learning Economies, Innovation Systems and European Integration', *Regional Studies*, vol. 31, no. 5, pp. 479-490.

Hadjimichalis, C. and Papamichos, N. (1991), '"Local" Development in Southern Europe: Myths and Realities', In E. Bergman, G. Maier, F. Tödtling (eds), *Regions Reconsidered: Economic Networks, Innovation, and Local Development in Industrialized Countries,* Mansell, London/New York, pp. 141-164.

Håkansson, H. (1992), 'A Model of Industrial Networks', In B. Axelsson and G. Easton (eds), *Industrial Networks: A New View of Reality,* Routledge, London, pp. 28-34.

Håkansson, H. (1993), 'Networks as a Mechanism to Develop Resources', In P. Beije, J. Groenewegen, O. Nuys (eds), *Networking in Dutch Industries,* Garant/SISWO, Leuven/Apeldoorn, pp. 207-223.

Hart, H.W. ter and Lambooy J.G. (1989), *Urban Economic Dynamics: An Introduction in Economic Geography* (in Dutch), Muiderberg, Couthino.

Lagendijk, A. (1997), *From New Industrial Spaces to Regional Innovation Systems and Beyond. How and from Whom Should Industrial Geography Learn?* EUNIT, Discussion paper 10, CURDS, Newcastle upon Tyne.

Lambooy, J.G., Wever, E. and Atzema, O.A.L.C. (1997), *Spatial Economic Dynamics* (In Dutch), Dick Couthino, Bussum.

Lundvall, B-Å. (1992a), 'Introduction', In B-Å. Lundvall (ed.), *National Systems of Innovation: Towards a Theory of Innovation and Interactive Learning*, Pinter Publishers, London, pp. 1-19.

Lundvall, B-Å. (1992b), 'User-Producer Relationships, National Systems of Innovation and Internationalisation', In B-Å. Lundvall (ed.), *National Systems of Innovation: Towards a Theory of Innovation and Interactive Learning*, Pinter Publishers, London, pp. 45-67.

Maillat, D. (1991), 'The Innovation Process and the Role of the Milieu', In E. Bergman, G. Maier, F. Tödtling (eds), *Regions Reconsidered: Economic Networks, Innovation and Local Development in Industrialized Countries*, Mansell Publishing Limited, London/New York, pp. 103-117.

Malecki, E.J. (1991), *Technology and Economic Development: The Dynamics of Local, Regional and National Change,* Longman Group UK Ltd, Burnt Mill, Harlow, Essex.

Marshall, A. (1961) (1st edn 1890). *The Principles of Economics*. London: Macmillan.

McDermott, Ph. and Taylor, M. (1982), *Industrial Organisation and Location,* Cambridge Geographical Studies, no. 16, Cambridge University Press, Cambridge.

Meeus, M., Oerlemans, L. and Hage, J. (1999), 'Sectoral Patterns of Interactive Learning: An Empirical Exploration of a Case in a Dutch Region', *ECIS Working Paper*, 99/5, Faculty of Technology Management, Eindhoven University of Technology, Eindhoven.

Morgan, K. (1997), 'The Learning Region: Institutions, Innovation and Regional Renewal', *Regional Studies*, vol. 31, no. 5, pp. 491-503.

North, D.C. (1994), 'Economic Performance through Time', *American Economic Review*, vol. 84, no. 3, pp. 359-368.

Oerlemans, L. (1996), *The Embedded Firm: Innovation in Industrial Networks* (In Dutch), Tilburg University Press, Tilburg.

Oerlemans, L., Meeus, M. and F. Boekema (1999), 'Learning, Innovation and Proximity: an Empirical Exploration of Patterns of Learning', in: F. Boekema, K. Morgan, S. Bakkers and R. Rutten (eds), *Knowledge, Innovation and Economic Growth. The Theory and Practice of Learning Regions*, Edward Elgar, Cheltenham.

Pfeffer, J. and Salancik, G.R. (1978), *The External Control of Organization: A Resource Dependency Perspective,* Harper and Row, New York.

Piore, M.J. and Sabel, C.F. (1984), *The Second Industrial Divide: Possibilities for Prosperity,* Basic Books, New York.

Pred. A. R. (1967), *Behavior and Location; Foundations for a Geographic and Dynamic Location Theory,* Lund Studies in Geography, no. 27, Lund.

Rosenberg, N. (1994), *Exploring the Black Box; Technology, Economics, History,* Cambridge University Press, Cambridge.

Saxenian, A. (1994), *Regional Advantage; Culture and Competition in Silicon Valley and Route 128,* Harvard University Press, Cambridge Mass./London.

Scott, A.J. and Storper, M. (1992), 'Regional Development Reconsidered', In H. Ernste and V. Meier (eds), *Regional Development and Contemporary Industrial Response: Extending Flexible Specialisation,* Belhaven Press, London/New York, pp. 3-24.

Siebert, H. (1969), *Regional Economic Growth: Theory and Policy,* Scranton, PA, International Textbook Co.

Smith, K. (1995), 'Interactions in Knowledge Systems: Foundations, Policy Implications and Empirical Methods', *STI Review,* no. 16, OECD, pp. 69-102.

Storper, M. (1995), 'The Resurgence of Regional Economic, Ten Years Later: The Region as a Nexus of Untraded Interdependencies', *European Urban and Regional Studies,* vol. 2, pp. 191-221.

Storper, M. (1997), *The Regional World. Territorial Development in a Global Economy,* The Guilford Press, New York/London.

Storper, M. and Harrison, B. (1991), 'Flexibility, Hierarchy and Regional Development: The changing Structure of Industrial Production Systems and their Forms of Governance in the 1990s' *Research Policy,* vol. 20, no. 5, pp. 407-422.

Turner, J.H. (1974), *The Structure of Sociological Theory,* Dorsey Press, Homewood, Ill..

Vaessen, P. (1993), *Small Business Growth in Contrasting Environments,* Nijmeegse Geografische Cahiers, no. 40, KU Nijmegen, Faculty of Administrative Sciences, Department of Economic Geography, Nijmegen.

Weick, K.E. (1976), 'Educational Organizations as Loosely Coupled Systems', *Administrative Science Quarterly,* vol. 21, no. 1, pp. 1-19.

Williamson, O.E. (1975), *Markets and Hierarchies: Analysis and Antitrust Implications,* The Free Press, New York.

Zeitlin, J. (1992), Industrial Districts and Local Economic Regeneration: Overview and Comment', In F. Pyke and W. Sengenberger (eds), *Industrial Districts and Local Economic Regeneration,* International Institute for Labour Studies, Geneva, pp. 279-294.

3 Accessibility versus Proximity in Production Networks

ANTJE BURMEISTER

Introduction

This chapter questions the conceptualization of 'accessibility', a well known concept in transport economics and geography. It deals, in particular, with the theoretical and methodological analysis of the role of accessibility in the efficiency and the dynamics of production systems. Transportation and communication systems are, of course, crucial to the efficiency of production systems and, more generally, to regional development. On this ground, accessibility is often considered as a determinant of regional development. We will argue that accessibility, as a merely spatial concept, does not deal adequately with the spatial and organizational dynamics of production systems.

The first part of the chapter will present a survey on accessibility as a concept of transportation economics and geography. Most approaches, especially in transport economics, are explicitly, or more often implicitly, based on the neo-classical framework. Accessibility is conceptualized by the means of distance, time, cost and location on the infrastructure network. Some larger and more comprehensive approaches recognize the need to include non physical aspects into their definition of accessibility: social distance, the possibility to participate in a given activity, determined by various factors beyond physical distance. In empirical work however, when the problem becomes one of measurement and of appropriate indicators of accessibility, only the spatial dimension (or the transport cost dimension) is usually taken into consideration.

We will then analyze the limits of accessibility as a merely spatial (or space-time) concept for understanding the efficient organization of the circulation of goods, information and knowledge in contemporary production systems. In our view, the efficiency of circulation loses more and more its strong correlation with geographical accessibility. Efficient organization of transportation of goods is less and less constrained by physical distance and more and more by organizational aspects. Analyses in terms of mere transport cost are also incomplete. At the very least, it is necessary to analyze a complete cost measurement, including inventory, opportunity costs, risk and other factors. Even then, the evaluation of access seems incomplete to us, since it lacks the dimensions of flexibility, reliability, controllability of circulation, which become more and more important, especially in just-in-time production systems.

The Concept of Accessibility and the Underlying Analysis of Space

Accessibility is a well-known and easily (at least intuitively) comprehensible concept in transport economics. It can be roughly defined as the ease of spatial interaction, the potentiality of contacts with activities of supplies or as the attractiveness of a node in a network taking into account the mass of other nodes and the costs to reach those nodes via the network (Rietveld and Bruinsma, 1998). According to Izquierdo and Monzon (1992), accessibility measures the separation of activities or locations linked together by a transport system.

The concept is thus meant to describe the quality of services provided by a transport system and has commonly been used in transport and regional planning for more than 30 years. What is more, accessibility is often used as a 'miracle word' in order to explain the need for transport investment.

The Conceptual Development of Accessibility

Accessibility is, initially, a geographical concept. Geographers define the concept as the capacity to reach customers, a service, or a message. The first conceptualization going further than the mere physical measurement of distance or access was made by Hansen (1959). The concept has then progressively been introduced in transport planning and evaluation of projects in the 1960s and 1970s.

We can identify, schematically speaking, three steps of increasing complexity of the concept:

- accessibility as a topological concept: physical measurement of the properties of space or the transport system;
- accessibility as a relationship between opportunities of interaction and cost, based on the gravity model of spatial interaction;

- accessibility as the net utility of the transport system, based on the neo-classical theory of consumer behavior.

Much of transportation research has been devoted to methodological aspects of accessibility. Measurement has thus been progressively refined and become more complex. The first indicators were strictly physical: distance, expressed in kilometers, time or transport cost. The service provided by an additional infrastructure or an improvement of the transport system is measured by the reduction in travel time or transport cost (or generalized transport cost).

Other topological indicators do not refer to Euclidean space, but to network analysis. In its simplest expression, accessibility means access to a network, expressed as a binary variable: accessibility equals either 1 (connected to the network) or 0 (not connected). This type of indicator is more relevant in networks such as telecommunications, where cost is almost independent from distance. A major improvement comes from the application of graph theory, which allows the modeling of the structure of a transport network and thus provides a more realistic representation of space structured by transport infrastructure.

The problem with topological indicators, from the point of view of transport planning, is that they only describe the *supply* of transport services, while they do not take into account demand. Accessibility is always positive, i.e. an improvement of accessibility is always an improvement of the quality of the transport system.

Demand for transportation is introduced through the application of the gravity model, well known in spatial analysis: the demand for spatial interaction is derived from the distribution of factors such as population, employment, or income.

The general form of gravity-based accessibility indicators is the following:

$$A_i = \sum_j O_j \, f\,(C_{ij})$$

Where O_j : motive for travel (opportunities of destination in zone j)
  C_{ij}: measurement of the journey from i to j
  f : weighting function, expressing the 'resistance function'

The third step in the development of an 'economic' theory of accessibility was the introduction of the 'utility' concept (Koenig, 1974). Measuring the service provided by an additional infrastructure or an improvement of the transport system through reduction of travel time or transport cost is

Table 3.1 A Classification of Alternative Indicators of Accessibility

Topological Indicators

Index	Definition	Remarks	Indicator
Acc1	A node has access to a network if a link exists between the node and the network.	Access, connectivity Binary variable: 1 or 0 Ex: the city X is connected to the highway network	Connectivity
Acc2	The distance one has to travel between the node and the nearest node on the network.	Ex: the distance between the city X and the nearest point of entry of the national highway system is 17 km.	Distance
Acc3	The accessibility of a node in a network is the total number of direct connections with other nodes.	Ex: From city X one can fly to 12 destinations without changing planes.	Connectivity
Acc4	The accessibility of a node to another node is the total number of links connected to this node.	Ex: From city X, the railway lines extend in 4 directions.	Connectivity
Acc5	The accessibility of a node to another node is measured as the travel cost between these nodes.	Accessibility is considered in a strictly bilateral way without summation between destinations.	Cost

Source: based on the survey of accessibility indicators in Rietveld and Bruinsma (19T8)

Table 3.1 Continued

Economic Indicators

Index	Definition	Remarks	Indicator
Acc6	The accessibility of a node is the weighted average travel cost between the particular node and all nodes in the network.	Weights may relate to the masses of the nodes, or to the total number of trips made to the nodes.	Interaction
Acc7	The accessibility of a node in a network is the expected value of the maximum utility of a visit to any node.	Utility of a visit to a certain node is assumed to depend on - the mass of the node - the travel costs of a trip to the node - a stochastic term	Utility
Acc8	The accessibility of a node in a network is proportional to the spatial interaction between the node and all other nodes.	The spatial interaction between nodes may be directly measured or computed by means of a spatial interaction model.	Interaction
Acc9	The accessibility of a node in a network is the total number of people one can reach from the node within a certain transport cost limit.		Interaction
Acc10	The accessibility of a node is the inverse of the balancing factor in a singly or doubly constrained spatial interaction model.	Interpretation given by many authors.	Interaction

Mixed Indicator

Acc11	Accessibility is measured by means of expert judgement.	No formal definition is given. Usually a ranking of cities.	Ranking

problematic. Topological and gravity-type measures implicitly assume total transport demand to be stable over time. However, it is well known that the addition of a new element to the transport system usually induces new demand, and that improvements of the transport system do not result in decreasing, but stable or even increasing overall transport times or transport costs.

The economic measurement of accessibility is *net utility*, the difference between the utility of the attracting motive (jobs or services, for example), and the global transport cost (the resisting element). This formulation supposes, of course, to introduce a utility function into the calculation scheme.

Although the formulation of utility is quite basic, it introduced a revolution in transport planning, dominated until then by the physical measurements of the engineering sciences. However, as shown in Table 3.1, most indicators developed for transport planning studies or even econometric models rely on the more basic formulations of accessibility.

The main conclusion that we can draw from this comparison of accessibility indicators in use in economic modeling as well as in project evaluation is that the theoretical background is hardly ever questioned, and that developments relate mainly to technical aspects of measurements. Accessibility is evaluated differently according to the subject (access to workplaces, access to services etc.), to the type of flows (goods or people) and to the spatial scale (local, urban, regional, national, European). Important developments have been made in the field of graph theory and spatial imagery. However, the framework of evaluation remains either a-theoretical (in the case of topological measures) or based implicitly on the neo-classical analysis in economics.

The Concept of Space: Space = Transport Cost

We will now examine the different types of accessibility measures as to their theoretical background, and particularly their conceptualization of *space* (Table 3.2). We can distinguish between indicators without an explicit economic theory and those that do refer to a form of economic theory, be it very basic.

The topological indicators of accessibility refer to the discipline of regional planning in geography. Their content belongs to the field of physical geography, in the sense that they do not have an explicit social or economic content. The (implicit or explicit) objective of these analyses is spatial equity. Accessibility indicators measure the differentiation of physical space created by the transport system.

Table 3.2 The Conceptual Development of Accessibility

Type	Measurement	Theoretical background
Topological indicators:		Topology of the transport network:
	-Distance -Time -Transport cost	➤Euclidean space
	Connectivity	➤Graph theory
Economic indicators:		
	Spatial interaction (attraction function / impedance function)	➤Gravity model
	Utility function (net utility: gross utility of nodes - transport cost)	➤Neo-classical theory of consumer behavior

The absence of an explicit economic theory in these formulations does not mean that they do not convey any conceptualization of space and its role in the economy. On the contrary, the use of such indicators in economic analyses of spatial organization or in evaluation studies of specific infrastructures confers them an implicit theoretical content. The spatial dimension of economic systems is derived either from Euclidean space, distorted by geographical constraints, or from network representations, and defined exclusively by transport costs. Space, in this view, is simply a constraint in economic interactions.

In all these indicators, space is considered as a 'friction' in interactions between economic agents, introducing some form of distance, cost or a negative utility. The intensity of this friction (or transport cost) is usually considered as proportional to distance (or connectivity). The gravity type indicators introduce weighting of accessibility by the interest attached to a specific location. The utility type indicators further develop this model of spatial interaction by integrating the friction of space into the optimization calculation of economic agents, not as distance in itself (or connectivity), but as the (negative) utility of distance.

We can thus conclude that what is commonly called the 'economic' theory of accessibility combines two major features of neo-classical economic theory: the theory of homogenous space and the theory of consumer behavior (marginal utility). Space is an exogenous resource, homogeneous and thus neutral to economic trajectories. Referring to Perroux's distinction between geonomic and economic space, this conceptualization does not take into account the space constructed by the interactions between economic actors.

The orthodox analysis of space integrates space either as a variable in a partial equilibrium analysis or as an exogenous parameter. Space can be considered as a good, for which a market exists. The cost of distance (usually transport cost, but eventually also transaction cost) can be integrated in optimization behavior of economic agents.

The implicit conceptual representation behind most models refers to the standard neo-classical framework of production. In this framework, the improvement of technologies meant to overcome space in interacting (i.e., transportation and telecommunication techniques) will lead to the abolition of spatial friction. This is based on two essential assumptions:

- production is a combination of generic production factors, exclusively procured through market transactions;
- space is a reservoir of generic resources that can be transferred (or are accessible) at a certain cost.

There are no analyses in the field of transport economics which refer to theoretical frameworks other than neo-classical economic theory. Theoretical developments on the theory of production and in regional science, which develop alternative assumptions, have been totally ignored in transport economics up to now. The evolutionist theories of production and innovation, for instance, adopt an approach in terms of resource creation (as opposed to resource allocation). Production is here based on specific resources created through organizational learning. The paradigm of neutral space, on the other hand, has been contested by a long tradition of heterodox research from industrial districts and growth poles to local systems of innovation (milieu) and production and, more recently, the concept of proximity related to organizational learning and innovation (Bellet et al., 1993). These analyses consider mere cost distance as a poor translation of the role of space in industrial dynamics. The focus is here on the role of space in the co-ordination of production.

On the whole, however, the relevance of the traditional conceptualization of accessibility is hardly ever questioned. Similarly, the coherence of such concepts with the assumptions of the neo-classical framework is taken as a given, even in a field such as transportation, where the basic assumptions such as constant returns to scale are not verified (Gramlich, 1994). This theoretical framework has important consequences, especially in the field of transportation, where concepts translate into public policies quite directly.

The Decreasing Relevance of Accessibility in the Spatial Organization of Production Networks

The fading of the correlation between geography and accessibility is nowadays widely recognized in the literature: geography is less and less a determinant for accessibility. In a spatial vision of the concept of proximity, one could even consider that accessibility replaces physical proximity in a world where transport cost is falling and immaterial interactions are growing fast.

However, we will attempt to show that accessibility, in its strictly spatial sense, is less and less a determinant of the efficiency of the circulation of goods, people and information. The organization of transportation is less and less constrained by spatial distance and more and more by organizational aspects. Connectivity, in the sense of being or not connected to an infrastructure network, is also insufficient for understanding the spatial organization of production. We will illustrate this thesis by three arguments: the absence of correlation between accessibility and regional development, firstly, and between accessibility and the possibility to implement Just-in-time production systems, secondly, and finally the specific problem of accessibility in the case of immaterial interactions.

The Relationship between Accessibility and Regional Development

In the field of regional science, there is abundant research work using the concept of accessibility as a determinant of regional growth. Authors such as Biehl (1986), Vickerman et al. (1995) and Spiekerman and Wegener (1996) conclude that the level of regional development in European regions appears to be clearly correlated to the different levels of accessibility.

However, the limitations of this concept are easy to demonstrate, since the direction of the causal relationship remains ambiguous here: infrastructure endowment can be interpreted as well as a cause as a consequence of regional development.

Moreover, the *dynamics* of regional development and their relationship to infrastructure investment remain impossible to explain. Vickerman et al. (1995), for instance, demonstrate that, whereas *levels* of GDP and *levels* of accessibility are usually correlated, *variations* in regional GDP over time cannot be clearly correlated to variations of accessibility. Their conclusions throw serious doubts on the theoretical foundations of policies using transport investments as a tool for regional development. What is more, the automatic nature of infrastructure effects in some of these theories leads to a dangerous vision of infrastructure investment as a universal tool of regional development strategies, as well as of European policies towards economic cohesion.

Thus, it appears to be problematic to establish a clear causal relationship between transportation and the performance of production systems within the traditional conceptual framework of transportation analysis. Access to generic resources does no longer appear as a determinant of regional development.

Just-in-time Production Systems and Accessibility

It is widely admitted that the expansion of just-in-time (JIT) production systems is related to the increasing overall performance of goods transportation (among others, falling transport costs). It is impossible, however, to deduce a direct relationship between the performance of such production systems and accessibility. Whereas a sufficient overall level of accessibility is necessary for JIT production to function efficiently, the explanation of the efficiency of organization of flows of goods lies elsewhere: in the organization of flows much more than in the spatial properties of transportation systems.

In order to explore the relationship between the diffusion of JIT production and deliveries and accessibility in terms of goods transportation, we use data from a survey of 110 production plants located in the Nord-Pas-de-Calais region, belonging to five industries (food, textile and clothing, chemicals, metalworking and machinery).

In our data base, JIT is defined from the point of view of what can be observed in the plant. We distinguish between JIT procurement (no input inventories: inputs are delivered to the plant according to the needs of the production process), JIT delivery (no output inventory: outputs are shipped as soon as they leave the transformation process), and total JIT (no inventories at all: inputs arrive at, and outputs leave, the plant synchronously to the production process). This definition, however, does not include the question of whether inventories are held elsewhere (the supplier, or the distributor). A cross-tabulation with the level of accessibility of the location of each plant gives the in Table 3.3.

The striking feature here is that there is no correlation[1] between JIT implementation and the level of accessibility. Among the plants that implement JIT at least partly, almost 40 percent have a level of accessibility less than

Table 3.3 Accessibility and Implementation of JIT

Accessibility: \ JIT:	Total JIT	Incomplete JIT	Inventories	**Total**
excellent	0	6	4	**10**
good	4	29	26	**59**
medium	4	14	13	**31**
weak	0	7	3	**10**
Total	**8**	**56**	**46**	**110**

Levels of accessibility (for goods transportation):
excellent: location on a node of several infrastructures
good :   location close to a major infrastructure
      (immediate access to a highway)
medium :   less than 40 km to a highway
weak :   more than 40 km to a highway
      (accessible only by small roads)

'good'. The plants that implement total JIT production and delivery are equally distributed among good and medium accessibility (not one of them has an 'excellent' accessibility).

One plausible explanation is the fact that the region of Nord-Pas-de-Calais, as many European regions have, on the whole, a good endowment in high-speed infrastructure such as highways and high-speed railways, as well as a central position in Europe (although peripheral in France). Thus, even a 'weak' accessibility here is still sufficient. Nevertheless, this analysis shows that location on the infrastructure network is not the main determinant for JIT implementation. The availability of infrastructure does, obviously, not constitute a bottleneck for high-speed deliveries and procurement.

Another, perhaps even more important explanation lies in the extreme quantitative and qualitative flexibility of goods transportation by road. The intense price competition in the trucking industry makes low-cost transportation available for a variety of products.

Many industry studies lead to similar conclusions. Industries such as the automobile industry, textile and clothing or the food producing sector illustrate the transformations in the organization of production and circulation and the relative weakening of the spatial constraint.

The textile industry, for instance, is undergoing a fundamental change towards the 'quick response' production system and short circuits of production, where the circulation of inputs and outputs induces higher standards of timeliness and reliability for transportation. Moreover, the trend towards almost real-time adjustment of production series to retail sales data necessitates appropriate communication systems between subcontractors and the principal. Our study of garment subcontracting demonstrates that the main obstacle for implementing quick response systems functioning over long distance does not lie in the insufficient performance of transport and communication systems, but in organizational difficulties of co-ordinating different production systems.

In the food industry, the larger geographic scale of procurement and distribution systems that goes together with the trend towards specialization of production plants on the European level is not only related geographical accessibility and the quasi-ubiquity and quality of infrastructure, but also includes many complex organizational aspects, such as the development of electronic data interchange (EDI) and real-time transmission of sales and production data between production plants in the food industry and firms of the distribution channels.

These industry cases clearly demonstrate that the transformations of production methods come with very different spatial forms, where accessibility in the spatial sense plays only a minor role.

The Problem of Accessibility in the Case of Immaterial Flows

Accessibility becomes, in the case of immaterial flows, a problem of being or not being connected to the telecommunication infrastructure network (or to certain types of high-performance networks), a binary variable, since spatial distance does no longer have a significant influence on the cost of transmission of information.

The increase of immaterial flows in production systems and the development of telecommunication technologies and their impacts on spatial patterns of development and the spatial organization of firms have been analyzed in a considerable amount of literature. The simplistic idea of the vanishing friction of space in the future leads to a vision of a virtual world, where immaterial interactions will replace material transportation. This utopia of ubiquity and virtuality relies on the neo-classical vision of space as a friction in the model of equilibrium and competition.

In this analysis, telecommunication and transportation are considered as intermediate resources for production. Technological developments in both fields improve accessibility and lower the cost of overcoming distance in production activities. New technologies of communication create positive network externalities and thus have positive impacts on economic development (Capello and Nijkamp, 1996). This type of approach can, however, be criticized as a model of technological determinism, the development of new technologies of transport and communication changing the spatial patterns and the behavior of firms in space (Capello and Gillespie, 1994).

Alternative approaches focus on the co-ordination of production systems and the media that support this co-ordination between actors. Transport and telecommunication are considered as alternative means of co-ordination between the members of the network (Brousseau and Rallet, 1997). The technological developments in both fields are instrumental to, but not the causes of, new organizations of production and new forms of spatial division of labor (Moati and Mouhoud, 1992).

Rallet (1997) considers telecommunication and face-to-face contacts as complementary means for the co-ordination of production. According to this thesis, more intensive use of telecommunication will not replace traveling for face-to-face interactions. The need for proximity will never disappear completely, because certain types of interactions cannot take place without spatial proximity.

The mere accessibility of information, which is, in the extreme vision of a virtual society, almost independent from spatial constraints, is not relevant explanation of the spatial dynamics of knowledge creation and diffusion. It puts aside the cognitive dimension, which is classically analyzed through the distinction between information and knowledge (Machlup, 1983) and between tacit and codified knowledge (Nelson and Winter, 1982; Polanyi, 1958).

Neo-classical economics generally adopts a more restrictive definition of knowledge: technology, for instance, is considered as a sum of information (private and public). Sociologists, on the opposite, consider knowledge as a social, collective phenomenon. The conservation, reproduction and transfer of knowledge are viewed as collective phenomena.

Heterodox analyses in economics analyze knowledge in a sense closer to the second definition. In the tradition of the evolutionist and institutionalist economics of innovation, the diffusion of innovation is modeled as a learning process, thus not comparable to a process of transmission of information, but of knowledge and know-how, which necessitate close interactions between individuals.

The cognitive distinction between information and knowledge leads to the assumption that only information can be exchanged in a market and travel in space independently. Knowledge, on the other hand, can only be partly standardized and codified. Tacit knowledge is embedded in people and thus cannot travel in space independently from people. Its transmission requires interactions between people.

The 'accessibility' of knowledge is thus not a mere problem of spatial accessibility, but an issue of creation of specialized resources through collective learning processes, which require organizational proximity.

Towards an Organizational Definition

We can summarize the main criticisms that we have addressed for the concept of accessibility in two points:

* the conceptualization of space as homogenous and neutral is far too poor to be able to describe properly the contemporary spatial dynamics of industrial development;
* the spatial differentiation measured by accessibility indicators is too weak to explain the role of transport systems. Fifty or one hundred years ago, accessibility was probably a good proxy of the spatial role of transport systems, whereas now, quasi-ubiquity of quality infrastructure leads to a decreasing differentiation of space in terms of accessibility.

The lack of a conceptualization of the organizational dimensions of transportation is an important limitation of economic theory of space, as well as of evaluation methods for transport infrastructure and systems. We will finally present some perspectives for the integration of the organizational dimension.

Access to Generic Resources or Creation of Specific Resources

Traditional location analysis refers only to generic resources and assets, which can be transferred in space. Space is viewed as a reservoir of generic resources, and territories are supposed to be differentiated only by their endowment in production factors such as differentiation of wage rates and the availability of skilled labor. The problem of transportation is thus one of access to generic resources at a minimum transport cost; in other words, accessibility measures access to generic resources.

In the alternative framework of regional economics, regional development trajectories are related to specific resources, which cannot be transferred and which are constructed by the actors of a territory in a path-dependent, cumulative process. Such an approach can draw on the heterodox approaches in regional science of socially constructed space, as well as on the Swedish network approach of innovation. The creation of products uses specific resources, such as knowledge, which can be tacit and non standardized and embedded in actors, organizations and collective learning processes.

Storper (1995) develops the idea of the '*region as a nexus of untraded interdependencies*'. These interdependencies are not transferable on a market and generate region-specific assets in production. According to this author, these assets are the central form of scarcity in contemporary capitalism, and not the availability of generic resources, as it is assumed in most location analyses.

Colletis and Pecqueur (1993) develop a similar approach by making the assumption that the main factor of differentiation of space does not lie in relative prices of production factors nor in transport costs, but in the supply of specific assets and resources, which do not compete directly on the market. They make a distinction between assets and resources: resources are potential production factors, whereas assets are production factors that are in use in a production process. A second distinction is made between generic and specific resources and assets. Generic production factors exist independently from their participation in a production process and can thus be transferred from one production to another. Specific assets are related to a specific production process and cannot be transferred to another without sunk costs. Specific resources are virtual and can thus not be transferred. These specific resources are critical factors in the process of technology creation.

These alternative analyses of regional development can be translated into the following assumptions:

- the development of production systems is mainly related to the path dependent process of creation of specific resources;
- transport infrastructure is, in most cases, a generic resource which can be used in different production processes.

The conjunction of these two assumptions would imply that industrial development is less and less directly related to the endowment in terms of generic infrastructure. Accessibility, as a merely spatial concept, measures only the access to generic resources, but is unable to take into account the construction of specific resources and the organizational dimension of geographical proximity in production systems.

Accessibility and the Concept of Proximity

Heterodox analyses focus on geographical proximity in order to explain alternative modes of production such as industrial districts, innovative milieux and various forms of localized production systems. Analyses of JIT systems such as Toyota city focus on the geographical concentration of subcontractors and suppliers around the assembly plant in order to explain the efficiency of the system. Spatial proximity is analyzed as improving horizontal circulation of information and reducing the costs associated to the high frequency of delivery of parts.

GEOGRAPHICAL PROXIMITY

Spatial dimensions
spatial propinquity
accessibility

Non spatial dimensions
organizational proximity
institutional proximity

Figure 3.1 Dimensions of Proximity

A deeper analysis, however, has to recognize the non spatial content of the concept of proximity. Proximity in production systems has organizational, institutional and cultural aspects (Figure 3.1) (Bellet et al., 1993). Although the two aspects are linked, we can analytically oppose spatial proximity, on the one side, and organizational and institutional proximity, on the other. Accessibility, in its strictly spatial sense, belongs to the first dimension. In its institutional dimension, proximity results in an institutional framework for interactions: shared representations, rules and norms, cognitive frameworks as well as formal institutions that stabilize the context of interactions (Kirat, in Bellet et al., 1993).

'CIRCULATORY' PROXIMITY

Spatial dimensions
accessibility
(distance, cost, time, speed ...)

Non spatial dimensions
reliability
flexibility
degree of control
adaptation to production rhythms
information flows
...

Figure 3.2 Dimensions of 'Circulatory' Proximity

Organizational proximity is a pre-condition as well as a result of networks of producers, since it can be defined as the capacity of putting together information and knowledge from different sources and organizations. Organizational proximity between the actors of a production network is as well a relation of *similarity* (actors who have similar organizations, who share similar knowledge and representation) and a relation of *membership* (actors who belong to the same organization and who interact build up a relation of organizational proximity).

The question then is whether, and how, the spatial notion of accessibility can be completed by a concept of proximity in the organization of flows of goods and information. Efficient circulation of goods and information requires, above mere accessibility, some form of organizational proximity between the firms.

Organizational Aspects of Accessibility: Strategies for Efficient Transportation

Efficient circulation of goods and information depends on the capacity to control flows, on their adaptation to production rhythms and constraints, on their reliability and flexibility, as well as on the efficiency of the associated flows of information (Figure 3.2).

The strategies used by producers to achieve organizational proximity in circulation of goods and information cover a variety of means. Among these strategies, accessibility is hardly ever a determinant or a strategic means. Only a few cases of very recent plants obey the logic of optimal location on the infrastructure network (location on a node). Accessibility is usually satisfying, and sufficient time accessibility is guaranteed even with locations that are, from the theoretical standpoint, far from optimal.

With regard to our industry survey, we can identify two major strategies in the field of circulation of inputs and outputs in production systems: the search for flexibility and the management of associated flows of information.

The search for flexibility in transportation and logistics As a matter of fact, strategies directed towards flexibility of production systems rely at least as much on the flexibility of transportation and logistics than on flexible production in the strict sense. The principal strategy used by producers is the total contracting out of generic goods transportation. This strategy relies on the extreme flexibility of goods transportation by road. Generic transportation services are available at very low cost, since the structure of the transport sector is atomistic and characterized by strong, partly even destructive, competition. The majority of firms in this sector are composed of only one driver, highly dependent in a hierarchical structure of subcontracting from first-tier large transportation or logistic firms. Price competition is fierce, partly due to deregulation on the European level.

Externalization of transport operations is thus the dominant mode of organization in most industries. The need for internalized, dedicated transport services applies only to a specific segment of the manufacturing firms (highly fragmented dispatching of goods that present specific constraints, totally non standardized, or impossible to standardize, shipments).

As for the organization of logistics in general (management of inventories, operation of warehouses, management of distribution systems, final packaging), the level of externalization is less advanced. In the food sector, however, there appears to be a trend towards externalization, especially in those firms that sell mainly to the large-scale distributors.

Logistics operations are more and more often contracted out to a logistic integrator, who is able to achieve high productivity of circulation of goods and information through the mix of products and destinations. This strategy is characteristic of the producers that combine the industrial type of transformation with a more flexible mode of circulation. The contracting out of logistics allows to achieve a level of reactivity and flexibility impossible to attain in the traditional industrial mode of production.

The case where transportation and logistics appear to be strategic for the competitiveness of firms is interesting to understand the minor role of accessibility. More and more producers use the flexibility of transport services in order to render their large-scale industrial production flexible and adapted to differentiated demand conditions. Flexibility is here achieved, first, through the total contracting out of transportation, either to a large number of small firms on a spot market basis in order to pressure prices down, or to a single contractor, who is generally highly dependent because of dedicated assets and market pressure. Contractual arrangements, instead of location strategies, appear as a major means of establishing control and flexibility of circulation.

Reliability of goods transportation and associated flows of information The reliability of goods transportation and its adaptation to production rhythms and constraints implies more and more the association of flows of goods and flows of information. One of the main strategies is based on standardization of the exchange of information, which takes the form of electronic data interchange (EDI) systems between manufacturers and distributors. The standardization of information flows, together with the progress in information technologies, allow circulation to take place in an extended geographical scale.

The implementation of EDI in the co-ordination of production and transport operations is not simply a technical issue. EDI requires organizational proximity and standardization of flows. It can be defined as the standardized transmission of information directly between computers of different organizations. The automation of data transmission makes the complete codification of information and transmission procedures necessary *ex ante*. Moreover, EDI is a non flexible co-ordination technique. In such, it appears to be more appropriate for situations of risk than for situations of radical uncertainty, where mutual adjustment and idiosyncratic interactions are vital.

Being a non flexible co-ordination technique, which requires investments in codification and standardization, EDI tends to be implemented bilaterally more often than multilaterally. Industries where intra-industry relations are more important than inter-industry relations tend to use EDI more often. The same goes for industries that do not have mainly international relations. The codification appears to be easier to implement on a national and an industry basis.

Brousseau (1994) shows that EDI cannot simply be considered as an alternative means of communication, compared to telephone, fax and e-mail. EDI does not replace other media in the co-ordination of production. It transforms co-ordination and the organization of production itself. The advantage of EDI for firms is not as much cost reduction or improved efficiency of electronic communication, but the necessary standardization of co-ordination procedures ex ante, which has many impacts on the overall performance of the firms beside cost reduction in communication.

According to our industry survey, about 30 per cent of plants use EDI with one or several partners. In the food and chemicals industries the use of EDI is above the average. In all industries, the use of EDI appears to be related either to the fact of selling to the automobile industry or the large-scale distribution chains, who impose their communication standards, or to the existence of one major customer, supplier or logistics provider, with whom the plant works on a long-term basis. The major determinant is thus not access to networks or technologies, but the adaptation of organization.

Conclusion

In this chapter, we have examined the traditional view of transport economics, as expressed in the concept of accessibility. Accessibility appears to be severely limited as a tool for analyzing the efficiency of circulation of goods and information in production systems. Conditions for efficient transportation go beyond time accessibility, which appears to be generally satisfactory. Circulatory strategies of firms mainly focus on achieving a high degree of reliability and control over a differentiated range of flows. In other words, 'proximity' in circulation of goods and information appears to be more of an organizational than a geographical nature.

We do not argue here that transport costs and the role of transport infrastructure in the differentiation of space and the spatial organization of production systems disappear completely. Their role remains strong in certain industries and subsectors. The error prevailing in transport economics is, in our view, to focus exclusively on this vision and to neglect a different role of transportation and space, prevalent in most of the more dynamic sectors of the economy.

Finally, we will have to address the question of possible integration of the organizational dimension into the concept of accessibility and, if possible, into comprehensive indicators. Two positions can be adopted in this respect: first, we can enlarge the concept of accessibility in order to include more organizational dimensions. On the opposite, the 'spatial' and the 'organizational' vision of accessibility can imply two antagonist theories of the role of space in economic interactions and thus remain incompatible.

Note

1   The results for the χ^2 test lead to the conclusion that the assumption of independence between the two distributions cannot be rejected: $\chi^2 = 4.354$; df = 6 ; p=0.629

References

Bellet, M., Colletis, G., Lung, Y. (eds), (1993), 'Economie de proximités',*Revue d'Economie Régionale et Urbaine*, no.3.

Bellet, M., Kirat, T. and Largeron, C. (eds) (1998), *Approches multiformes de la proximité*, Hermès, Paris.

Biehl, D. et al (1986), *The contribution of infrastructure to regional development*. Final Report, Brussels: European Commission.

Brousseau, E. (1994), 'EDI and inter-firm relationships: toward a standardization of coordination processes?' *Information Economics and Policy,* vol. 6, pp. 319-347.

Brousseau, E. and Rallet A. (1997), 'Le rôle des technologies de l'information et de la communication dans les changements organizationnels', In B. Guilhon, P. Huard, M. Orillard, and J. B. Zimmermann (eds), *Economie de la connaissance et organizations*, Paris, L'Harmattan, pp. 286-309.

Capello, R. and Nijkamp, P. (1996), 'Telecommunications technologies and regional development: theoretical considerations and empirical evidence' *Annals of Regional Science*, vol. 30, no. 1, pp. 7-30.

Capello, R. and Gillespie, A. (1994), 'Communication infrastructure and possible future spatial scenarios', In Cuardrado-roura, J.R., Nijkamp, P., Salva, P., *Moving Frontiers: Economic Restructuring, Regional Development and Emerging Networks,*: Avebury, Aldershot, chapter 10, pp. 167-191.

Colletis, G. and Pécqueur, B. (1993), 'Intégration des espaces et quasi-intégration des firmes: vers de nouvelles rencontres productives', *Revue d'Economie Régionale et Urbaine*, no. 3, pp. 489-508.

Gramlich, E.M. (1994), 'Infrastructure investment: a review essay' *Journal of Economic Literature*, vol. 32, pp. 1176-1196.

Hansen, W.G. (1959), 'How accessibility shapes land-use', *Journal of the American Institute of Planners*, vol. 25, pp. 73-76.

Izquierdo and Monzon (1992), *Infrastructure capacity and network accessibility*, Paper presented at the 12th International Symposium of the ECMT, Lisbon, May.

Koenig, G. (1974), 'Théorie de l'accessibilité urbaine', *Revue Economique* no. 2, pp. 275-297.

Machlup, F. (1983) 'Semantic Quirks in the Study of Information' In F. Machlup and U. Mansfield (eds) *The Study of Information*, John Wiley, New York.

Moati, P. and Mouhoud, E. M. (1992), *Les transports et les télécommunications dans l'arbitrage entre modes d'organization de la production*. PREDIT Research Report, Decembre, Paris.

Nelson, R. and Winter S. (1982), *An Evolutionary Theory of Economic Change*, Belknap Press, Cambridge.

Polanyi, M. (1958), *Personal Knowledge. Towards a Post-critical Philosophy.*, Routledge and Kegan, London.

Rallet, A. (1997), *L'impact des technologies de l'information et de la communication sur la coordination spatiale des activités de recherche et d'innovation*. Paper presented at the 33rd Congress of the French speaking section of RSA (ASRDLF), Lille, September 1-3, 15 pp.

Rietveld, P. and Bruinsma, F. (1998), *Is Transport Infrastructure Effective? (Transport Infrastructure and Accessibility: Impacts on the Space Economy)*, Springer, Heidelberg.

Spiekermann, K. and Wegener, M. (1996), 'Trans-European Networks and Unequal Accessibility in Europe', *EUREG*, vol. 4, pp. 35-42.

Storper, M. (1995) The resurgence of regional economies, ten years later: the region as a nexus of untraded interdependencies, *European Urban and Regional Studies*, vol. 2, no. 3.

Vickerman, R., Spiekermann, K. and Wegener, M. (1995) 'Accessibility and economic development in Europe', Paper presented at the ESF/EC Euroconference European Transport and Communication Networks: Policies on European Networks, Espinho, Portugal, April.

4 Industrial Districts and Social Capital

ROD B. McNAUGHTON

Introduction

The industrial districts literature evokes an image of dense local relationships between numerous small firms, usually specialising in different stages of a production process (e.g., Becattini, 1989 or Harrison, 1994). A similar image is evoked by descriptions of groups of related firms in 'clusters' (Porter, 1990), and by the external image and internal representation of an industrial 'milieu' (Camagni, 1991). At the core of these concepts is the argument that firms co-locate to take advantage of external economies. These advantages are supposed to be realized through a complex balance of co-operation and competition in flexible networks of socially embedded production relationships. Proximity and the shared history, culture and frequent face-to-face interchanges that it brings about, facilitate these networks (Dei Ottati, 1994, p. 530). Co-location is also thought to enhance flows of technical and market information, contributing to both innovation, and the diffusion of skills and competencies.

The embeddedness of economic exchange in dense local networks is often identified as a defining characteristic of districts (Staber, 1998, p. 702). However, embeddedness is idiosyncratic to place and time, contributing to variability in the organization of industrial districts. The theory of industrial districts is indeterminant in the sense that embeddness is portrayed as a cause of both inertia and change. Moreover, while the industrial districts literature generally '...conjures up images of order and cohesiveness', relationships within districts can be chaotic, and are often characterized by conflict and disintegration (Staber, 1998, p. 702). By examining twenty-four industrial districts in Italy over 40 years, Paniccia (1998) recently illustrated the diversity of district organisation processes and outcomes, as well as the apparently conflicting rules that can govern inter-firm relationships.

The theoretical indeterminancy of industrial district theory can be traced to a similar problem in economic sociology. The understanding of social embeddedness in the industrial districts literature is strongly influenced by the work of Granovetter (1985), and other economic and structural sociologists who have built on this seminal foundation (e.g. Zukin and DiMaggio, 1990). The empirical literature in Economic Sociology provides considerable evidence of the often-contradictory ways in which the behavior of agents in economic exchange is influenced by embeddedness (For examples, see the reviews of this literature in Uzzi, 1997, and in Portes and Sensenbrenner, 1993). However, a well-defined theory of embeddedness has yet to emerge. As Uzzi (1997, p. 35) points out: 'The fundamental statement that economic action is embedded in ongoing social ties that at times facilitate and at times derail exchange suffers from theoretical indefiniteness.' Thus, the under-developed state of embeddedness theory contributes to the indeterminancy of industrial district theory.

It is clear that the result of embeddedness is contingent, and this presents particular difficulties for local policy-makers who, having observed the success of some industrial districts, seek to stimulate similar districts in their own region. The result is a variety of publicly supported programs in several countries and regions that build industry associations, broker networks of small firms, and promote industrial clusters. However, these programs have largely been established without an explicit model of when and how embeddedness leads to improved economic performance, or of why public intervention might be required and how public welfare benefits might accrue (McNaughton and Bell, 1999).

Some industrial district researchers have started to explore alternative interorganizational theories that may help to explain the contingent outcomes of embeddedness. Staber (1998), for example, argues that neo-institutional and ecological perspectives can be combined to illuminate the relationship between district size and change. This chapter contributes to the exploration of interorganizational theory for insight into the functioning of industrial districts by examining the ways in which social capital theory enhances understanding of the outcomes of embeddedness. It also provides a theoretical structure that enhances understanding of policy initiatives aimed at promoting the emergence and success of networks and local clusters of firms.

What is Social Capital?

Social capital is the resources, tangible or not, that are available through a set of social relationships, and facilitate the attainment of goals (Bourdieu and Wacquant, 1992, p. 119). Thus, social capital refers not solely to a network of social relationships but also to the assets (and liabilities) embedded in, and available through, a network (Leenders, 1999, p. 2). Social capital contributes to the formation of obligations, expectations, trust, and sanctions, all of which assist economic exchange by mitigating contracting costs (Routledge and von Amsberg, 1996, p. 1).

The contemporary literature on social capital theory is closely identified with the work of Bourdieu and Passerson (1990), Coleman (1988), and Putnam (1993). However, the antecedents are numerous, extending back nearly a century, and to disciplines as diverse as education, anthropology, sociology, economics, business, and law. The history of influences in this literature is described in detail by Woolcock (1998, pp. 159-167), and by Wall, Ferrazzi, and Schryer (1998). Wall et al also illustrate the growing use of the term in academic literature by counting articles listed in various bibliographic databases in which the term appears for the period up to 1995. They note that usage of the term 'social capital' has several distinct variants, and that this pluralism, along with widespread and indistinct usage in the popular media, has hindered the emergence of a unified theory. Portes and Landolt (1996) further argue that the term has been 'stretched' by this extensive use, and is often inappropriately applied by:

- casting it as a ptoperty of groups rather than individuals,
- confusing social structure with the benefits facilitated by that structure,
- and focussing on the positive aspects of social participation without acknowledging potential negative effects.

The writings of Bourdieu, Coleman and Putnam all share some commonalties of understanding about the nature of social capital. In particular, that social capital facilitates the use of resources, is goal oriented and exerts a form of control through norms and standards (Wall et al, 1998, pp. 312-313). Within this broad understanding, however, each author differs in his emphasis. Further, they disagree on both the social unit at which social capital is seen to operate, and the way in which social capital should be measured. One reason for this is that the problems addressed by these authors are quite different. For example, Coleman was concerned about the way in which social capital enhances returns to education, while Putnam used the concept to explain regional differences in the political and economic performance of Italian regions. Bourdieu emphasized the importance of 'field' both in his definition of social capital and method of measurement. That is, that the appropriate type and measure of social capital is dependent on the endeavour being studied (e.g., the economic performance of firms versus the educational achievement of individuals).

The context of industrial districts places the emphasis very much on the social capital of corporations and of the private and public organisations that support them. Leenders (1999, p. 3) recently outlined the nature of social capital between firms, and defined corporate social capital as 'The set of resources, tangible or virtual, that accrue to a corporate player through the player's social relationships, facilitating the attainment of goals.' This definition is similar to Bourdieu and Wacquant's definition quoted above, and makes a distinction between social structure (a 'player's' social relationships) and the outcomes of social structure, allowing for the possibility of both social assets and social liabilities. Thus, this definition is precise and avoids the second and third inappropriate applications of the term identified by Portes and Landolt. With regard to the appropriate unit of analysis, Leenders (1999, pp. 5-10) argues that the full influence of social capital is only realized by examining multiple levels of analysis, including the individual, department, and organisation. This view of social capital encourages exploration of the interaction between personal and organisational networks, and the resulting pattern of opportunities and constraints.

Social capital is distinct from other forms of capital in that it is intangible, and not easily transferred. It is also distinguished by its ability to enhance the productivity of other forms of capital. Thus, investment in social capital is a complement, rather than a substitute, for investments in physical, human or technological capital. Social capital is created when relationships are formed, and it appreciates through use in repeated interactions. Since relationships are affected by each transaction, social capital can quickly appreciate or depreciate. Further, when an entrepreneur makes use of social capital to facilitate an exchange, a debt is incurred in the form of expected reciprocity. Most importantly, social capital exists as the goodwill between individuals and firms. It is idiosyncratic and not easily transferred. Therefore, individual ownership cannot appropriate its benefits. The result is that individual entrepreneurs and firms have little incentive to invest in social capital as it is essentially a public good (Coleman, 1990). Some authors such as Chirinko (1990) argue that social capital influences the relative bargaining strength between altruistic and egoistic tendencies in decision-making, and can lead to the private provision of public goods. However, Routlege and von Amsberg (1996) demonstrate that social capital can be modelled using only reference to self-interest, consistent with the assumption of most economic theory.

Social Capital and the Contingent Effect of Embeddedness

The image of the spatial organization of economic activity evoked by social capital theory is very similar to that conjured by the industrial district literature. For example, Walker, Kogut, and Shan (1997, p. 11) visualise inter-organizational social capital as a series of shaded 'patches' of localized relationships that vary in density (Walker, Kogut, and Shan, 1997, p. 111). Firms in a dark patch are embedded in a region with dense relationships and the potential for externalities from the formation of social assets. Social assets are essential for the emergence of production systems based on either flexible specialisation or extensive subcontracting (Nanetti, 1988).

The external economies that drive flexible or subcontract based production systems are facilitated by 'co-operative cultural norms widely diffused in the local population', and 'local governments and sectoral associations emphasising the servicing of the local production units' (Leonardi, 1996, p. 170). This enables the collective allocation of both production and input services for the benefit of firms within the district, creating a locally specific economy of scale. Thus, social capital is a key to the emergence of an industrial district. Without it, firms must internalize economies and individually meet the costs of operating in a particular region or sector. There are, of course, any number of circumstances where the ability to generate revenues exceeds these costs, explaining the empirical reality that many successful firms are located outside of districts.

Vatne (1995, pp. 66-70) provides a model that nicely summarizes the relationship between external/internal economies and firm performance in the specific context of growth through internationalisation. This model sees internationalisation as an entrepreneurial process that is embedded in a network of social and institutional relationships. These relationships can be used to gain knowledge, and seek out new partnerships that help the firm to grow and expand into foreign markets. For the network to be useful in this way, however, it must be rich in appropriate resources. If a firm is located in a region that is critically short of an important factor, or populated by non-dynamic firms that are weak in terms of their own internationalisation, local networking will not in itself overcome these limitations. However, in some industries there is little need for local support, and some small firms have specialized internal resources that make them almost independent of their local environment. These firms can grow and internationalize through internal economies, even when those firms around them are not similarly successful. Firms that cannot generate sufficient economies either internally or externally are unlikely to internationalize. The implication for understanding the effect of embeddedness on firm performance in general is clear: embeddedness can only enhance performance when it enables access to appropriate resources. This is evident in the definition of social capital, which includes not only social structure, but the resources that can be mobilized within that structure.

The ability to access appropriate resources explains the operational value of embeddedness to the firm. Embeddedness also has an intrinsic value expressed through the quality of relationship norms. These norms are not always positive from a broader societal perspective. Rubio (1997), for example, discusses the case of youth in Columbia whose relationships with family and friends can positively support a decision to engage in criminal activity - a form of 'perverse' social capital. For a firm, the analogous situation is participation in a network that reinforces poor or unethical business practices. (See Scott's, 1998, p. 10 discussion of the Los Angeles jewellery industry for an example.) Thus, the effect of embeddedness is also contingent on the quality of the norms that guide the social structure.

The issue of norms is closely related to the 'purposefulness' of the embedded relationships, or the ability to strategically direct the network of relationships. This issue has not been widely addressed at the level of industrial districts, but the literature on inter-firm networks reveals that systems of network relationships involving co-ordination and a clear strategic intent are relatively rare (Benson-Rea and Wilson, 1994, pp. 25-27; Field, Goldfinch and Perry, 1994). Even in regions such as Silicon Valley, where networking has made an acknowledged contribution to economic growth, the lack of 'administrative co-ordination' can make the network vulnerable to environmental changes over time (Saxenian, 1990, p. 105). In fact, the primary examples where embedded exchange exhibits strong co-ordination and strategic direction are in networks formed around a large focal firm, and often involve subcontracting relationships.

Lack of strategic direction and administrative co-ordination potentially impacts the stock of social capital and its usefulness in levering the productivity of other forms of capital (Bennett, 1997a, p. 332). As a response, institutions are often created in business communities to both foster and direct social capital (See Bennett's 1997a, 1997b, 1998a, 1988a, 1988b, 1988, 1999 stream of research for a discussion and examples of the potential for voluntary business associations to increase 'institutional thickness'). Examples include industry and trade associations, federations, commissions, Chambers of Commerce and the like. These associations are hierarchical inter-organisational systems (Alexander, 1992, p. 194). Formal associations, and their governance structure of positions, committees, and task forces, help to foster and appreciate social capital by mitigating transaction costs, and articulating common goals. This is analogous to the mechanisms used to harness social capital within the hierarchical structure of large organisations (e.g., Lipnack and Stamps, 1994).

Market forces do not organize densely embedded exchanges; rather they are structured by patterns of trust and opportunity. When the transaction costs of informal relations and spontaneous adjustment to environmental changes are low, a 'feudal' form of inter-organisational governance characterized by limited interaction between firms, and bilateral information co-ordination is often sufficient. Chisholm (1988) refers to this as 'co-ordination without hierarchy'. However, in an industrial district where networked firms constitute a value chain or flexible production system, the relationships between them are more frequent, complex, and interdependent. They may also require more idiosyncratic investments, which increases transaction costs. The result is a need for inter-organisational hierarchical governance and co-ordinative planning to '...design strategies for deploying the relevant organisational resources ensuring the commitment of each to its assigned role in the common undertaking. This can involve sanctions, monitoring and control (Alexander, 1992, p. 195).' The effects of embeddedness are thus contingent on the ability to co-ordinate firms and administer the network within a district toward a common purpose.

A final consideration is that embeddedness yields both social assets and social liabilities (Leenders, 1999, pp. 3-5). The bulk of the extant literature focuses on the positive side of social capital - social assets. However, a number of potential liabilities have also been identified. (For examples, see the discussion by Portes and Landolt, 1996.) The first liability is that strong ties can be used to exclude outsiders. In some cases this might constitute a barrier to start-up or in-migrating firms by preventing access to an important resource controlled by a network. A second problem is that membership in a network brings demands for conformity that may limit creativity and stifle entrepreneurial behaviour. Third, existing relationships may limit the extent to which firms have the time or inclination to search further afield to acquire resources. Thus, they may fail to identify important new suppliers and customers, or to import new technologies. Finally, reliance on dense local ties may limit growth. Informal local networks are limited in size as transaction costs within networks increase sharply as members are added and more resources must be devoted to measurement and enforcement (North, 1991, p. 99). Firms that rely solely on locally embedded exchange may fail to develop the contacts and skills necessary to move into larger more sophisticated markets co-ordinated by formal institutions and the rule of law (Woolcock, 1998, p. 163).

The fact that embeddedness produces both social assets and social liabilities suggests that the development of an industrial district may depend on the net of these two effects. In particular, the extent to which assets can be maximized and liabilities minimized. This can be thought of as the 'social profit' of embeddedness. The inclusion of relatively heterogeneous participants within a district and the maintenance of a portfolio of both embedded and autonomous relationships can mitigate the social liability of embeddedness. White, Gorton and Chaston (1996, pp. 38-40), for example, argue that successful networks bring together heterogeneous skills, allowing embedded firms to fill gaps in competencies and learn skills required for long-term development. Heterogeneity also lends itself toward an informal system of checks and balances that help to ensure accountability and integrity within relationships. However, depending on the source of the heterogeneity, it could also inhibit the formation of trust and lead to unhealthy conflict.

Autonomous relationships are links to organizations outside of the local network. These serve as a benchmark of norms and practices in other communities, and as a conduit for importing new information. Autonomous relationships cost more to monitor but should also be more valuable as they yield non-redundant information. Ideally, social capital reduces the cost of maintaining existing embedded relationships so that more resources can be put into establishing new (initially) autonomous ones (Walker, Kogut and Shan, 1997, pp. 111). Thus, both stability and dynamism are affected by the balance between embedded and autonomous ties formed by firms in a district.

Public Facilitation of Social Capital

The widely documented success of some industrial districts such as the Prato district in Tuscany, the Herning-Ikast area in Denmark, Baden-Wurttemberg in Germany (Grotz and Braun, 1993), and Silicon Valley (Saxenian, 1990, 1992) and Route 128 (Todtling, 1994) in the United States has attracted the attention of policy-makers. The success of these districts led many policy-makers to surmise that the key to facilitating district development is investment in 'thickening' the embeddedness of local firms. The result is a proliferation of programs to facilitate network formation.

Network brokering programs are generally based on a model developed by the Danish Technological Institute which advocates the external facilitation of networks by trained brokers who identify prospective networks and guide their formation. Brokers are usually independent management consultants who receive special training for the program. The Danish program has been adopted and adapted by a number of countries including Norway, Finland, several US states and Canadian provinces, Brazil, Australia, New Zealand, Portugal, Spain and Britain. In most of these countries a multi-pronged strategy is used in which co-operation between firms is first promoted through soft networks of trade associations, then specific networks are brokered, and finally strategic clusters of co-located firms are identified. In New Zealand, for example, these initiatives are called joint action groups, hard business networks, and cluster musters.

The basic assumption of these programs is that firms tend to under-invest in co-operative relationships. This assumption is confirmed by a number of studies. For example, Curran, Jarvis, Blackburn and Black (1993) found that small firms shunned 'voluntary relationships', and made little use of networking even to overcome problems that threatened the survival of the firm. Curran et al. suggest this is because of the independent attitude of entrepreneurs, coupled with the time constraints created by having to deal with many day-to-day management problems. In addition, the entrepreneurs studied were sometimes fearful of outside interference, loss of control, and the potential for local competitors to gain inside knowledge. In another example, Human and Provan (1997) compared firms in two relatively large networks with a control sample of 'market firms', and found that market firms made only minimal use of inter-firm relationships. Managers explained this in terms of limited time, no perceived need, and fear of losing proprietary information.

A belief among many managers (and indeed policy-makers) that networks are anti-competitive or collusive also impedes the formation of deeply embedded production relationships (Harper, 1993; Benson-Rea and Wilson, 1994). This view is fostered by emphasis on the benefits of competition in moves toward deregulation, and enforcement of anti-competition laws. In most cases, networks are not anti-competitive, but do require a change in business culture, from being competitive as individual firms, to being competitive collectively (Martinusson, 1994). Finally, Fukuyama (1995) suggests that cultural differences are also an influence, as high trust societies tend to view competition collectively and have an advantage in the formation of social capital.

The same considerations that inhibit network formation also mitigate the development of mechanisms for co-ordination within networks. Namely, the benefits of co-ordination are difficult for an individual firm to appropriate, and to collectively achieve benefits, firms must give up some autonomy and call on uncommon managerial skills (i.e., managing between firms rather than within them). This is particularly difficult for small firms with few slack resources, and owner/managers that have limited experience outside their own firm.

A few authors have used game theory, in particular the prisoner's dilemma, to explain this failure of the market for relationships (e.g., Jarillo, 1988; White, Gorton and Chaston, 1996). However, sound theoretical reasoning for public funding of network brokers, or the welfare benefits of brokering programs is generally absent from the extant literature and public discussion of brokering programs. In this regard, policy implementation is ahead of a clear understanding of how embeddedness can enhance (or hinder) economic performance.

The stress placed by some authors on the public good nature of social capital offers additional insight into the tendency to under-invest in relationships, and the potential role of public intervention. For example, Coleman (1993a, 1993b) clearly identifies social capital as a community resource that is of benefit to all members of a closed network, and constitutes a by-product of activities not specifically designed for its production. As a result it is under-produced. He recommends the restoration of primordial organisations within society to encourage a richer stock of social capital.

Olson's (1965, pp. 22-36) classic analysis of collective action in small groups sheds light on the conditions under which investments in a communal resource like social capital will occur. He argues that in some small groups at least one member will find that personal gain exceeds the total cost of providing some amount of a collective good. Thus, this member is better off providing the good even if they have to meet the entire cost. Olson concludes that the provision of common goods is most likely in smaller groups with members of unequal size (or extent of interest in the public good). This is because where an individual participant is likely to gain a disproportionate advantage from the common good, they are more likely to invest in that good. However, because self-interest and the potential for free riding limit investment, it is unlikely that an optimal amount of the good will be produced. Olson's argument is a particularly good explanation for the social capital of districts built on subcontracting relationships, where the formation, governance and strategic direction of the district falls disproportionately on a large focal firm.

While he does not describe them in detail, Olson (1965, p. 35) also refers to 'certain institutional or procedural arrangements' that may stimulate investment in common goods. Public sector initiatives are a likely example. Certainly the failure of the market for social capital suggests that there may be a role for public intervention as sub-optimal levels of social capital have broader social welfare implications in terms of reduced productivity, innovation, employment, et cetera. However, public investment in social capital formation is problematic as:

- the nature and extent of social relationships varies between sectors;
- the tasks performed by social relationships change as exchange becomes more sophisticated; and
- either a paucity or a surfeit of social capital at a particular institutional level can impede economic development (Woolcock, 1998, p. 167).

An implication of these problems is that an economic development policy based on the facilitation of social capital must help firms to overcome both the static dilemma of collective action, and the dynamic one that results from organisational change when successful collective action begins to influence social relationships. To accomplish this, policies must achieve a complex dynamic between 'top-down' and 'bottom-up' incentives to the formation of social capital (Woolcock, 1998, p. 180).

Woolcock (1998, pp. 167-182) provides a framework of the different levels, dimensions, and combinations of social capital that succinctly illustrates the necessary dynamic. This model articulates the interplay between embeddedness and autonomy at both the micro- and macro-levels. At the micro-level it distinguishes between high and low states of both 'integration' (embeddedness) and autonomy, and at the macro-level between high and low states of 'synergy' (state-society relations) and 'organisational integrity' (institutional coherence, competence and capacity). Thus, with two states for two dimensions at both micro- and macro-levels, there are sixteen outcomes that characterize the possible dynamics of social capital. The case where levels are low across all four dimensions characterizes the extreme situation of 'anarchic individualism' where there is no trust, self-interest guides all economic and social exchange, and individual actors are all isolates. A business community with these characteristics would be bereft of social capital. The other extreme, having high levels across all dimensions, is termed 'beneficent autonomy'. This ideal community would have a large endowment of social capital, forged at both the macro-and micro-levels by integrated and purposeful actors that are accountable through their connections both within and between diverse groups. The development of industrial districts, both organic and planned, can be analysed within this framework. Bottom-up development proceeds from the development of local ties, to the inclusion of extra-community relations, to the development of organisations that assist in more complex institutionalized types of exchange. Top-down development starts with the provision of institutional structures, and fostering state-society relations that hopefully promote both greater integration, and shared connections between diverse groups at the micro-level. Either too much or two little integration at either the macro- or micro-levels can impede development, and the balance between top-down and bottom-up must constantly shift for development to be sustained. In effect, there are four types of social capital, the presence or absence of which, and their interaction with each other, influences economic outcomes.

Conclusions

This chapter began by identifying a dilemma in our understanding of industrial districts: embeddedness, a central characteristic of districts, can lead to very different economic outcomes. Emeddedness is credited as an agent of both inertia and change. The diversity of ways in which emeddedness can influence economic behaviour is now widely documented in empirical studies of districts (Harrison, 1994). However, industrial district theory is indeterminant in the sense that it does not currently explain the contingent effect of embeddedness. Identification of the conditions and processes that lead to one outcome or another are an emerging issue in the study of districts, and researchers are exploring various inter-organisational theories in a search for insight (e.g., Staber, 1998). I contribute to this search by reviewing the theory of social capital, and discussing how the concept can be used to analyse both the contingent effect of embeddedness, and public policies designed to influence economic development by fostering embeddedness.

Social capital theory hinges on a metaphor that maps the commonly understood concept of economic capital onto the social domain. In doing so it provides a language for describing and communicating many of the consequences of the local embeddedness of firms. This language is familiar to both policy-makers and the owners/managers of the small firms they seek to assist. Woolcock (1998, p. 188) similarly argues that the common language of social capital unites the various academic disciplines that independently address socio-political issues of development. The attractiveness of the social capital metaphor has led to its wide usage, and those who adopt it to explore industrial districts will need to carefully articulate the particular theoretical stream that underpins their use of the term.

I adopt a definition of social capital in the corporate domain suggested by Leenders (1999). This definition emphasizes that social capital is not only the structure of a network of social relationships, but that it also includes those resources available through that structure, and the outcomes in terms of assets or liabilities. This definition, and the implications that flow from it, suggests that the influence of embeddedness on the development of industrial districts is contingent on at least five things:

- the extent to which appropriate resources are available through local relationships;
- the quality of the norms that govern the embedded relationships;
- the strategic governance and direction of the embedded relationships;
- the balance of social assets and liabilities created through embeddedness;
- the heterogeneity of participants, and their portfolio of embedded and autonomous ties.

The nature of social capital as a public good, as emphasized by Coleman (1993a, 1993b) and others, highlights that the concept is also useful for analysing the potential of public programs to influence the development of industrial districts by facilitating embeddedness. A variety of programs have been implemented in a number of countries. In general, they seek to stimulate economic development by brokering networks of firms, and increasing their 'institutional thickness'. A theory that clearly articulates the rationale for public intervention in the market for inter-firm relationships, and the potential welfare outcomes of such intervention, is lacking in the extant literature. Such a rationale can logically be developed from social capital theory, and is also enhanced by the theory of collective action (e.g., Olson, 1965). Woolcock (1998) offers a compelling argument and a well-developed framework within which top-down and bottom-up social capital based programs can be designed and evaluated.

An important next step is to apply social capital theory directly to interpret empirical observations about the contingent outcomes of embeddedness in industrial districts. A large collection of existing data about the apparent contradictory outcomes of embeddedness might be meaningfully re-interpreted in this way. Similarly, social capital theory (and in particular Woolcock's policy framework) might be used to evaluate the myriad of programs that attempt to influence embeddedness. (Interestingly, few of these programs have had a formal evaluation of their outcomes. See McNaughton and Bell, 1999, pp.

72-74 for a related discussion.) Future research may also collect data in industrial districts specifically to test hypotheses generated from social capital theory.

References

Alexander, E. R. (1992), 'A Transaction Cost Theory of Planning', *Journal of the American Planning Association*, vol. 58, no. 2, pp. 190-200.

Becattini, G. (1989), 'Sectors and/or Districts: Some Remarks on the Conceptual Foundations of Industrial Economics', In E. Goodman and J. Bamford (eds), *Small Firms and Industrial Districts in Italy*, Routledge, London, pp. 123-135.

Bennett, R. J. (1997a), 'Administrative Systems and Economic Spaces', *Regional Studies*, vol. 31, pp. 323-336.

Bennett, R. J. (1997b), 'The Relations Between Government and Business Associations in Britain: An Evaluation of Recent Developments', *Policy Studies*, vol. 18, pp. 5-33.

Bennett, R. J. (1998a), 'Explaining the Membership of Voluntary Local Business Associations: The Example of British Chambers of Commerce', *Regional Studies*, vol. 32, pp. 503-514.

Bennett, R. J. (1998b), 'Business Associations and Their Potential to Contribute to Economic Development: Re-exploring an Interface Between the State and Market', *Environment and Planning A*, vol. 30, pp. 1367-1387.

Bennett, R. J (1998c), 'Business Associations and Their Potential Contribution to SMEs Competitiveness', *Entrepreneurship and Regional Development*, vol. 10, pp. 243-260.

Bennett, R. J. (1999), 'Explaining the Membership of Sectoral Business Associations', *Environment and Planning A*, vol. 31, pp. 877-898.

Benson-Rea, M. and Wilson, H. I. M. (1994), *Networks in New Zealand*, Final Report to the Ministry of Commerce, University of Auckland, Auckland.

Bourdieu, P. and Passeron, L. (1990), *Reproduction in Education, Society and Culture*, Sage, London.

Bourdieu, P. and Wacquant, L. (1992), *Invitation to Reflexive Sociology*, University of Chicago Press, Chicago.

Camagni, R. (1991), *Innovation Networks*, Belhaven Press, London.

Chirinko, R. S. (1990), 'Altruism, Egoism, and the Role of Social Capital in the Private Provision of Public Goods', *Economics and Politics*, vol. 2, pp. 275-290.

Chisholm, D. (1988), *Coordination Without Hierarchy: Informal Structures in Multiorganisational Systems*, University of California Press, Berkeley.

Coleman, J. S. (1988), 'Social Capital in the Creation of Human Capital', *American Journal of Sociology*, vol. 94, pp. 95-120.

Coleman, J. S. (1990), *Foundations of Social Theory*, The Belknap Press of Harvard University, Cambridge.

Coleman, J. S. (1993a), 'The Decision of Organisations and the Right to Act', *Sociological Forum*, vol. 8, pp. 527-546.

Coleman, J. S. (1993b), 'The Rational Reconstruction of Society', *American Sociological Review*, vol. 58, pp. 1-15.

Curran, J., Jarvis, R., Blackburn, R. and Black, S. (1993), 'Networks and Small Firms: Constructs Methodological Strategies and Some Findings', *International Journal of Small Business*, vol. 11, no. 2, pp. 13-25.

Dei Ottati, G. (1994), 'Trust, Interlinking Transactions and Credit in the Industrial District', *Cambridge Journal of Economics*, vol. 18, pp. 529-546.

Field, A., Goldfinch, S. and Perry, M. (1994), *Promoting Small Business Networking: An Agency Comparison*, Research Report # 2, Social Research and Development, Christchurch.

Fukuyama, F. (1995), 'Social Capital and the Global Economy', *Foreign Affairs*, vol. 74, no. 5, pp. 89-103.

Granovetter, M. (1985) 'Economic Action and Social Structure: The Problem of Embeddedness', *American Journal of Sociology*, vol. 91, pp. 481-510.

Grotz, R. and Braun, B. (1993), 'Networks, Milieux and Individual Firm Strategies: Empirical Evidence of an Innovative SME Environment', *Geografiska Annaler B*, vol. 75, no. 3, pp. 149-162.

Harper, D. (1993), *An Analysis of Interfirm Networks*, Report prepared for the New Zealand Ministry of Commerce, Contract No. 584, New Zealand Institute of Economic Research.

Harrison, B. (1994), *Lean and Mean, The Changing Landscape of Coroporate Power in the Age of Flexibility*, Basic Books, New York.

Human, S. E., and Provan, K. G. (1997), 'An Emergent Theory of Structure and Outcomes in Small-Firm Strategic Manufacturing Networks', *Academy of Management Journal*, vol. 40, no. 2, pp. 368-403.

Jarillo, J. C. (1988), 'On Strategic Networks', *Strategic Management Journal*, vol. 9, pp. 31-41.

Leenders, R. Th. A .J. (1999), 'CSC: The Structure of Advantage and Disadvantage', In Leenders, R.Th. A. J. and Gabbay, S. M. (eds) Corporate Social Capital and Liability, Kluwer Academic Publishers, Boston, pp.1-14.

Leonardi, R. (1996), 'Regional Development in Italy: Social Capital and the Mezzogiorno', *Oxford Review of Economic Policy*, vol. 11, no. 2, pp. 165-179.

Lipnack, J. and Stamps, J. (1994), *The Age of the Network: Organizing Principles for the 21ˢᵗ Century*, Omneo/Oliver Wright Publications, Essex Junction, Vermont.

Martinusson, J. (1994), 'More then an End in Itself, The Export Network as a Stepping Stone', *Firm Connections*, May/June.

McNaughton, R. B. and Bell, J. (1999), 'Brokering Networks of Small Firms to Generate Social Capital for Growth and Internationalistion', *Research in Global Strategic Management*, vol. 7, pp. 63-82.

Nanetti, R. Y. (1988), *Growth and Territorial Policies: The Italian Model of Social Capitalism*, Pinter Publishers, London.

North, D. C. (1991), 'Institutions', *Journal of Economic Perspectives*, vol. 5, no. 1, pp. 97-112.

Olson, M. (1965), *The Logic of Collective Action: Public Goods and the Theory of Groups*, Harvard University Press, Cambridge.

Paniccia, I. (1998), 'One, a Hundred, Thousands of Industrial Districts. Organizational Variety in Local Networks of Small and Medium-sized Enterprises', *Organization Studies*, vol. 19, no. 4, pp. 667-699.

Porter, M. E. (1990), *The Competitive Advantage of Nations*, MacMillan Press, London.

Portes, A. and Landolt, P. (1996), 'The Downside of Social Capital', *The American Prospect*, vol. 26, pp. 18-21, 94.

Portes, A. and Sensenbrenner, J. (1993), 'Embeddedness and Immigration: Notes on the Social Determinants of Economic Action', *American Journal of Sociology*, vol. 98, no. 6, pp. 1320-1350.

Putnam, R. D. (1993), *Making Democracy Work,* Princeton University Press, Princeton.

Routledge, B. R. and Von Amsberg, J. (1996), *Endogenous Social Capital*, mimeograph.

Rubio, M. (1997), 'Perverse Social Capital – Some Evidence from Columbia', *Journal of Economic Issues*, vol. 31, no. 3, pp. 805-816.

Saxenian, A. (1990), 'Regional Networks and the Resurgence of Silicon Valley', *California Management Review*, vol. 33, no. 1, pp. 89-112.

Saxenian, A. (1992), 'The Origins and Dynamics of Production Networks in Silicon Valley', *Research Policy*, vol. 20, pp. 423-437.

Scott, A. J. (1998), *Regions and the World Economy: The Coming Shape of Global Production, Competition and Political Order*, Oxford University Press, Oxford.

Staber, U. (1998), 'Inter-firm Co-operation and Competition in Industrial Districts', *Organization Studies*, vol. 19, no. 4, pp. 701-724.

Todtling, F. (1994), 'Regional Networks of High-Technology Firms – The Case of the Greater Boston Region', *Technovation*, vol. 14, no. 5, pp. 323-343.

Uzzi, B. (1997), 'Social Structure and Competition in Interfirm Networks: The Paradox of Embeddedness', *Administrative Science Quarterly*, vol. 42, pp. 35-67.

Vatne, E. (1995), 'Local Resource Mobilization and Internationalization Strategies in Small and Medium Sized Enterprises', *Environment and Planning A*, vol. 27, pp. 63-80.

Walker, G., Kogut, B. and Shan, W. (1997), 'Social Capital, Structural Holes and the Formation of an Industry Network', *Organization Science*, vol. 8, no. 2, pp. 109-125.

Wall, E., Ferrazzi, G. and Schryer, F. (1998), 'Getting the Goods on Social Capital', *Rural Sociology*, vol. 63, no. 2, pp. 300-322.

White, J. E., Gorton, M. J. and Chaston, I. (1996), 'Facilitating Co-operative Networks of High-Technology Small Firms: Problems and Strategies', *Small Business and Enterprise Development*, vol. 3, pp. 34-47.

Woolcock, M. (1998), 'Social Capital and Economic Development: Toward a Theoretical Synthesis and Policy Framework', *Theory and Society*, vol. 27, pp. 151-208.

Zukin, S. and DiMaggio, P. (1990), *Structures of Capital: The Social Organization of the Economy*, Cambridge University Press, New York.

5 Industrial Districts: Measuring Local Linkages

BOYOUNG LEE, LIN LIU and HOWARD A. STAFFORD

Introduction: Agglomeration and Industrial Districts

Important developments have occurred in industrial location theory and in regional economic development policy. A cumulative causation with regional advantage model has gained ascendancy over the classical least-cost equilibrium development model, and regional or local economic environments are accorded great significance. A fundamental theoretical notion is that agglomeration economies (external economies of scale) and competitive advantages accrue to firms through co-location. Agglomeration is thought to be more important than ever before in determining an area's economic fortunes.

In addition to the lower costs via transportation or transactions costs and shared public goods, competitive advantage adds economic dynamics as a result of continual innovation and transfers of new knowledge within clusters of firms (Doeringer and Terkla, 1995). Competitive advantage is argued to be based on collaboration among specialized firms (Piore and Sable, 1984), and the interaction of competition with innovation (Porter, 1990), and the agglomeration economies of clusters of large firms with local suppliers (Krugman, 1991). These are not new ideas in industrial location. Wheat, for example, discusses agglomeration;

> agglomeration is the term for the tendency of industry to attract industry. The term has been applied to the clustering of industry in the Manufacturing Belt. However, it can be applied to any state with a large metropolitan area where industry is clustered. Such clustering could result from intermediate markets and external economies. Firms are said to congregate in order to buy from, and sell to, each other. At the same time this clustering leads to skilled labor pools, business services, transport facilities, and other economies external to the firm. These external economies attract still more industry. (Wheat, 1973, p. 207)

This direct and compact paragraph is useful. It highlights what in this chapter are referred to as vertical, or supply chain, linkages ('firms...congregate in order to buy from, and sell to, each other') and horizontal linkages ('skilled labor pools, business services, transport facilities...'). It also indicates that the concept must operate within a specified spatial context (e.g., 'state with a large metropolitan area where industry is clustered'). These are the basic elements of the 'industrial district' conception. The mention of 'metropolitan area' seems to suggest that not only is manufacturing primarily an urban activity, but also that the metropolitan geographic scale may be somehow important (among other things, this chapter examines horizontal and vertical linkages at the metropolitan scale). There is another significant issue connected with Wheat's discussion of agglomeration. In his 'Synthesis and Conclusions' chapter, he discusses locational influences, in order: markets, climate, labor, thresholds, and other influences. Agglomeration is in the 'other influences' section. Wheat wrote almost thirty years ago; a similar chapter today might move 'agglomeration' up to center stage, perhaps as an 'industrial district' topic.

An 'industrial district' is an area with a group of economic activities connected by functional linkages and spatial proximity. The 'industrial cluster' model focuses on supply chain (input-output) linkages, producer services linkages, informational linkages and labor force linkages between producers. The 'industrial district' model adds spatial proximity to the industrial clusters conception. Factories located in an 'industrial district' presumably are able to enjoy the localization and urbanization advantages of co-location. Thus, an 'industrial district' is (a) a relatively small region, (b) with above average horizontal and vertical links with other economic activities in the region. However, the industrial district concept has no significance if the spatial clustering is not greater than normal ('more than expected', or 'above average'). In other words, to be designated an 'industrial district' the area should have significant groupings of activities that have especially strong ties with the local area. The concept is clear, but how are especially strong real-world industrial linkages to be recognized, at what spatial scales, and what are their characteristics?

Linkages, Networks, and Local-ness

The more a region can be both a supply and a market area, the stronger and more attractive it is. These supply chain linkages are central to regional development theory. They still are the most important linkage elements in regional development models. As important as production linkages are, expertise and information sharing also are important to economic success. Social, institutional and labor force linkages are critical in the rapid communication of industrial expertise, and in enriching the contents. The importance of informational agglomeration has long been recognized (e.g., Chinitz, 1960), but it now has a much more important role in economic growth models (Rees and Stafford, 1986). For example, Saxenian (1994) persuasively argues that the current differences in economic health between Silicon Valley and its once more mighty rival area, Route 128 in Boston, are in large part a consequence of differences in regional industrial cultures in the previous decade. Silicon Valley's competitive edge seemed to be in a network of firms that constantly interacted, both formally and informally, economically and socially, with much trading of employees, in an information rich environment which encouraged experimentation. In contrast, the Route 128 electronics firms were much more self-sufficient and did not produce the same levels of creative tension in their region. Informational agglomeration was superior in the modern Silicon Valley industrial district.

Modern information and communication technologies permit the development of flexible production systems. Flexible production is an important adjunct to the logic of industrial districts (e.g., Scott, 1988). To the

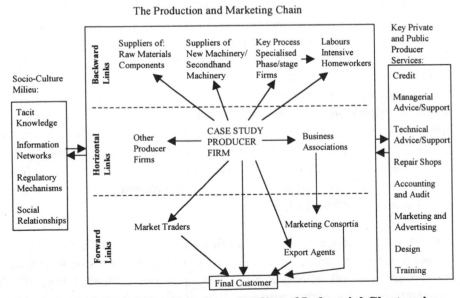

Figure 5.1 Relational/Network Case Studies of Industrial Clusters in LDCs

extent that producers are able to move from mass production to more customized operations--to temper economies of scale with economies of scope--they are better able to cope with market volatility. Another aspect is increasing outsourcing of functions from companies to suppliers, and closer ties between producers and suppliers. Superior communication and transportation capabilities also allow the development of Just-In-Time production systems. All these developments enhance the advantages of spatial proximity. It is now contended that regional economic development favors areas with strong large firms, long-standing industrial cultures, and service-rich environments, which together create a positive 'spatial symbiosis' effect (Capello, and Nijkamp, 1997). In other words, in spite of the potentials of advances in communications to help overcome the friction of distance and enable rapid and almost cost-less transmission of data, modern technologies seem to be favoring spatial agglomeration, at least at the regional scale. Production systems in the information age increasingly rely on knowledgeable individuals, who in turn maintain their competitive edge via intense, and often informal professional and social contacts. Face-to-face contact is important, and it happens at the local level (Malecki et al., 1995).

Figures 5.1 and 5.2 illustrate the arguments. No firm (or manufacturing plant) operates in isolation. All have interchanges up and down the production and marketing (supply) chain, and horizontally with producer services and with their socio-cultural milieu (Figure 5.1). In addition, there must be a spatial context, since the agglomeration arguments require spatial boundaries. Figure 5.2 puts the concept in terms of local and nonlocal space. This research examines interchanges in terms of their degree of *local-ness*. *Local-ness* should be a measure of the consequences of the efficiency of agglomeration, or of the supply or opportunity for local acquisition of the commodity or service or information. For example, the use of printing services would be expected to have a higher *local-ness index* than a highly specialized and infrequently used manufacturing input. Labor would be expected to have a high local-ness index when the region is defined as the metropolitan area, but a lower index if the spatial context is intra-urban neighborhoods.

Of course, each company, industry, and region may be expected to exhibit some uniqueness. For example, not all firms can benefit equally from Just-In-Time production systems; while they work well in the automobile industry, they do not serve oil refiners at all (Laulajainen and Stafford, 1995). 'Each manufacturing industry depends on a different mix of economic resources and costs for its success. What makes a community an ideal place for chicken processing is different from the resources required for the production of plastic

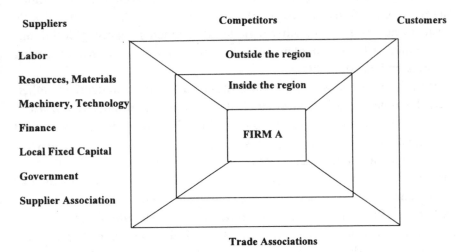

Suppliers   Competitors   Customers

Labor

Resources, Materials

Machinery, Technology

Finance

Local Fixed Capital

Government

Supplier Association

Outside the region

Inside the region

FIRM A

Trade Associations

Figure 5.2 Firm Mapping Onto Local and Nonlocal Space

Source: Markusen, 1994

feedstocks, plastic end-use products, automobiles, or computer chips' (Hill, 1998). Different regions with different industrial specializations presumably benefit differently from local linkages and networking. This research uses empirical data from a long-established and reputedly well-rounded region, which may give some benchmarks for a 'normal' region.

The Identification Problem: Degree of Local-ness?

For some observers 'clusters' are simply plants of similar type or size that have some relatively close spatial arrangement. For example, Sweeney and Feser note that they 'are not interested in whether businesses cluster, per se; this can be verified by viewing any map of economic activity' (1998, p. 50). They are defining clustering only in terms of spatial proximity. Not captured are the horizontal or vertical linkage aspects; these cannot be verified just by map viewing. Another frequent use of the term cluster focuses on industries of the same and/or closely related types; here the operational definition is by prior classification rather than either functional interactions or spatial proximity. Even when the industrial district concept includes space, there is no consensus on how large the space should be; in different studies it ranges from city sub-areas to multiple countries. Finally, in the majority of studies there is emphasis on the supply chain linkages but too little attention is given to the horizontal linkages (Held, 1996). In regional development practice there is little consistency among states or other regional governments regarding definitions or operational criteria or implementation of procedures to enhance clustering (Doeringer and Terkla, 1995).

Research rarely focuses on the **identification** of industrial districts; rather, almost all studies examine **assumed** clusters and **assumed** industrial districts. Research on the 'medical devices industry cluster' in the Minneapolis-St. Paul region illustrates the normal approach; both the cluster and the region were **predefined** (Maki and Maki, 1994). The abundant research literature on industrial districts consistently uses the concept to explain the outstanding or unusual economic performance of such predefined regions.

Sforzi's (1989) Italian study is a rarity. He does **not** assume a pre-determined industrial district. He attempts to **find** industrial districts (while everyone else works the other way around). We follow his lead by not assuming an industrial district (but we do not use his methodology). Also, most of the literature has no empirical content. In those studies which look at real places, almost always a fast growth and specialized place is selected for examination before the industrial district concept is applied. The place is then named some sort of industrial district, which presumably explains the already documented unusual performance of the place. The implication is that the growth is explained by the 'specialized industrial district' characteristics of the place, but this is analytically unacceptable. The definition must be separated from the explanation. Gertler neatly expresses the difficulty:

> How do we recognize a true industrial district when we see one? How big or small, in terms of area extent, can these be? What proportion of transactions involving producers within such districts need be wholly contained within the same area? And what kinds of social relations between producers in the area in question qualify as being representative of the unique behaviour believed to take place in such districts? Here there is no real consensus (1992, p. 263).

This research develops methodologies to answer these questions. The application of the procedures can provide empirical benchmarks to judge 'unique' or above average. The common procedures are partially reversed. The industrial districts are **not pre-defined**. Nor is the metropolitan area examined especially noted for recent unusual economic performance. Measuring the magnitudes of vertical and horizontal linkages in a seemingly 'normal' regional economy begins to develop benchmarks that may be used in any area. The empirical application is in accord with Harrison's observation that there is not much readily available data, so there is little alternative to 'scholars rolling up their sleeves and going out and conducting original surveys...[on] how firms located at different sites within a metropolitan region interact...' (1998, p. 25).

Methodology

As noted, there is no consensus on an operational definition of 'industrial district', but the concept clearly involves 'nearby' transactions between economic actors. Malmberg notes that 'proximity matters' but asks the basic empirical question 'to what degree are linkages local?' (Malmberg, 1996, p. 194).

This research develops indices that measure *local-ness*. Such measures can assist in identifying the degrees to which areas are or are not industrial districts. The economically mature Greater Cincinnati Metropolitan Area is used to illustrate the calculation of the indices.

This research suggests that an area with manufacturing must meet the following criteria to be considered an industrial district:

- there exist high degrees of spatial proximity between plants;
- there exist strong local vertical linkages, represented as input-output linkages;
- there exist strong local horizontal linkages, represented as producer services linkages, informational linkages and collaboration linkages;
- there exist strong local labor force linkages.

A composite Industrial District Index (IDI) can then defined as a function of spatial proximity (SP), vertical linkages (VL), horizontal linkages (HL), and labor force linkages (LL).

A larger SP value indicates a higher degree of spatial proximity, and larger

$$IDI = f(SP, VL, HL, LL) \qquad (5.1)$$

values of VL, HL and LL point to stronger local linkages.

Following the above criteria, the value of IDI indicates the degree to which an industrial region can be regarded as an industrial district. The following sections describe the calculation of each of the four factors.

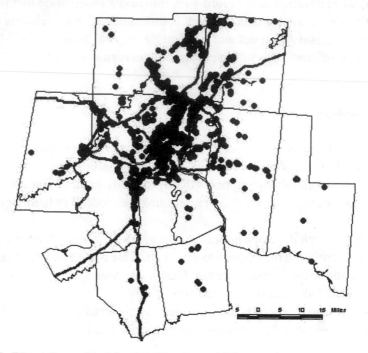

Figure 5.3 Plant Locations in the Cincinnati Metropolitan Area: Plants With 15+ Employees

Spatial Proximity

A standardized nearest neighbor index R is to used determine the difference in the degree of clustering among plants. The R index is the ratio of the average nearest neighbor distance between plants over the corresponding value for a random distribution with the same point density. With the standardized index, a perfectly clustered pattern produces a R value of 0.0, a random distribution 1.0, and a perfectly dispersed arrangement (a triangular lattice) generates the maximum R value of 2.149 (Taylor, 1977, p.157).

This index has been calculated for all manufacturing plants of 15 or more employees in the Cincinnati Metropolitan Area (N = 1,500). The type (by SIC code) and location (by latitude and longitude) of each plant (Figure 5.3) is known (Industrial Map Company, 1993). For the nearest neighbor calculations straight-line distances between plants were used.

Nearest neighbor indices show that manufacturing plants are located in close spatial proximity to each other. For all manufacturing, the R index is 0.22, showing strong clustering (as graphically revealed in Figure 5.3). Likewise, the plants within each of the two digit Standard Industrial Classification (SIC) groups are highly spatially clustered (Figure 5.4).

For this study, the R index is converted to the SP index so that larger SP values indicate higher degrees of clustering.

$$SP = (2.149 - R) / 2.149 \qquad (5.2)$$

The value of SP ranges from 0 to 1. For a perfect clustering pattern (all points are at the same location), SP will be 1. For a triangular lattice pattern, SP will be 0. For all manufacturing, the R index of 0.22 is converted to the SP index of 0.90.

Local-ness of Vertical Linkages and Horizontal Linkages

The point pattern analysis cannot reveal the important interactions (linkages) between individual plants. For these it is necessary to gather information from manufacturers. Local-ness has been examined for inputs to plants, and outputs from plants, and the distances from which producer services and information are obtained, and the relative location of employees for a sample of manufacturers in the Cincinnati Metropolitan Area. A questionnaire was sent to managers of manufacturing plants within the thirteen county metropolitan

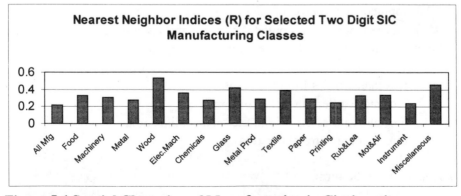

Figure 5.4 Spatial Clustering of Manufacturing in Cincinnati Metropolitan Area

regions. Five of the counties are in southwest Ohio, six are in northern Kentucky, and two are in southeast Indiana.

The managers were asked questions about their specific plant at a specific location. Of particular relevance to this research, they were asked to list the major material inputs which came into the plant, and to make informed guesses about the percentage of each which came from a source:

- less than 2 miles from the plant;
- 2 or more miles but less than 5 miles;
- 5 or more miles but within the Cincinnati metropolitan area or;
- from outside the Cincinnati metropolitan area.

They were asked to list the main products shipped from the plant, and again for each to indicate how far away it was shipped, using the same four distance categories as for inputs. For informational contacts there were questions regarding frequency of use and distance away from the plant to the place of work of the contact. A list of producer services was presented and respondents were asked to rank them by volume of purchases, and to indicate the distance between the plant and the source of the producer service, using the four distance categories. The managers were asked to make an informed guess about the radius (in miles) of a circle around their factory that encloses the residences of seventy-five percent of their employees. There were 71 usable responses. This is a small portion of the manufacturing plants in the region, and we cannot say that it is a representative sample. However, as discussed later, the results generally accord with theoretical expectations so we are encouraged to believe that they are realistic. They are certainly sufficiently realistic for illustration of the development and interpretation of local-ness indices.

A *local-ness* index is computed for each plant's interaction with each other economic actor. The four distance ranges used are:

- less than 2 miles from the plant;
- 2 or more miles but less than 5 miles;
- 5 or more miles but within the metropolitan area;
- outside the metropolitan area.

The index is of the form:

$$LI = .01*(\% < 2 \text{ miles}) + 0.0075*(\%2\text{-}5 \text{ miles}) + 0.0025* (\%5\text{miles-Metro. Area}) \quad (5.3)$$

This produces local-ness index values that range from one to zero. If, for example, a plant obtains all of its payroll services within 2 miles of the plant, it has a local-ness index of one for that service. If all of the service is obtained outside the metropolitan area, the index is zero. If 50 percent of the service is obtained within five miles, and the remainder from outside the metropolitan area, the index is .375. The absolute values of the indexes provide evidence on the robustness of the 'local industrial district' argument. The relative values indicate if a plant or service, an input or output is especially well connected locally.

The data from the 71 individual manufacturing plants in the Cincinnati Metropolitan Area whom responded to the questionnaire allow tests of local vs. non-local interactions.

Table 5.1 and Figure 5.5 reveal that material outputs have the lowest the local-ness index, and the next lowest is material inputs. This leads to low local-ness index (0.16) for vertical linkages.

Producer services have the highest local-ness index (0.47), followed by collaborations and information contacts. The local-ness of horizontal linkages as a whole can be represented as the average ([0.23+0.24+0.47]/3 = 0.31) of the above three indices. Obviously, horizontal linkages are more locally oriented than vertical linkages. Table 5.1 also shows that significant amounts of

Table 5.1 Linkage Structures Based on Distance from Plants: Local-ness Indices

Regional Scale	Material Input	Material Output	Total Input/output	Information	Collaborations	Producer Services
Within 2 miles(%)	3.9	0.99	2.45	5.03	2.51	6.35
2-5 miles (%)	16.13	6.93	11.53	18.21	22.67	49.22
5 mi-metro area (%)	19.34	18.25	18.79	18.31	18.64	14.33
Within 5 miles(%)	20.03	7.92	13.98	23.24	25.18	55.57
Within metro area (%)	39.37	26.17	32.77	41.55	43.82	69.9
Out of metro area (%)	60.63	73.83	67.23	58.45	56.18	30.1
Local-ness	0.21	0.11	0.16	0.23	0.24	0.47

interactions occur within the metropolitan area, but do not occur at sub-regional scales within the Metro Area.

Local-ness of Labor Force

Local-ness of labor force can be measured by the average distance between workplace and residence of employees, which in turn can be converted to a

Table 5.2 Labor Linkages by Employment Size

Employment Size	Total # of Plants	Subtotal (miles)	Average (miles)	Ranges (miles)
Total	70	1409	20.42	5~50
Less than 50	46	927	19.72	5~50
50~100	9	189	21.00	5~42
100~500	12	203	16.92	8~30
500~1000	2	60	30.00	10~50
Greater than 1000	1	30	30.00	30

local-ness index. Information from 71 individual manufacturing plants of the Cincinnati Metropolitan Area allows a test of the degree of local-ness of labor force.

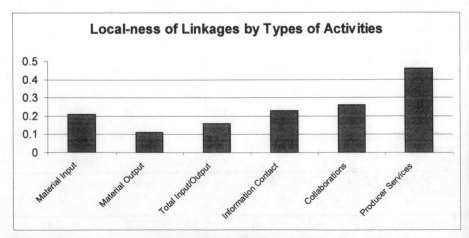

Figure 5.5 Local-ness of Vertical Linkages and Horizontal Linkages

In terms of labor force, most employees commute to work between fifteen to thirty miles (Table 5.2). It can be concluded that the 'labor shed' is the metropolitan region, which is approximately a circular region centered on downtown Cincinnati with a radius of thirty-five miles.

The fifteen to thirty miles distance (average distance from residence to workplace) range is in the 'more than five miles but within the metropolitan area' category. Using formula (5.3), the local-ness index of labor force is approximately 0.25.

Calculation of a Composite Industrial District Index

A general definition of the industrial district index is given in equation (5.1). The function **f** in equation (5.1) is unknown. In this study, we use a weighted linear combination:

$$IDI = W_{SP}*SP + W_{VL}*VL + W_{HL}*HL + W_{LL}*LL \qquad (5.4)$$

Subject to: $W_{SP} + W_{VL} + W_{HL} + W_{LL} = 1$
where W_{SP}, W_{VL}, W_{HL} and W_{LL} are the weights of their corresponding factors

Since the range of SP, VL, HL and LL is 0 to 1, the value of IDI will range from 0 to 1. A larger IDI value indicates a higher degree to which an industrial region can be viewed as an industrial district.

Following the calculations in the above section, the SP for all-manufacturing is 0.90, the local-ness of vertical linkages is 0.16, the local-ness of horizontal linkages is 0.31, and the local-ness of labor force linkages is 0.25. Assuming the weight is 0.25 for each of the four factors, we can calculate the IDI for the Cincinnati Metropolitan Area as

$$IDI_{Cincinnati} = 0.25*0.9 + 0.25*0.16 + 0.25*0.31 + 0.25*0.25 = 0.41 \quad (5.5)$$

Results

Simply looking at the spatial proximity of plants and inferring that such simple 'clustering' reveals anything about the interactions between the factories is not valid. **All** manufacturing within the metropolitan area **is highly spatially clustered**. There is no evidence of special spatial clustering by type of manufacturing. Simple spatial clustering is not unusual and does not vary significantly by type of manufacturing.

The distances between plants and the different economic actors with whom they interact, however, are useful data. The empirical evidence from the Cincinnati metropolitan area is in accord with expectations. Industrial location theory and experience indicate that the average travel distance for inputs and outputs will decline as the elements become more widely spatially available, or the friction of distance involved in the delivery of the product or service increases. Material inputs and market locations are most likely to be specialized and spatially scattered. Producer services are spatially more widely available, and there often are personal contact components involved in vendor selection or service use involved. Personal contacts often are also important for collaborations and information transmission. Labor faces high friction of distance. Thus, the results in this research that the local-ness index for supply chain (vertical) linkages is lower than for the producer services, information and collaborations (horizontal) linkages, and for labor are expected. These reasonable results indicate that the sample data are realistic and also that the methodologies employed are useful.

Metropolitan Scale and Industrial Districts

The appropriateness of thinking of a metropolitan sized or smaller region as an industrial district is questionable:

- the industrial district concept has no validity at a **sub-metropolitan scale**;
- the interactions between firms and those with whom they do business often are beyond the metropolitan area, so it is difficult to make a strong argument for the metropolitan region as an industrial district;
- the metropolitan region is **too small** an area to show industrial districts as traditionally measured via material inputs and product sales **vertical (supply chain) linkages**;
- the within-metropolitan linkages are more apparent in the exchange of information, the utilization of local contacts, and the use of local producer services. At the metropolitan scale, the **horizontal** links are much **more important** than the vertical links between firms;
- of the firm-to-firm linkages, **only producer services** are mainly sourced (70 percent) within the metropolitan region;
- **an exception is labor**. The metropolitan region is the appropriate

spatial frame for analysis when the focus is labor supply or employment opportunities.

If the major concern is for labor, and there is evidence that labor skills and availability and technology transfer among workers are the most critical factors now determining regional economic prosperity, then the metropolitan region is an appropriate size for designation as an industrial district. This, of course, might have been expected since in the United States metropolitan regions are defined by labor force journey-to-work patterns. Others have found this scale useful in regional economic development analyses (Bartik, 1991; Hicks and Rees, 1993). The relatively high local-ness index for producer services reinforces these arguments for the metropolitan area as an industrial district in these restricted dimensions.

The metropolitan area is not a satisfactory scale for industrial district designation when the emphasis is on traditional supply chain linkages. Inputs and outputs have spatial fields far beyond the city. Somewhat surprisingly, the informational contacts and collaborations also appear to be mainly beyond the metropolitan region. This may be a data deficiency, or it may be a consequence of specialized intra-industry knowledge fields, which operate nationally or even internationally. More careful exploration of this issue is necessary.

Coe and Townsend argue that 'localized' agglomerations are a myth, and that the service economy of Southeast England operates on a large region basis (1998). The results of this research generally support their position. There is **no** evidence that 'local' has any real operational meaning at the **within** metropolitan scales. The smallest viable region is the metropolitan, and only for certain types of interactions. Most linkages operate beyond the metropolitan area. McLean (1996) observes that 'defining a region is one of the most difficult tasks planning practitioners face' (1996, p. 189). This research confirms why it is so difficult. There is no one spatial scale that fits all circumstances. We probably cannot answer Gertler's question 'how do we recognize a true industrial district when we see one?' because there is no such thing as a true industrial district with a single and simple geographic boundary.

This research provides something more important than identification of simple single bounded industrial districts. It provides methodologies to conduct analyses of regions regarding their varying degrees of local-ness for horizontal and vertical linkages or labor, collectively and independently. Thus, analysts can approach questions such as 'Do more successful regions have higher degrees of local-ness for supply chain linkages than less successful regions, or vice-versa?' or 'Are local-ness indices for vertical linkages inversely related to horizontal indices?' It also is possible to systematically address the relationships between changes in local-ness and changes in spatial scale.

Local-ness Indices

The local-ness indices objectively identify components of industrial districts. The Industrial District Index (IDI) is a function of spatial proximity (SP), local-ness of vertical linkages (VL), horizontal linkages (HL) and labor force linkages (LL). It has paved the way for future large-scale comparative studies to establish baseline values for IDI, SP, VL, HL and LL. These can be used to indicate the degree to which any area demonstrates industrial district characteristics, and/or to determine the relative local-ness of the components.

Comparative studies are needed to establish benchmarks for baseline values of spatial proximity (SP), vertical linkages (VL), horizontal linkages (HL), labor force linkages (LL), and the Industrial District Index (IDI).

In this research, IDI is represented as a weighted linear combination of SP, VL, HL and LL. Other expressions of IDI may be useful as well. Comparative studies are needed to test the stability and sensibility of the function for IDI.

Acknowledgment

The support of the Institute of Advanced Manufacturing Sciences, Cincinnati, Ohio is gratefully acknowledged.

References

Bartik, T. J. (1991), *Who benefits from state and local economic development policies?*, UpJohn Institute, Kalamazoo.

Capello, R. and Nijkamp, P. (1997), 'Telecommunications network externalities and regional development: empirical evidence', In Bertuglia, Lombardo and Nijkamp, *Innovative Behaviour in Space and Time*, Springer, Berlin.

Chinitz, B. (1960), 'Contrasts in agglomeration: New York and Pittsburgh', *American Economic Review: Papers and Proceedings*, vol. 40, pp. 279-289.

Cincinnati Industrial Pinpointer (1993), Industrial Map Co, Alexandria, KY.

Coe, N. M. and Townsend, A R. (1998), 'Debunking the myth of localized agglomerations: the development of a regionalized service economy in South-East England', *Transactions of the Institute of British Geographers*, vol. 23, no. 3, pp. 385-404.

Doeringer, P. B. and Terkla, D. G. (1995), 'Business strategy and cross-industry clusters', *Economic Development Quarterly*, vol. 9, no. 3, pp. 225-237.

Gertler, M. S. (1992), 'Flexibility revisited: districts, nation-states, and the forces of production', *Transactions of the Institute of British Geographers*, vol. 17, pp. 259-278.

Harrison, B. (1998), 'It takes a region (or does it?): the material basis for metropolitanism and metropolitics', Paper prepared for the conference Urban-suburban interdependence: new directions for research and policy, co-sponsored by the Great cities Institute of the University of Illinois, the Lincoln Institute of Land Policy, and the Center on Urban and Metropolitan Policy at the Brookings Institution, Chicago, IL, September 24-25.

Held, J. R. (1996), 'Clusters as an economic development tool', *Economic Development Quarterly*, vol. 10, no 3, pp. 249-261.

Hicks, D. A. and Rees, J. (1993), 'Cities and beyond: a look at the nation's urban economy', In J. Sommer and D.A. Hicks (eds), *Rediscovering Urban America: Perspectives on the 1980's,* US Department of Housing and Urban Development, Washington, DC.

Hill, E. W. (1998), 'World-class productivity: Basis for the *Industry Week* formula', *Industry Week*, April 6.

Krugman, P. (1991), *Geography and trade*. MIT Press, Cambridge, MA .

Laulajainen, R. and Stafford, H. A. (1995), *Corporate geography: business location principles and cases,* Kluwer Academic Publishers, Dordrecht.

Maki, J. and Maki, W. (1994), 'Economic role of university-industry collaboration in a regional medical devices industry cluster', Paper prepared for the North American Meeting of the Regional Science Association.

Malecki, E. J., Tootle, D. M. and Young, E. M. (1995), 'Formal and informal networking among small firms in the USA', Paper prepared for the Annual Meeting of the Association of American Geographers, Chicago.

Malmberg, A. (1996), 'Industrial geography: agglomeration and local milieu', *Progress in Human Geography*, vol. 20, no. 3, pp. 392-403.

Markusen, A. (1994), 'Studying regions by studying firms', *The Professional Geographer*, vol. 46, no. 4, pp. 477-490.

McLean, B. M. (1996), 'Studying regional development: The regional context of development', *Economic Development Quarterly,* vol. 10, no. 2, pp. 188-198.

Nadvi, K.and Schmidz, H. (1994), *Industrial clusters in less-developed countries: a review of experiences and research agenda*, Institute of Development Studies, Discussion Paper 339.

Piore, M and Sable, C. (1984), *The second industrial divide*, Basic Books, New York.

Porter, M. E. (1990), *The competitive advantage of nations*, Free Press, New York.

Rees, J. and Stafford, H. A. (1986), 'Theories of regional growth and industrial location: their relevance for understanding high-technology complexes', In J. Rees (ed), *Technology, regions, and policy*. Rowman and Littlefield, Totowa, NJ.

Saxenian, A. 1994. *Regional advantage: culture and competition in Silicon Valley and Route 128*. Harvard University Press, Cambridge, MA.

Scott, A. J. 1988. *New industrial spaces: flexible production, organization and regional development in North America and Western Europe,* Pion, London.

Sforzi, F. 1989. 'The geography of industrial districts in Italy', In Goodman, E. and Bamford, J. (eds.). *Small firms and industrial districts in Italy*. Routledge.

Sweeney, S. H. and Feser, E. J. 1998. 'Plant size and clustering of manufacturing activity', *Geographical Analysis*, vol. 30, no. 1, 45-64.

Taylor, P. J. 1977. *Quantitative analysis in geography: an introduction to spatial analysis*. Houghton Mifflin Company, Boston.

Wheat, L. 1973. *Regional growth and industrial location*. D. C. Heath & Co, Lexington, MA.

6 Micro Business Networks in Rural Canada: The Case of Peer Lending and Micro Credit Circles

DAVID BRUCE and ROGER WEHRELL

Introduction

The micro enterprise literature identifies, among other things, the importance of peer lending circles and micro credit networks as important vehicles for helping emerging micro businesses become established or helping them make important decisions about the future direction their businesses might take (Aspen Institute, 1995; Bornstein, 1995; Boshara et al., 1997, Clark and Houston, 1993). Participants in such networks identify the networking, sharing of ideas, peer group support, and business skill development as important, often even more important than the small amounts of business capital they receive.

Peer lending and micro credit networks are found in many different geographical contexts; in both urban and rural areas within countries, and in both developed and developing countries. These networks sometimes differ in the specific clientele they target, such as women, youth, Aboriginals, or those on social assistance.

This chapter focuses on the utility of peer lending circles as a means of stimulating and supporting small business development, and creating a link to broader community and regional development. It also focuses on their relative success in providing business development opportunities for members of groups traditionally outside the business world.

This chapter also explores several dimensions of 'network' relationships, including: relationships among participants, relationships between participants and their network 'coordinator', relationships between businesses inside the networks and those outside the network, and relationships between the network and the supplier or guarantor of credit.

Two case studies are used to illustrate the dimensions of network relationships within micro credit lending circles in a rural Canadian context: Red Ochre Micro Business Lending Service, located on the Great Northern Peninsula of western Newfoundland; and Microentreprise Restigouche Micro Entreprise in northern New Brunswick. These examples offer different models or approaches to the provision of micro credit, including differences in economic context, clientele, financial partnerships, range of services, and degree of success in meeting organization objectives. The common link between the two is the community-based nature of the programs. Locally based lending circles create clusters of emerging entrepreneurs in small rural communities, encouraging cooperation and shared learning and development in a business environment.

The analysis provides a discussion of the importance of trust-based social capital in rural communities. It also provides a discussion of appropriate public policy and programs which support local innovations in small business development.

Micro Credit and Micro Enterprise Defined

'Micro credit' is used to describe a variety of forms of credit in small amounts. There is not complete uniformity in the way the term is used. Typically it refers to small amounts of credit to finance income generating activity including part-time, casual, or ad hoc enterprises; informal and underground businesses; and owner operated formally organized and registered businesses with fewer than five employees. The amounts of credit are small enough so that conventional financial institutions (CFIs), such as banks, using standard business credit instruments and conventional loan administration techniques find such small business loans unprofitable and avoid them. In Canada, depending on which lending officer and which CFI one talks to, this could mean business loans and lines of operating credit in a range as low as CDN$3,000 and less or as high as CDN$25,000 and less.

Our interest in this chapter is business loans provided in the very smallest amounts, usually beginning at CDN$500 and stepping up incrementally from there. There are two typical approaches to providing this credit: directly from an organization (known generally as a micro loan fund) to an individual; or indirectly to an individual through a business planning and business loan approval process within what is generally referred to as a peer group lending circle. Our interest in this chapter is in exploring network dimensions relative to micro credit provided through a peer group lending model. Micro credit and the manner in which it is provided is of interest and importance because it is the single most important tool for micro enterprise development.

Micro enterprise development in turn is one important aspect of community economic and social development. Micro enterprises are very small businesses owned and operated by one or two individuals. They typically have few assets. Formal definitions typically specify that they employ five or fewer persons. Usually their employees, other than the owners, are part-time or seasonal. The majority are home-based businesses. They include many seasonal businesses and enterprises involving part-time activity on the part of the owner/operator. Micro enterprises include more variation than any other category of business (Wehrell et al., 1998).

Micro enterprises are important to community business and economic development for several reasons. They are a source of new businesses that will grow and eventually establish themselves in the small and medium sized business sector. They are often a source of supplemental income for families otherwise at or well below the poverty line. They are a laboratory for experimentation with new business ideas at low risk levels. They are a real learning centre for individuals otherwise lacking business skills and business experience to acquire them through self-employment opportunities. They offer possibilities for personal development through self-employment to individuals in situations of social dependence and isolation who have not developed self-esteem, confidence in interpersonal relations, and socially supportive networks (Wehrell, 1996).

Social Capital in a Rural Setting

The development of social capital is central to socio-economic change and development. Social capital or social infrastructure, as described by Flora et al. (1992), is really all about the collective will of local communities to provide for their social and economic well-being. It is comprised of three elements - social institutions (such as schools or local service clubs), the human resource base (the skills and abilities of people), and social networks (the linkages within communities and with other communities).

The development of social capital is primarily built through an ongoing process of establishing norms and building trust. How communities learn, and how they approach the concept of what learning is all about, determines the degree to which social capital is built and the extent to which communities respond to and adapt to change. Networks in this context play an especially important role relative to micro enterprise development in general and peer lending micro credit programs specifically. Communities and regions where trust, kinship, connectedness, and informal networks through social and other settings are highly visible and active, are more likely to accommodate and facilitate the norms of a peer lending circle. These include, among others, the willingness to share ideas, to support one another, and to work collectively for the success of each other's businesses.

Rural Considerations Respecting Network and Proximity

An overarching theme in business literature is the role of agglomerations and the ensuing spinoffs that result from firms within a sector sharing ideas, technology, and benefiting from economies of scale and access to supportive and linked activities (Gertler and DiGiovanna, 1997; Gertler, 1995; MacPherson, 1994, 1991, 1988). In a rural context, this is less likely to be the case, given the tyranny of distance and the lower density of population and consequently, the subsequent smaller local and regional consumer markets. However, networks become important for overcoming those barriers, even if the distances between the network members is reasonably large. In a rural micro credit context, bringing together people under the common element of their business size only, regardless of sector, has the potential to achieve some positive outcomes, some of which are direct business outcomes, while others are personal and social outcomes. Examples of possible business outcomes include shared ideas about market opportunities and supply sources, development of cross-sector business partnerships for retail and marketing projects, and establishing a credit history for the purpose of securing larger loans at conventional lending institutions should the need arise. Examples of possible personal and social outcomes include improved personal confidence and self-worth among the members, decreasing the dependency on social programs for economic support, and enhancing the existing stock of trust and community togetherness. While these impacts may not be the same as in urban settings, the range of potential network outcomes is equally important.

Dimensions of Micro Credit

In this section we discuss the different dimensions in which micro credit operates, specifically its role or place in the spectrum of business capital, urban versus rural dimensions, its role in developed countries versus its role in un- and under-developed countries, and the spectrum of clientele accessing micro credit or to which micro credit programs have been targeted, in a developed country context.

Role of Micro Credit in the Spectrum of Business Capital

The range of business credit tools and financial capital for business startup and expansion is staggering and diverse, and we do not attempt to catalogue all of them here. However, it is sufficient to say that from a business credit perspective there are typically five conventional tools: term loans or business demand loans; lines of operating credit; business credit cards; and overdraft protection on business accounts.

Typically, the application and administration procedures require formal business plans and periodic financial statements from the enterprise. Since the application evaluation and the loan monitoring procedures are more extensive than those associated with personal credit instruments, typically the fees associated with business credit instruments are also higher. However, credit to micro enterprises, even if incorporated, usually must be secured through the micro entrepreneur's personal guarantee (or that of a co-signer), and this means assessment of the personal net worth and assets of the micro entrepreneur.

The cost of lending with conventional business credit instruments is high, especially for small amounts of business credit. It is estimated that between CDN\$15,000 and CDN\$20,000 is the lowest amount of credit that can be issued on a break even basis. The costs consist mainly of the loan officer's time in assessing the credit application and in monitoring the enterprise's performance and credit repayment. The returns on the small loan amounts micro enterprises require do not justify the high costs of processing the loans using conventional loan administration procedures. Thus it often becomes impractical for these institutions to provide very small business loans.

Obtaining access to these conventional sources of business credit is a significant obstacle to micro enterprise development, thus the need for micro credit programs to fill the gap. Both the individuals and their enterprises are problematic. A high proportion of the entrepreneurs are from groups that are not deemed credit worthy by conventional lending institutions. Their credit history is often poor. Sometimes, in case of homemakers for example, it is non-existent. The enterprises usually do not have fixed assets that can serve as collateral for loans. They may not have a long history of operations. Many micro entrepreneurs have less business sophistication than other business people and consequently find it difficult to navigate the formal loan application procedures employed by most conventional financial institutions and even by most alternative business credit granting agencies. The small amounts involved do not justify their employing accountants and other experts to help them.

The public sector at both provincial and federal levels of government, concerned with financing of all small businesses, has developed a series of programs and agencies to provide business credit to small businesses having trouble qualifying for conventional business financing from banks. The Business Development Bank of Canada (BDC) is an example of such an agency, as are the community business development centres (community based organizations originally established under the Community Futures Program by the federal government in the most economically depressed regions of the country) and the recently formed SOLIDE (Sociétés locales d'investissement dans le développement de l'emploi) in the Province of Quebec. Provincial programs like the New Brunswick Entrepreneur Loan Programme provide business credit to small businesses through existing provincial and regional economic development agencies. Almost none of these sources of alternative business credit is explicitly targeted at micro entrepreneurs and the provision of micro credit. Yet because they provide loans in amounts smaller than those normally considered by the conventional lenders, they typically serve some micro entrepreneurs as clients.

Thus, the establishment of a micro credit program in general, and more specifically a peer group lending model, is a means of addressing a gap in the range of business credit supply. It is a technique employed by MFIs (micro finance institutions) for loan assessment and administration procedures designed to reduce lending costs while managing the extra risks incurred by lending to many of the special groups that they target--groups of potential borrowers that CFIs avoid. Peer group lending is a common strategy for cost reduction and risk management. The strategy calls for borrowers to be organized in small groups varying in size from four to ten members, with each group member bearing some form of responsibility for the loans issued to other group members. Each group undertakes some of the administrative functions in screening its members' loan applications and administering their loans. A natural extension of this is that social networks and social relations play an important part in assessing and managing lending risk.

In systematically constructing a system of business credit relying on these borrowers' groups, MFIs introduce social networks and social relations into their calculations for assessing and managing lending risk. The assessment techniques and calculations employed by CFIs typically treat the business borrower as an isolated and independent entity. The soundness of the business loan is assessed in terms of the borrowing business's capacity for repayment.

This capacity is determined in terms of the business's estimated future cash flows and the market value of business assets that serve as collateral in case projected cash flows fail to be realized. Sometimes the lender introduces social and legal relations into the calculations in a narrow way by requiring cosignatories or guarantors to the loan, but the focus of the assessment is the business and business owner as an independent entity whose social obligations and social networks are irrelevant.

Peer group lending techniques direct their calculation and assessment of risk associated with the business lending toward the social network which the borrower brings with him/herself to the peer group lending program and which the program compels the borrower to elaborate and develop insofar as he/she and his/her peers follow the procedures laid down in the program. At the same time, in part by design and in part as an unplanned byproduct, the borrower develops a network of business relationships:

- with his/her peers in the borrower group;
- with micro entrepreneurs in other borrower groups;
- with established businesses in the community; and
- with the MFI and partner credit providers.

This business network rests upon and is fostered by the social networks just mentioned.

Movements in Developed and Undeveloped Economies

Tools and techniques for micro credit were invented and refined in the 1970s and 1980s in the developing world. In developing countries the formal financial sector of banks and other well-known lending institutions often is insufficiently developed. Often there is insufficient coverage to provide credit and other financial services, such as savings facilities, to large parts of the population. Micro finance institutions (MFIs) were often established as nonprofit institutions, to provide credit and other financial services to clients not serviced by CFIs. The savings deposit facilities offered by MFIs also allowed the MFIs access to reasonably priced loan capital which they could use to support their micro credit services.

The micro credit movement gained significant attention first in 1976, with the Grameen Bank in Bangladesh providing small amounts of capital to mostly poor women in rural areas (Bornstein, 1995). Business operations were typically agricultural in nature and provided some means of independence for women. Loan repayment rates were excellent. This has largely been the case elsewhere in other underdeveloped economies (Berenbach and Churchill, 1997; CIDA, 1995). In developing countries these programs typically encompass an entire village, where pre-existing kin, family, and social networks are highly developed, but where most of the people are extremely poor. Peer lending is the typical approach, although some direct lending from an organization to an individual does occur.

The success of the Grameen Bank experience in a developing country context led to its replication in the United States and Canada in many jurisdictions by the late 1980s (Taub, 1998). While the objectives in underdeveloped countries focussed on getting people who had never been part of the economy into the economy, and the clientele was quite large in numbers, the focus in developed countries became much different. In addition, society is much more highly stratified in a developed country, with fewer strong social and family networks and connections pre-existing in a community. The multitude of micro lending groups quickly became focussed on narrowly defined target groups in narrowly defined geographic locations: women in a poor section of the city; Aboriginals; the disabled; recently unemployed in a resource town. Thus the pre-existing conditions of broader networks and more homogenous population from an economic status point of view within a given community found in a developing country simply are not present, thus making it more challenging to achieve the same outcomes in a developed country context.

Furthermore, these groups and others were recognized as having access to the highly formalized system of financial institutions for the purpose of savings and some other financial services However, they were largely unable to access business credit from these same institutions. In North America the formal system of financial institutions is much more extensive and provides access to a variety of financial services to most of the population. Typically, even MFI clients in North America have access to savings services from CFIs including credit unions. However, the same CFIs may not offer them access to credit to finance either personal consumption or income generation activity. North American MFIs typically concentrate on the provision of credit for income generation activity and do not act as deposit taking financial intermediaries.

Another limiting success factor in the developed country context is the presence of and a culture of relative dependency on a social welfare system or safety net (Taub, 1998). This 'fall-back' position gives people an 'out' from an economic perspective if they choose not to undertake a micro enterprise activity, or if they fail to succeed in their micro enterprise venture. The debate about this issue is broad and lengthy, but we point to this factor in a general sense as a contextual issue for consideration in assessing the relative experiences in our case studies.

Urban and Rural Dimensions of Micro Credit

Micro credit programs operate in both urban and rural settings (Burrus and Stearns, 1997; Calmeadow Foundation, 1997; Himes and Servon, 1998; Women's World Banking, 1996). In an urban setting, the programs quite often serve a very narrowly defined group of people, and are often tied to, in a formal or informal way, other programmatic efforts to assist people - housing programs, education or literacy programs, and much more. Moving people off social assistance is a much desired outcome (Taub, 1998). However, in rural areas, micro credit program objectives and outcomes can be quite different. In some areas, they help to address the lack of presence of any financial institution in the area. In other cases, the target may be cottage or craft businesses as part of economic development strategy to exploit the culture and heritage of a region. In other cases where incomes have become depressed in a resource-based economy, the program might provide a vehicle for a household member to start a business for the purpose of supplementing household income.

In rural areas, however, there are special challenges. Rural areas have smaller local markets with fewer immediate new business opportunities for micro entrepreneurs than in urban areas. And persons in rural communities may feel more isolated from and less connected to areas of economic activity. On the other hand, micro lending programs and the networks they create might have a better chance of sustaining themselves in rural communities where it is perceived that social relations and community ties are much stronger, and people are more likely to work together to ensure mutual success.

The Micro Credit Clientele and Supportive Organizations

The private non-profit sector has spawned organizations like Calmeadow whose explicit mission is credit provision to micro entrepreneurs. This sector includes organizations that are church based. It includes community loan funds that embrace a variety of social objectives of which micro enterprise development through micro credit is but one. Some of these organizations target micro entrepreneurs in specific groups, such as women or Aboriginals or the disabled, requiring special attention in order to foster micro enterprise development and self-employment. Although lagging the United States in the development of micro credit initiatives, Canada has developed an array of efforts including a significant number in rural areas (Wehrell et al., 1998).

Dimensions of Micro Credit Networks

Network development is a critical element of peer group lending. The range of networks, at a primary and secondary level, and at a business and social level, are illustrated in Figure 6.1.

Peer group lending strategies in effect use social networks to assess and administer loans cost effectively while reducing risk. First, they exploit existing social relationships among borrowers. Second, they introduce rules and procedures for borrowers to follow which reinforce existing relationships and create new ones. Most of these rules and procedures are centered around the requirement that borrowers undertake some form of joint or collective

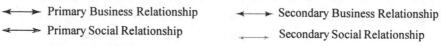

⟵⟶ Primary Business Relationship   ⟵┄┄► Secondary Business Relationship
⟵⟶ Primary Social Relationship   ┄┄┄► Secondary Social Relationship

(Nature of Relationship from Micro Entrepreneur Perspective)

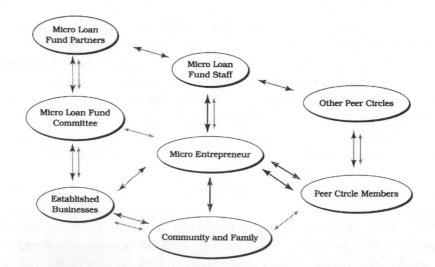

Figure 6.1 Business and Social Network Construction in Peer Lending Micro Enterprise Programs

responsibility for the repayment of each other's loans with regard to everyone in a borrower group.

The group is established in part by putting individuals in it who already have some social relationships with each other. Perhaps they are members of the same village. Where borrowers form their own groups they are likely to seek fellow borrowers that they already know through some social network, and this means that each borrower may well be familiar with some family members or friends in the wider social networks of his or her fellow borrowers. The social networks existing prior to group formation will increase the likelihood of social factors including peer pressure among group members influencing loan repayment behavior so that likelihood of delinquency and default is reduced.

In addition to relying on the influence of prior social relationships among group members, many MFI's establish systems and rules and training and indoctrination procedures that strengthen the social networks among borrower group members. For example, groups undergo orientation at group meetings where microcredit program staff instruct them in how to assess each other's loan applications. They learn the details of each other's businesses and financial situations. Once loans are issued, there are required monthly borrower group meetings at which the members make their monthly repayments of interest and principal. Because the personal and business financial situations of small owner/operators are almost impossible to disentangle, borrowers become familiar with the family situations of fellow borrowers whose loan applications they are assessing. Often they enter into business relationships and business alliances with each other where the nature of their business activities are complementary to each other in some way. The group activities required by the formal procedures the MFI establishes for borrowers groups increase the social interaction and strengthen the social ties among group members.

Where MFI's entertain social and economic objectives beyond the provision of microcredit MFI clients may find themselves in evolving social networks outside their immediate borrowers group. Some MFIs attempt to increase their clients' income generating capacity through business training. Borrowers may find themselves in training occasions with members of other borrower groups. Some MFIs seek to organize all their borrowers to undertake particular business functions collectively or cooperatively. For example, the MFI may try to organize trade shows for its members to promote business dealings among members. Or it may try to organize its members into marketing or purchasing cooperatives. Finally, many MFI's rely on clients to fill many of the governance and administrative roles of the MFI. Clients may hold some of the seats on the board of directors of small community based MFIs. They may also hold the majority of seats on the MFI's working committees, such as a Fund Raising Committee or the Recruiting Committee. Any such initiatives and arrangements will draw members into increasingly elaborate and strong social networks with each other. Such strengthened social ties and felt social obligations to fellow borrowers and to the MFI will further reduce probabilities of loan default and delinquency. The average borrower's sense of commitment and obligation to repay, the possibilities of exerting peer pressure on him/her to repay, and his/her capacity to repay are strengthened. And these factors are part of the system the MFI devises for managing the lending risk behind each loan in a very calculated way.

Levels of Business Networking

The clients served by many MFIs have a narrow horizon of business contacts. They are micro enterprises with limited numbers of customers and suppliers. They are often isolated from the traditional business community. As individuals they have limited economic power. However, their membership in borrower groups typically leads to inclusion in wider business networks whether or not the MFI explicitly encourages this networking. As mentioned above, four types of business-to-business networking occurs.

At the first level, when the members of a borrower group learn more about each others' products and plans for additional products and services, as they must do in assessing each other's loan applications, they often form both ad hoc and longer lasting strategic alliances for the purpose of selling or promoting each other's products. They may also refer customers to each other and advise each other on new marketing opportunities. Besides the normal social motives and business motives for forming these alliances and acting in a cooperative fashion, there is the motive of needing their peer borrowers to succeed in repaying loans so that other group members can maintain access to credit from the MFI or so that the others avoid increasing their repayment obligations in order to cover for defaulters and delinquents in the group.

Peers within a borrower group may also generate ideas for reducing costs by sharing resources. There are examples of two MFI clients moving their micro enterprises into the same storefront location to share the rent. In other examples, two crafts enterprises share a table or booth at crafts fairs in order to reduce expenses.

At the second level, micro entrepreneurs in one borrower group may extend their business networks to include micro enterprises in other borrower groups.

The types of alliances that develop are similar to those at the first level. They are based on the small scale of the enterprises. Micro entrepreneurs can deal with each other as peers with many similar needs related to their small scale. Their tendency to develop at this second level depends on the MFI's efforts to facilitate contact among the peer borrower groups it services. For example, some MFIs explicitly encourage clients to conduct business with other. They may publish newsletters or directories describing the products and services of all their clients. They may organize business ventures, such as marketing cooperatives or trade fairs, involving all their members from the various borrower groups. On the other hand, even MFIs that do not deliberately construct business networks among their clients foster their creation by the very nature of business to business and group to group interaction that tends to occur once borrower groups have been established. These relationships develop naturally even if more slowly than in circumstances where they are deliberately constructed by the MFI.

On a third level of business-to-business networking MFI clients form alliances with businesses and business persons from the established business community. Some MFIs recruit volunteers from the established business community to serve on committees and boards in the governance and operation of the MFI. Through their participation these volunteers learn about and come into contact with the micro enterpreneurs and their enterprises. Familiarity with each other's products and services and business needs leads to the possibility of business interchange between the two. Some MFIs arrange formal mentor relationships between business persons from the established business community and MFI clients. The idea is to help the micro entrepreneur develop his/her business skills and judgement and his/her enterprise so that it is more likely to succeed and to repay loans to the MFI. Such relationships increase contact between the micro entrepreneurs and the established business community and the likelihood that other business relationships develop between the two.

The fourth and final level on which MFI clients expand their business-to-business networks is with business credit providers. Access to credit is the issue that brings micro entrepreneurs to MFIs in the first place, and their borrower-lender relationship with the MFI is already a major expansion of their business networks. However, in North America the story is more complex than that. Many North American MFIs establish partnerships with established financial institutions and other business credit providers to provide their service. Sometimes the partner is a bank or a credit union. Sometimes it is a government funded or owned small business lending and development agency.

The MFI does this in order to reduce its operating costs. The partner may actually disburse loan funds and receive client repayments. It may track the repayments with its information system and provide reports to the MFI. In short, whatever the origin of the loan funds, the partner may bear many of the costs of administering the MFI's loans. If the partner is a bank or other deposit taking financial institution, the MFI client may be required to open an account with the partner and to receive funds and make repayments through that account. These sorts of arrangements mean that the micro entrepreneur expands his/her network to credit providers.

Many North American MFIs deliberately make network expansion at this level an objective. The assumption is that a successful client using microcredit productively will eventually expand his/her micro enterprise and therefore expand his/her credit needs beyond what the MFI can supply. Because of expanded contacts and networking with the partner financial institution or other credit provider, the successful client will be able to access more conventional sources of business financing in the future when required. If the partner financial institution is a bank or credit union, the MFI borrower without a credit rating when first accessing a microloan may be able to build a credit rating through repayment of the microloan. Some North American MFIs hope that their clients thereby 'graduate' to the established business community.

Any such partnerships and arrangements with established institutions and enterprises in the community may bring about interactions between MFI clients and members of the community they would not normally interact with. MFIs whose mission is poverty alleviation and which target disadvantaged social groups outside the economic mainstream may explicitly design their system to maximize such interactions. For example, MFI clients are often required to open deposit accounts with a partnering bank and to interact with its staff including account managers. The idea is get the clients to begin to form banking relationships and expand their sphere of business and social contacts in ways that support an expansion of their income generating activities or enterprises. Encouraging their entry into wider social and business networks is part of the process that will lead such MFI clients, in theory, to graduate from dependence on the MFI for business credit to dependence on CFIs to satisfy their business credit needs.

Case Studies

In this section we provide two case study examples of rural peer lending micro credit networks in rural Canada (Figure 6.2). One provides the example of establishing many of the interconnected networks necessary for a successful peer lending program. The second provides the example of how weak prior social relationships among MFI clients due to geographical and linguistic distance can undercut the effectiveness of a peer lending program. In spite of that it is still an example of how such a program still fosters business networks among micro enterprises.

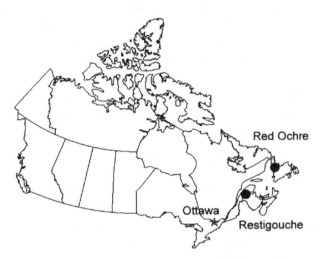

Figure 6.2 Case Study Locations (Canada)

Red Ochre Micro Business Lending Service, Western Newfoundland

The study area in Newfoundland is defined by the area serviced by the Red Ochre Micro Business Lending Service. The fund is operated by the Red Ochre Regional Board Inc., which is responsible for Economic Zone 7, covering most of the western side of the Great Northern Peninsula. Other credit providers in the region cover some of or all of Economic Zone 7 as one part of a wider area of coverage in Western Newfoundland (Red Ochre, 1997).

The geography The Red Ochre Region covers an area of 17,500 km², stretching 363 kilometers from north to south. There are 36 communities in the region with a combined population of 11,000. This is a relatively isolated and sparsely populated area of Newfoundland. It is off the main Trans-Canada Highway running through the central part of the province. Deer Lake (population 4,300 with an airport) is located about one hour's drive from the southern part of the region. Corner Brook (population 22,400) is located another forty minute drive south of Deer Lake and is the regional service centre for western Newfoundland.

The economy The strategic economic plan for the Red Ochre Region identifies it as one of the most economically challenged zones in the province. The unemployment rate has remained at approximately 33 percent since the early 1980s. Only 20 percent of the men and 17 percent of the women have full-time employment. Seasonal employment with low wages is the norm. This has led to a steady out-migration of people, particularly since the closure of the ground fishery in the early 1990s. Challenges in fostering new business development, as identified in the strategic plan, include: lack of capital, lack of technical knowledge, lack of business knowledge, lack of coordination among government departments, lack of entrepreneurship, a high illiteracy rate, and lack of local business data. The strategic plan identifies developing home-based, micro, and small businesses, building a stronger tourism industry, securing better access to business capital, and fostering youth entrepreneurship among the priority areas for action in business development.

The business credit supply network There are only two bank branches located within the entire Red Ochre Region – one in the south and one in the north – and they do not service business credit clients. They are serviced primarily by branches located in Deer Lake and Corner Brook, outside of the region. There are three alternative sources of business credit beyond banks and the micro loan program. NORTIP, a community business development centre, is the largest and provides higher risk loans of up to CDN$75,000. The Business Development Bank of Canada (BDC) has a branch which services this area, and the provincial government's Department of Development and Rural Renewal (DDRR) offers some business lending programs. To a large extent there is very little formal networking among these suppliers of credit, except for that between NORTIP and each of the other suppliers as NORTIP actively seeks referrals from the others.

The micro loan fund The Red Ochre Micro Lending Service (MLS) partners with NORTIP to provide small business loans and micro enterprise support services to micro entrepreneurs and would-be micro entrepreneurs organized into peer lending groups of four to seven borrowers. Between 1997 and the present five peer lending groups have been established, and two have completed two round of loans and their repayment. Red Ochre MLS provides the loan security and administers the loan application and repayment process. NORTIP makes the actual loans to borrowers.

The Red Ochre MLS is managed by an Area Committee, appointed by the Red Ochre Regional Board. The Newfoundland-Labrador Federation of Cooperatives (NLFC) acts as a provincial partner for this and other micro loan funds operating in the province, providing resources, training materials, a framework for delivery, and a CDN$1 million reserve fund to guarantee loans provided by banks or other credit programs through the micro loan funds.

The Red Ochre MLS provides a micro entrepreneur a first-time loan of CDN$500 and subsequent loans in increasing amounts at CDN$500 increments to a maximum of CDN$5,000. Interest rates are currently at prime plus two percent. Loans are made to an individual micro entrepreneur although the peer lending group must approve the loan first. Red Ochre MLS also provides business training courses, business planning assistance, mentoring, and peer exchange and support.

Only term loans are available. Terms range from three to eighteen months depending on the size of the loan. Loans are amortized over the term. Peers evaluate the worthiness of credit applications by using four criteria – credit history, cash flow, capacity or capability to manage a business, and personal character. Borrowers complete an application by following a workbook.

The clientele can be characterised as part-time, home-based, start-up enterprises. In the first year the program targeted youth 18–29 years of age, but now there is no targeting and about two-thirds are women and about one-third are youth. Most of these people are interested in running only small enterprises for the purpose of supplementing family income. Most are using the financing from Red Ochre MLS for materials, supplies, equipment, and a little bit of marketing or advertising.

Network Elements

The relationship **among individual micro entrepreneurs** has been extremely positive. This region has a rich history of family closeness and communities working together. The peer groups were strategically established to have people from the same or neighbouring communities within one group. This eliminates significant travel time and cost for people, and builds on community and family history. Additionally, people have been supportive of others' business ideas and have contributed to the development of plans, provided contacts for supplies, and much more.

The relationship **between individual micro entrepreneurs and the program coordinator** has also been extremely positive. The coordinator is a young male in his early thirties with a business degree from a university. He and his family are lifetime residents in the region, so he knows many people personally and has used that approach to encourage and facilitate involvement. Although the distances are large, the coordinator meets personally with the peer groups on a regular basis, and maintains office hours in both the northern and southern parts of the region. The coordinator has also been important, through facilitating group discussions and assessment activities, in helping would-be entrepreneurs determine their real financing needs and their other needs, such as training. This helps sort out who can benefit from the micro loan program and who can really benefit from other credit providers.

The relationship **between individual micro entrepreneurs and established businesses** has been slow to emerge. Although the Area Committee, which consists mainly of established business people, meets the clients on annual basis through a social event and business plan presentation, few direct business spinoffs have developed. This is not a negative item, since many of the micro entrepreneurs are operating seasonal tourism and craft related businesses, and are filling a gap or niche in the business circle. This is also explained by the relatively small number of established businesses in the region, and their relative lack of coverage across many business sectors. It is expected that over time some of the micro entrepreneurs will establish formal networks with some of these established businesses.

The relationship **between the loan fund and other agencies** has been mixed. The relationship with NORTIP is extremely positive and mutually beneficial: Red Ochre MLS has a loan partner, NORTIP develops a potential client base once those businesses grow. The relationship with the NLFC, which provides the loan guarantee and significant resource support, has also been positive. Red Ochre MLS has benefited from the administrative efficiencies of this larger organization, and NLFC in turn is making a positive contribution to community development while building a strong base of independent micro loan funds across the province. The relationship with conventional lending institutions has been almost non-existent since there are only two branches in the whole region, and neither was willing to serve in the capacity as the lending agency, as NORTIP now does. Funding to cover the cost of the coordinator position is provided by an annual government employment program, and coordinated by the NLFC on behalf of all micro loan programs operating across the province. This has resulted in some tensions as the department requires an annual application for funds, and has also expressed some concerns about the true economic value and outcome of the micro loan programs. Red Ochre MLS is promoted through brochures, fact sheets, newspaper advertisements, mailouts to all 4,000 households in the region, and columns in the Red Ochre Regional Development Board's quarterly newsletter, which also goes to all households. Referrals are received from government departments social services, rural community councils, the banks, the BDC and NORTIP, and local churches.

Microentreprise Restigouche Microenterprise, Campbellton, New Brunswick

In May 1995, officials in the Department of Economic Development and Tourism of the government of the Province of New Brunswick became interested in a pilot project for a microloan fund in Restigouche County in northern New Brunswick. Using government funding to finance operations in the first two years and to provide security for the initial loan capital, four institutions partnered in establishing the loan fund. These were a credit union, a regional economic development commission, a regional non-profit quasi public sector small business lending agency, and the Rural and Small Town Programme of Mount Allison University. The MFI was christened Microentreprise Restigouche Microenterprise (MRM). Its name was designed for the bilingual population it was meant to serve. It served Restigouche County, the area coincident with that served by the small business lending agency. MRM commenced operations in September 1995 and ceased operations in January 1998 when its lending operations and clients were absorbed by the small business lending agency.

The geography Restigouche County is one of the two northernmost counties of New Brunswick. It lies on the Bay of Chaleur, an extension of the Gulf of Saint Lawrence. It also borders Québec to the north. Its principal municipality is Campbellton (population 8,600). The nearest urban centres and markets are Moncton, 332 kilometers to the south, and Fredericton, 362 kilometers to the southwest. Its other two towns (populations under 5,000) and seven villages (populations under 2,000) are spread out over an region stretching from 260 kilometers east to west and 100 kilometers from north to south. However, most lie close to the coast of the Bay. The area is mostly forested; wide forested areas separate many of the small towns and the dispersed population of just under 40,000. Besides the topography and physical distance, language divides the population, which is 60 percent Francophone and 40 percent Anglophone. Most of the towns are predominantly either one or the other.

The economy Restigouche is heavily dependent on the forestry industry for harvesting, processing, and business service sector jobs. Its two largest employers, after the public school system and the Restigouche Health Services Corporation, are the pulp mills in Atholville and Dalhousie. The former has been opened and closed several times over recent years. The latter has been in continuous operation but has steadily downsized its workforce with constant improvement to production technology. The fishery has steadily declined in importance due to the shrinking resource, and there is no agriculture of significance. Tourism and recreation including winter recreation have potential given the area's climate and scenery and the topography of the Restigouche River system and the Bay of Chaleur. However, the region is distant from urban markets. Self-employment is quite low compared to the national average. The region's labour force has a mentality fashioned from a long history, prior to the 1990's, of plentiful high paying jobs in forest-based industries. One important source of self-employment for men has been the provision of business services (e.g., hauling and truck or equipment sales and maintenance) to forestry companies and contractors.

The business credit supply network Restigouche has a rudimentary but operative business credit supply network. Six of Canada's chartered banks offer credit service in Restigouche. All of them have branches in Campbellton. Two of them operate a branch each in the next largest town, Dalhousie. However, of these eight branches, only three of them in Campbellton seriously pursue the market for business credit. In addition to the chartered banks there are nine autonomous credit unions, known as Caisses Populaires, operating in nine of the county's towns and villages. Only the largest in Campbellton puts any priority on the business credit market. Besides these CFIs, there is one small business lending agency already mentioned operating out of Campbellton and a Federal Business Development Bank operating from the city of Bathurst in the neighbouring county to the south.

The microloan fund MRM was established to provide small loans from CDN$500 to CDN$5,000 to micro entrepreneurs whose business credit needs were too small and whose business and personal profiles were too risky to be attractive as business credit clients to other sources of business credit in Restigouche. It used a peer group lending method. Its board of ten volunteers and its loan coordinator (a paid staff position) oversaw the formation of the borrower groups of from two to six members each. MRM clients were required to become members of the credit union that was one of the four partner institutions establishing MRM and to hold an account at the credit union. The credit union actually lent the money to MRM's clients over terms of three months to a year. MRM placed funds on deposit with the credit union to secure the loans. Delinquency or default by one member in a borrower group meant that other group members would be denied access to further credit until repayment obligations were covered.

By June 1997 MRM had seven borrowers groups ranging in size from two to five members for a total membership of thirty-two members. Many of the groups had some members who did not have a loan outstanding at that time. After the members of a borrowers group approved a member's application for a first loan of CDN$500 and after MRM's executive board confirmed that the group had followed the prescribed loan assessment procedures by meeting with a representative of the borrower group and sometimes with the loan applicant, the credit union actually disbursed the loan. By June 1997, many of the borrower groups had members who were working on repayment of second or third loans. These were of larger size than the first one; some were for as much as CDN$2,500.

Network Elements

When the program was initiated, officials in the Department of Economic Development and Tourism lacked first hand experience of peer group lending. Nor were staff in the development commission, the credit union and the small business lending agency familiar with it. They were enthusiastic about the idea of extending small loans to micro entrepreneurs and cutting down the costs of lending by using peer group lending techniques as they understood them. These officials assumed that **social networks** on which the techniques were built would be easy to exploit in Restigouche County and would ensure the success of the program. In fact, the difficulties arose at this level because of the strategy MRM used for recruiting clients in conjunction with the nature of the region from which they recruited them.

MRM began the peer group lending process of forming client groups by advertising its product of micro-business loans among the groups it targeted as most likely to be interested in developing income generating activities and small enterprises to supplement a low individual or family income or to fill an income void created by job loss. Such groups included clients of government programs for the unemployed and several women's groups. Ads and other marketing communications tools encouraged interested potential clients to come forward and declare their interest as individuals. After several months of marketing the program and the product, the loan coordinator had received 266 expressions of interest. Between sixty and seventy of these were judged to be reasonable prospects given their interest and commitment to their enterprise and their difficulties accessing business credit. However, the process of group formation proceeded painfully and slowly. The expressions of interest had come from individuals dispersed over a wide geographic area and from two linguistic communities. MRM employed the prevalent theory among peer group lenders that borrower groups should be self forming and self policing to the greatest extent possible. Potential borrowers naturally wanted to form groups with other members from the same municipality and language group to make it possible to satisfy MRM's requirements for regular and frequent borrower group meetings. Searching for three suitable peers (initially minimum group membership was set at four among the pool of sixty recruits proved frustrating for many.

Nevertheless, once groups formed and loan applications were made and processed, the social networks that were constructed in the process proved effective in minimizing probability of default. Peer pressure on the relatives of one borrower who moved to Toronto in search of work three months after taking out a loan seemed effective in getting the borrower to honor repayment obligations after some delinquency. Many of the peer groups reported strong social bonds forming among their members.

The development of **business networks among the micro enterprises** occurred in all groups, even in groups where social networks among members were constructed from scratch during the group formation and orientation process. For example, one member of the first borrower group to form carried on a part-time enterprise making picnic tables and wooden lawn furniture. The three other members of that group each took one of these tables and placed it on their lawns with a for sale sign, thereby generating several sales during the first summer.

The development of **business networks among micro entrepreneurs across borrower groups** was less apparent but some did occur during the life of the project. In part it was linked to deliberate efforts by MRM's loan coordinator to promote such business networking. For example, one of the borrowers was a graphic artist and operated a home-based graphic design business. MRM itself used her services in designing and producing some of its own marketing material during the project's second year. It thereby acquainted micro entrepreneurs in borrower groups outside hers with her service. Several board members who ran their own businesses also became familiar with her work through this process and subsequently used her service thus providing examples of **business networks between micro entrepreneurs and members of the established business community**.

Finally, at the fourth level of **business networks with sources of business credit** all of MRM clients took out accounts at the Caisse Populaire de Campbellton, the credit union that partnered with MRM, and met its manager. Having to deal with this credit union was a source of annoyance to those coming from municipalities far away from Campbellton with their own credit unions. However, it did extend their business network. MRM clients also became familiar with the staff at the small business lending agency which was one of the four partners establishing MRM. When MRM was dissolved in late 1998, many of the clients continued as borrowers at the small business lending agency.

MRM as an exercise in micro enterprise business network development around the provision of micro credit showed how the mechanics of such formation can work, even in less than optimal circumstances. The government agencies funding MRM expected it to grow its client base more rapidly than it did to the point of becoming financially self-sustaining over a two or three year period. When those expectations were not met, further funding was refused. Without assessing the soundness of those expectations, it is fair to say that one reason the client base grew more slowly than expected is the difficulty of exploiting prior social networks among borrowers in forming and operating groups given the way MRM initially recruited clients. It recruited them over a wide geographical area from a dispersed population and then expected the clients to form groups from among the pool of recruits most of whom had no common social network. However, even in these unfavourable circumstances one sees the development of business networks among the clients who did manage to form borrower groups and business networks between these micro entrepreneurs and players in the established business community. One sees it happening on the basis of the social networks that were constructed as a result of MRM's lending system and of some of the deliberate strategies of its loan coordinator.

Discussion and Conclusions

Micro enterprise networks established through peer lending circles are important because they have a strong social dimension, both from the foundation on which they are built (the more pre-existing social networks, the better), and from the point of view of outcomes (achieving intangible social benefits such as building individual confidence and skills, and tangible benefits such as moving people off their dependency on social welfare programs).

Conclusions may be drawn from the case studies about the ways in which micro credit programs using peer group lending can foster business network formation among micro enterprises they serve. Both MRM and Red Ochre in fact fostered such business network formation. The latter may have been more effective in accomplishing this objective due to the effect of some contributing factors present in its case and absent from the Restigouche case. The following factors appear to be influential in fostering business network formation.

Prior social networks among the micro entrepreneurs entering borrower groups and accessing micro credit

MRM was wanting in this regard for half of its groups due to the way clients were recruited as individuals across a wide geographic area without consideration for prior social relationships with other clients until after they had been recruited. Red Ochre, on the other hand, deliberately undertook to build small borrower groups within specific limited targeted geographical pockets to take advantage of preexisting social networks and to reduce travel costs. Red Ochre focussed on geographical issues and employed local thinking at the outset.

Detailed procedures for borrower group formation, operation, and loan application assessment rigorously administered by a loan coordinator and/or MFI board

The peer group lending method has, as a by-product the strengthening of preexisting social networks among borrowers or the construction of new social networks for borrowers with no common pre-existing social network. Both Red Ochre and MRM employed the method rigorously and fostered such networks among the micro entrepreneurs and other participants in the micro credit project, such as volunteer board members.

Deliberate and imaginative strategies on the part of the MFI for fostering alliances among the micro entrepreneurs served by the MFI

The presence of this factor is in part dependent on the time and resources that MFI staff and board have left over to devote to it after dealing with operational issues essentially connected to running a business credit service. In the case of MRM the problem of satisfying expectations of the project's funders and of countering the lack of commitment from some of the partners meant that the loan coordinator and board were usually absorbed in trying to expand the client base and to increase revenues from interest and fees through recruiting, group formation and orientation, and loan administration. Credit was the primary objective. Business network building was a low priority. Even so, some limited explicit efforts to foster alliances among micro enterprise clients had appreciable results.

A financial institution partnering in the establishment of the micro credit program and playing an operational role in the program

Red Ochre lacked such a partner during the first year of operation, and had limited effectiveness in some aspects of business network building as a result during this time. During its second year it partnered with a regional small business lending agency. MRM had two such partners, a credit union and a small business lending agency. Business network building for the micro entrepreneurs at the fourth level, between them and sources of business credit, was very effective. This was so true that when the project was terminated for other reasons, these networks endured well beyond the life of the project.

Policy Questions and Opportunities

Micro enterprise development must be seen in the context of the range of small business opportunities and should receive the same kind of programmatic support aimed at the upper end of the small business sector, where there tends to be more capital and more jobs involved. This translates into the need for a commitment on the part of an appropriate public agency to assist in defraying the operational expenses of peer lending programs.

Micro enterprise development must also be seen as a tool for social development, for helping to ease people into the labor force and off social welfare programs. It has the further benefit of developing practical and real skills among people even if the business does not succeed. A small investment in these programs can go a long way to reducing the overall cost of social welfare programs.

Obtaining a partner to supply loan capital is not a problem, as most CFIs or community based organizations are willing to do so. The challenge is in securing a partner to provide operational financing, and this is necessary because the quality of the network developed between the micro entrepreneur and the coordinator, between the coordinator and the peer lending circles, between the coordinator and board/committee, and between the coordinator and other potential partners will determine the success of the program.

References

Aspen Institute (1995), *Micro enterprise Assistance: What are we Learning About Results?* Aspen Institute, Washington, DC.

Berenbach, S., and Churchill, C. (1997), *Regulation and Supervision of Microfinance Institutions: Experience From Latin America, Asian and Africa*, Occasional Paper No. 1, MicroFinance Network.

Bornstein, D. (1995), 'The Barefoot Bank with Cheek', *The Atlantic Monthly*, vol. 276, no. 6, December.

Boshara, R., Freidman, R., and Anderson, B. (1997), *Realizing the Promise of Micro enterprise Development in Welfare Reform*, AEO Exchange, Chicago.

Burrus, W., and Stearns, K. (1997), *Building a Model: ACCION'S Approach to Micro enterprise in the United States*, ACCION International.

Calmeadow Foundation (1997), *Calmeadow's Operational Review: A Tool for Documentation and Analysis of Microfinance Organizations*, Calmeadow Foundation, Toronto.

Canadian International Development Agency (CIDA) (1995), *Summary of Proceedings: International Forum on Microenterprises*, Canadian International Development Agency, Ottawa.

Clark, P., and Houston, T. (1993), *Assisting the Smallest Businesses: Assessing Micro enterprise Development as a Strategy for Boosting Poor Communities*, Aspen Institute, Washington, DC.

Flora C., Flora J., Spears, J., and Swanson, L. (1992), *Rural Communities: Legacy and Change*, Westview Press, San Francisco.

Gertler, M. (1995), 'Being there: proximity, organization, and culture in the development and adoption of advanced manufacturing technologies', *Economic Geography*, vol. 71, pp. 1-26.

Gertler, M., and DiGiovanna, S. (1997), 'In search of the new social economy: collaborative relations between users and producers of advanced manufacturing technologies', *Environment and Planning A*, vol. 29, pp. 1585-602.

Himes, C., and Servon, L. (1998), *Measuring Client Success: An Evaluation of ACCION's Impact on Microenterprises in the United States*, ACCION International.

MacPherson, A. (1988), 'New product development among small Toronto manufacturers: empirical evidence on the role of technical service linkages', *Economic Geography*, vol. 64, pp. 62-75.

MacPherson, A. (1991), 'New product development among small industrial firms: a comparative assessment of the role of technical service linkages in Toronto and Buffalo', *Economic Geography*, vol. 67, pp. 136-46.

MacPherson, A. (1994), 'The impact of industrial process innovation among small manufacturing firms: empirical evidence from western New York', *Environment and Planning A*, vol. 26, pp. 453-70.

Red Ochre Regional Development Board Inc. (1997), *Strategic Economic Plan 1997-2001*.

Taub, R. (1998), 'Making the Adaptation Across Cultures: A Report on an Attempt to Clone the Grameen Bank in Southern Arkansas', *Journal of Developmental Entrepreneurship*, vol. 3, no. 1, pp. 53-69.

Wehrell, R. (1996), *The State of Home Based Business in Atlantic Canada*, Rural and Small Town Programme, Sackville.

Wehrell, R., Bruce, D., Harold, J., and Joyal, A. (1998), *Evaluation of Demand for Micro Credit in Rural Canada*, Agriculture and Agri-Food Canada, Ottawa.

Women's World Banking (1996), *Institution Building in Microfinance: Lessons From Funders and Practitioners*, Women's World Banking, New York.

7 Organizational Clusters in a Resource Based Industry: Empirical Evidence from New Zealand

MICHÈLE E.M. AKOORIE

Introduction

Rediscovering the importance of location is a prominent theme in the realm of current management and economic literature. Long neglected by management theorists and economists alike, the role of geography has often been reduced to assessment of cultural and other differences in doing business in various countries and corporate location has been treated as a narrow sub-speciality of operations management. In the area of international business where globalization allows companies to source capital, goods and technology from anywhere and to locate operations wherever it is most cost effective, the tendency has been to see location as diminishing in importance (Porter, 1998a).

This is arguably not the case. International business scholars have pointed out that more attention needs to be given to the importance of location as a variable affecting the global competitiveness of firms (Dunning, 1998). Firms who seek to become globally competitive need to pay close attention to the importance of location as they seek to acquire new areas of firm specific competence and/or simultaneously more efficiently deploy their home based assets. The development of their home based assets, in turn, are in part a function of the strength of the knowledge-related infrastructure in which these 'created assets' are fostered and nurtured.

Empirical evidence supporting this rediscovery of location in the management literature is distinguished by its absence. The objective of this chapter is to fill this gap, by offering evidence on the development of an organizational cluster in a resource-based industry in New Zealand. The chapter is organized in the following manner. In the first section, the literature relating to the antecedents and current management exponents of 'clustering' is discussed. We then offer a brief overview of the context in which resource-based industries have developed in the New Zealand economy. The following section examines the dimensions of the resource-based industry chosen for inclusion in this chapter - the bloodstock (or thoroughbred breeding industry). A cluster map of the industry is then developed. We then discuss the role of spatial proximity in promoting the competitiveness of these firms through knowledge creation, collaboration and the dissemination of information within the cluster firms. Some conclusions and comments on the future of the industry are offered in the final section.

Clusters: Antecedents and Overlaps

The objective of this section is to examine the extant literature in relation to clusters. We draw a distinction between networks and clusters here. Networks may exist within a cluster, but they are not the same as clusters of geographically proximate firms. Networks are loosely defined as forms of collaborative activity between firms, not necessarily in the same geographic space. Modern telecommunications makes possible the development of virtual networks, which are linked through electronic means. Clusters are geographic concentrations of interconnected companies, specialized suppliers, service providers, firms in related industries and associated institutions (for example, universities, standards agencies and trade associations) in particular fields that compete but also co-operate (Porter, 1998a, 1998b).

Clusters in the Management Literature

Commonalities and complementarities link clusters of interconnected firms. The geographic scope of a cluster can range from a single city or state to a country or even a network of neighboring countries. Porter's 1990 work, *The Competitive Advantage of Nations* put forward a theory of national, state and local competitiveness within the context of a global economy. Critics of the 'Diamond' of International Competitiveness have focused their attention on *inter alia*, the inappropriateness of the model for resource-based economies (Rugman, 1992; Cartwright 1993). However, they paid limited attention to the evidence that it is the competitive *clusters* of firms at the regional level, which contributes to the national competitiveness of an economy. Porter (1990) may also have given less emphasis to the regional context, but his subsequent work (1994; 1996; 1998a; 1998b) together with that of Enright (1995) has refocused attention on the phenomena of regional clusters of innovative activity within a country, using these examples to explain the economic income divergence within an economy.

Porter (1998a; 1998b) in describing clusters as the 'new economics of competition' refers to the historical and intellectual antecedents of cluster theory. The antecedents of cluster theory represent two divergent streams in the literature, economic geography and the 'new geographical economics' (Martin 1999). In essence, Martin (1999) suggests that what the new geographic economists are saying is not new, and 'it is most certainly not geography' (p. 67).

The New Geographical Turn in Economics

The 'geographical turn' in economics embraces two main research programs, concerned respectively with increasing returns and spatial agglomeration of economic activity and the dynamics of regional growth convergence. The first area is particularly associated with the work of Krugman (1991;1993; 1994a; 1995) and Arthur (1994; 1996) and Venables (1996a; 1996b). The argument suggested here is that increasing returns, economies of scale and imperfect competition are far more important than constant returns, perfect competition and comparative advantage in causing trade and specialization. The market technological and other externalities underpinning these increasing returns arises through a process of regional and economic agglomeration. Martin's (1999) main criticism of this line of reasoning, is that first, such work has been done (and discarded) by geographers who were busy analyzing industrial location back in the 1960s and 1970s. A resurgence of interest in industrial districts has focused on a new body of work on industrial districts, in particular the unevenness of development, the role of history (path dependence) and the consequences of inertia effects on the rise and decline of urban economies.

Second, Martin (1999) opines that 'new economic geography' is long on mathematical modeling and short on empirical application. Martin ascribes this deficiency to the abstract, oversimplified and idealized nature of the models themselves. Furthermore, limited attention is paid to the forces that influence the geographical distribution of industry and economic activity (such as local infrastructure, local institutions, state spending and intervention, regulatory arrangements and foreign investment and disinvestment). In this sense the limitations of the studies are that the architecture of policy to stimulate and encourage the development of economic agglomeration, is missing.

The second major stream of the 'new economic geography' focuses on long run growth and convergence, rather than on industrial and urban location. Interest in this area has been stimulated by the 'new growth theory', based on a reformulation of the neo-classical growth model. Barro and Sala-i-Martin (1995) suggest, that unlike the standard neo-classical growth model which assumes diminishing returns to capital and labor, the neo-classical convergence growth model is more applicable at the cross-regional than at the cross-national level, because of greater uniformity of structural, technological, institutional and social characteristics, within nations than between them. Again Martin (1999) critiques the regional convergence models on the grounds that the empirical studies examine only one aspect of convergence, that is income or output per head. There have been few attempts to unravel the relative role of capital flows, labor migration or technological spillovers in the evolution of cross-region income distribution.

The lack of empirical evidence is not the only concern; what is of more concern is that the 'mathematical modeling' of new economic geographers gives social, cultural and institutional factors involved in spatial economic development a secondary, or even marginal role. This, assumedly, is because such factors cannot be reduced or expressed in mathematical form.

Neo-Marshallian Industrial Districts

The third strand of theory that Martin (1999) identifies is the work based on neo-Marshallian industrial district economics. This approach is marginalized in the literature because it has little impact on mainstream economics. Yet, if the 'institutional thickness' which is the geographers' idea of studying 'real people in real places' is the ideal, then the neo-Marshallian focus on the industrial districts of 'Third Italy" should have a prominent place in the management literature (Antonelli, 1990,1994; Beccatini, 1990; Garofoli, 1991). The contribution from this area is that the detailed empirical work on specific regions emphasizes the embedness of the social, institutional and cultural foundations of local industrial growth. These foundations are built on the networks of trust, co-operation, competition and governance that characterize such areas.

Not surprisingly, the Marshallian concept of industrial districts has been most influential in the development of the management literature. In the management literature, like economics, attention to geography or location has been minimal. Globalization has created a tendency to regard location as of diminishing importance (Porter 1998a). However, as Dunning (1998) points out more attention needs to be given to the importance of location as a variable affecting the global competitiveness of firms. There are two reasons for this.

First, with the gradual dispersion of created assets, the structure and content of the location portfolio becomes more critical to firms who seek to acquire new assets and simultaneously more efficiently deploy their home based assets. Second, the role of government becomes more critical as they need to understand the growing importance of knowledge-related infrastructure and with it the idea of sub-national spatial units as a nexus of untraded interdependencies. Government's role is to promote the dynamic comparative advantage of their resource-capabilities and to work in partnership with firms to improve or replace markets in the cases of those markets where endemic market failure is most widespread (Dunning, 1998).

The role of location then, is becoming more widely recognized for its importance in the management literature. There is an enduring theme of 'rediscovering Marshall' that is the work of Alfred Marshall (1919; 1920). The symbiosis between knowledge and organization is the driving principle behind the idea that a mutually beneficial relationship is produced in the industrial environment between the creation of new information and organizational improvement of related firms (Zaratiegui, 1997). While Marshall's concept of 'industrial districts' has its contemporary expression in the new industrial districts of Silicon Valley and the industrial districts of Third Italy, most emphasis is given to his insights regarding the importance of technological spillovers and the role of externalities rather than how these districts grow. Marshall (1919) suggests that each new period takes advantage of advances made in previous periods on three levels. First, the businesses own internal organization serves as a source of internal data. Second, the organization of businesses within an industrial district gives each the access to a fund of common knowledge and third, the knowledge imparted by suppliers and consumers serves to improve the internal organization of each business.

Porter (1998a) emphasizes the importance of government policy in developing economy wide competitiveness. This policy goes beyond the traditional, although not unimportant roles of government policy. These traditional roles are, first, to achieve macroeconomic and political stability, second, to improve the general microeconomic capacity of the economy by improving the efficiency and quality of the general-purpose inputs into the economy.[1] The third role for government is to establish the overall microeconomic rules and incentives governing competition that will encourage productivity growth.

In relation to the role of government in facilitating cluster development, Porter (1998a) requires that governments accept the way of organizing thinking about many policy areas that go beyond the common needs of the entire economy. This is not only essential at the national level, but at the sub-national level (regional and state agencies). Cluster-based thinking will help to guide policies in science and technology, education and training, and the promotion of exports and foreign investment. Governments should focus on cluster upgrading and reinforcing, rather than the creation of new clusters. Most clusters form where there is a foundation of locational advantages to build on and often form independently of government action (and sometimes in spite of it). Understanding cluster dynamics requires acceptance of the concept. However, it is by no means clear how this shift in thinking is to take place, apart from offering evidence of successful cluster-based initiatives in different countries.

In summary therefore, the preceding section suggests that there is a respectable body of complementary literature from different disciplines that examine the same phenomena. The phenomena is that the competitiveness of that a firm is a nexus of treaties, between interdependent entities, grounded in a unique location 'space' which is firmly rooted in the historical, cultural and institutional context in which it develops. What is new in the management literature is the recognition of the importance of location, paradoxically, since it requires the recognition that the most enduring advantages in a global economy will be local. Recognizing the importance of location and the individual initiatives of entrepreneurs helps explain the shifting dynamics of clusters.

Resource Based Economies

This next section relates cluster development to New Zealand's predominantly resource-based economy – highly dependent on export income, principally derived from revenue generated from the outputs of a pastoral economy. New Zealand's export dependence is a function of its small size (3.8 million population) and the need to meet a high proportion of intermediate and final demand from imports.

It has been long recognized that to derive economic rent from natural resources requires the application of capital, technology and know-how to produce a marketable commodity or product. In this regard, location, created assets (knowledge) and capital triangulate to form a core of firm specific advantages, which arise from the interactions of these components (Akoorie, 1998). Yet, resource based industries are regarded as the weaker dimension of a country's economic base for a number of reasons.

First, commodity-based products, which form the bulk of resource outputs have suffered from a steady deterioration in world prices since World War II, coupled with a pervasive protectionism in most developed countries' markets for agricultural products in particular. For countries like New Zealand this has resulted in the deterioration in the terms of trade – the amount that a country has to export to pay for imports. Since New Zealand is highly dependent on exporting, with agricultural earnings still contributing to over one-half of export income, this has become a critical issue in the debate over future economic directions.

Second, countries such as the newly industrializing economies (NIEs) of North and South East Asia have benefitted from the growth of trade in manufactured products, relative to agricultural commodities. Yet, as Krugman (1994b), pointed out, with considerable prescience, the economic growth rates of these economies was fragile, and owed more to the mobilization of previously under-utilized resources, than to improvements in productivity. More recently, the rates of growth in the trade in services have overtaken trade in manufactured goods. Those countries who have developed competencies in a few key technology fields, such as information technology, telecommunications, biotechnology and advanced materials are experiencing high growth rates as a consequence of growing global demand for these advanced interdisciplinary technologies. One example is the Republic of Ireland, which has positioned itself as the e-hub for the European Union.

Third, the resource-based economies such as New Zealand are bound by the limitations of small size. It follows from this that firms of small average size will dominate small economies. Small firms operating internationally suffer from a number of weaknesses, primarily financial and managerial resource constraints (Akoorie and Enderwick, 1992), which affect their ability to acquire knowledge of the external international environment which in turn influences the creation of internal knowledge within the organization. Overcoming the weaknesses of resource constrained internationalization is an initiating force for small firms to engage in collaborative activity (forming networks) or to co-operate within a specific industrial sector (cluster formation).

Over the last three decades the response of the New Zealand economy to the changing dimensions of international trade and investment has been a limited one. The response in the 1960s to deteriorating economic conditions for agricultural commodities was to diversify the base of the economy.

Diversification has meant finding alternative uses for agricultural land, rather than producing the traditional primary commodities of butter, cheese, wool and meat (which were the basis of the economy from the 19th century). Market diversification was to find alternative outlets to its traditional markets of the United Kingdom and the United States. The limitations of restructuring to include the development of an internationally competitive industrial manufacturing base, late entry into world markets, the pervasive legacy of protectionism (over a period of 50 years) and the financial and resource constraints of small firm size (Akoorie and Enderwick, 1992).

Agricultural diversification in the 1960s promoted the establishment of a number of new agricultural industries – among which were kiwi fruit, soft fruits, deer farming, wine, and thoroughbred breeding. None of these industries were 'new' – wine making had been carried out in New Zealand since the middle of the 19th century, principally for fortified wines for domestic consumption and horses were imported to New Zealand at about the same time.[2] However, the potential of these industries to contribute to the export-earning base was recognized and promoted through a number of government-funded financial incentives (Enderwick and Akoorie, 1996). The international orientation of these industries dates from that era. Although these industries have a national dimension, they are a collection of sub-national clusters of regional districts, arising out of specific locational variables, such as climate and soil type coupled with the created assets of industry specific knowledge, technology and capital. Unlike the industrial districts of Modena, Silicon Valley and Route 128, these New Zealand based industries are resource-based and like the neo-Marshallian industrial districts, depend on the institutional, historical and cultural 'thickness' that explains the robustness of many of these districts. This type of thickness is found in naturally occurring clusters of firms, in geographic proximity. These forms of collaboration, may be partial, informal or periodic, but they share a common industry framework and knowledge, a web of commercial, social and technical agreements which unites the entrepreneurs with rivals, and innovations that foster incentive and information (Zaratiegui, 1997).

In New Zealand, evidence of naturally occurring resource-based clusters suggests that there is a long history of collaborative activity in specific industries. The dairy industry in New Zealand was founded on the principles of co-operatives, and still remains so today. Encouraging collaboration in the New Zealand context has been a response to both environmental factors (distance from markets, isolation of industry) and the capital requirements for processing. Collaboration has been institutionalized in New Zealand, through the acceptance of the principle of statutory authority for Producer Boards, who act on behalf of the industry. The restructuring of the Boards, initiated by government policy, but carried out by the Board's themselves, seems to indicate that there is an industry preference for the principles of co-operation (Akoorie and Scott-Kennel, 1999). The creation of a mega co-operative in the dairy industry, will be the first serious challenge to the Commerce Commission as a test of market power. As far as small firms are concerned, the issue of collaboration creating market dominance has never yet been tested, since in reality, collaboration does not take place on any significant scale to be perceived as a threat to open competition.

The Industry Cluster: Thoroughbred Breeding

This industry, the breeding of thoroughbred horses for flat racing, hurdling and steeplechasing has been selected as an example of a resource-based industry that has a national dimension, but is also sub-national (regional) in character and location. The industry has been long established in New Zealand; it has well-developed institutional, historical and cultural characteristics and it developed initially to meet domestic demand before becoming internationally oriented. The thoroughbred industry makes a significant contribution to export earnings. In 1998 (year ending December) the industry exported NZ$132 million worth of thoroughbred horses for racing and as breeding stock. The principal market is Australia, followed by the United States, Macau, Singapore, Malaysia and South Africa. In the same year, New Zealand exported sport horses (of thoroughbred or thoroughbred cross origin) worth NZ$11.6 million. These horses are bought by foreign buyers as eventers or show jumpers (Anderson, 1998).

The thoroughbred breeding industry is an example of *cluster convergence*. The principal thoroughbred studs were historically located in the Canterbury (South Island), Hawkes Bay and Wairarapa regions of the North Island. In the last fifty years the thoroughbred breeding industry has converged into the central North Island (the Waikato region). The greater Waikato area has twenty-six of New Zealand's major stud farms and seven of these studs are recognized by their yearling sales results as being the top ten New Zealand breeders. There are 258 registered thoroughbred stallions in New Zealand of whom 160 covered more than ten mares in the 1997 season. There are 9,400 registered brood mares in New Zealand, but only 2,400 of these were covered (used for breeding) in the 1997 season. The Greater Waikato region has 35 percent of the country's thoroughbred stallions and over 40 percent of New Zealand's broodmare population, making the area the largest pool of thoroughbred breeding stock in New Zealand (New Zealand Thoroughbred Breeders Association, 1997/1998). The reasons for this concentration of related clusters in the Central Waikato are discussed later.

A study of this industry is undertaken using a cluster mapping technique (derived from Porter, 1998a). This cluster map shows the dimensions of the core firms, the related and supporting industries, and the shared industry inputs (shared in terms of inputs into other related industries). It also shows the dimensions of the physical and social infrastructure that support the core and the related and supporting industries, and finally, the industry intersections, where the core industry crosses over to another (often related) industry. The mapping techniques shows how one competitive industry can help another in a mutually reinforcing process and that "improving the productivity of all industries enhances prosperity both directly and through the influence one industry has on the productivity of others" (Porter, 1998a, p. 10).

While tracing the development of an industry cluster can show how the resource cluster has grown, how clusters can be 'spun-off' to create new clusters forms in other locations, and identify the probable triggers of cluster formation and development. It cannot identify one of the key features that contributes to cluster evolution. If proximity in geographic, cultural and institutional terms, allows special access, special relationships, better information, powerful incentives and other opportunities for advantages in productivity and productivity growth that are difficult to tap from a distance, then a key element of the research is to try to define how these interactions occur. This in our view is the most difficult dimension of cluster based research. Since most knowledge is created and reproduced through some sort of social interaction, often embodied in the organization of the firm, it is very difficult to identify exactly where in the organization the knowledge and the skills are embodied and how the embodiment has taken place (Maskell and Malmberg, 1999). Nevertheless our cluster case research has enabled us to identify the specific forms of knowledge intrinsic to both industries, how they are generated, and codified in what form and how that contributes to spatial reproduction in clusters of sub national industries.

Identifying the Components of a Cluster

A cluster can be described as a complete system, where groups of firms have established a relatively high degree of collaboration over time (Enright, 1995).

Clusters are usually based on local/historical/sectoral agglomerations of firms in which the different elements of the system (e.g. specialized suppliers, toolmakers, machine builders and services) are present in a relatively restricted geographical area. The institutional, cultural and historical 'thickness' of a cluster is reinforced by the physical and social infrastructure in which the cluster is embedded. Ffowcs Williams (1997) suggested that the elements of a 'high performance' cluster could be presented as shown in Figure 7.1.

The Layers of the Cluster

Four layers of activity can be differentiated in the cluster. The first is the 'cluster core' which contains a critical mass of highly specialized similar and related firms within close geographic proximity and amongst whom there is both strong competition *and* cooperation. Vertical and/or horizontal integration is achieved through participation in networks – either informal or

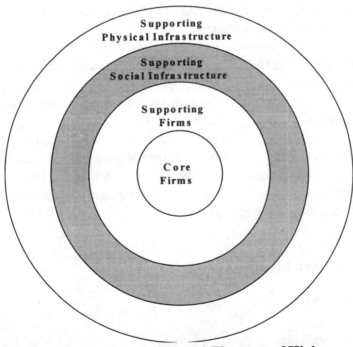

**Figure 7.1 The Four Integrated Elements of High
Performance Clusters**

Source: Ffowcs Williams (1997)

formal. This core is also characterized by the interchange of knowledge and information at both the domestic and international level.

The next layer consists of an array of specialist supporting firms. These include specialist service providers such as financial services, legal and design services and insurance services as well as providers of materials and equipment servicing needed for the core to function effectively. This layer is also characterized by high levels of rivalry and cooperation but with the added dimension of very tight linkages between firms in this layer and those at the core of the cluster.

The third layer contains the supporting social infrastructure which includes secondary and tertiary educational institutions, industry training organizations, local sources of business and technology advice, and professional and trade associations. A key element in the performance of the cluster is the capability of the individual elements comprising this layer and the linkages between them. Within this layer there are opportunities for members of the core to meet regularly for discussion and information exchange. It also ensures that the workforce utilized by the core is well informed and skilled in the specific areas of expertise required by the industry.

The final layer comprises the physical infrastructure. It is suggested that this layer should include highly specialized and integrated facilities such as transport, utilities and waste disposal. Members of this layer can be either public providers or private sector but they must be flexible enough to identify and speedily address capacity constraints (Ffowcs Williams, 1997).

In the next section of the chapter we utilize the diagram of the four integrated elements of the cluster to discuss the development and growth of the thoroughbred-breeding cluster in Cambridge, New Zealand. The elements of the cluster are described and a discussion of how knowledge and information is a key component of the competitiveness of this cluster is offered.

The Thoroughbred Breeding Cluster in Cambridge

Birth and Evolution

The town of Cambridge (population (1992) 10,530) is in the Waikato region of New Zealand, approximately 130 kilometres from Auckland, its largest city. Cambridge and nearby Matamata are two towns at the centre of the New Zealand thoroughbred breeding industry. The greater Waikato region has 35 percent of the country's stallions and over 40 percent of New Zealand's broodmare population, making it the largest pool of thoroughbred breeding stock in New Zealand.

The Cambridge area has developed as a center for thoroughbred breeding for several reasons. The first significant stud in Cambridge was the Trelawney Stud, purchased by Senton Otway in the 1930s. Otway stood the highly successful sire Foxbridge (Foxlaw-Bridgemount) bred in England and imported into Cambridge in 1935. Foxbridge dominated the New Zealand racing and breeding scene during the 1940s and 1950s, capturing eleven successive general sire premierships and eleven broodmare financial premierships. His broodmares proved magnificent influences for superior ability up to two miles on the flat (du Bourg, 1980). Otway had a remarkable collection of stallions at Trelawney[3] and bred or owned the sires of seven Melbourne Cup Winners (the premier Australasian Group 1 race).[4] More recently the presence of one of the most successful stud masters in New Zealand, Patrick Hogan of the Cambridge Stud has reinforced this preeminence. Hogan stood one of New Zealand's most prominent multimillion dollar sires of recent years, the now deceased Sir Tristram [Sir Tristram (1971, Sir Ivor – Isolt)]. Sir Tristram, dominated the New Zealand breeding industry from 1980 until his death in 1996. Sir Tristram sired 658 winners and nineteen Group one race winners and was Champion Australasian Sire of Broodmares three times. One of his sons, Zabeel, is also standing at the Cambridge Stud to carry on the Sir Tristram line. Zabeel has sired 144 winners (1998) including the 1997 winner of the Melbourne Cup, Might and Power, as well as the Auckland Cup winner for 1998, Jezabeel.[5] Jezabeel also won the Australian Melbourne Cup in November, 1998, the world's most prestigious staying handicap, valued at NZ$3.32 million.[6]

Location

Desirable factor locations for the breeding of thoroughbreds include a temperate climate and fertile 'well-draining' soil. The temperate climate means that stock can be reared out of doors, rather than being stabled. This offers a benefit in two ways. First, the cost of rearing an animal out of doors reduces the input in terms of capital and manpower. There are significant cost savings in farm construction and consumption of feed, which provides breeders with a comparative cost advantage over competitors. Second, the New Zealand thoroughbreds are considered to be hardier, developing muscles and ligaments under natural conditions and are less susceptible to diseases such as respiratory illnesses, which is one of the inherent disadvantages of indoor stabling.

The area has excellent free draining sandy loam soils, which are ideal for horse breeding. Free draining soils are essential for carrying stock out at pasture all year round, important because horses are heavy animals and damage pasture lands. Having free-draining soil allows more horses to be kept per hectare than most other places in the world. The strip of land where the Cambridge studs are concentrated (beside the Waikato River to Lake Karapiro) is rated in the top one percent of arable land in the country. The mild climate with adequate rainfall encourages the growth of good pasture, with high levels of protein and essential trace elements for growing young bloodstock. Apart from the soil type, farmland in the greater Auckland region has increasingly come under pressure from the pace of relentless urban development. Substantial land area required for bloodstock made the Waikato area an attractive alternative. With the move of the national yearling sales from Wellington (Trentham) to Auckland in the 1990s, the traditional center for thoroughbred breeding in the Manawatu (north of Wellington) became less important.

The third element in location advantages for Cambridge is proximity and accessibility to customers. The advantage of accessibility to sales outlets (the Karaka auction venue – two hours away) is that transporting a yearling over a lesser distance reduces the risk of damage in transfer. The Karaka sales venue is also close to the major airport (Auckland) which handles airfreight of horses overseas. Not all of the thoroughbred sales occur at public auction. Sales by private treaty are common, and international buyers have the advantage of being able to visit New Zealand's top studs in a single day, only 130 kilometres from the major gateway to New Zealand at Auckland.

Elements of the Cluster

Figure 7.2 presents a schematic diagram of the Cambridge thoroughbred cluster. The cluster includes an extensive complement of supporting industries to the breeding of thoroughbreds. On the input side the cluster shares commonalities with the wider agricultural cluster of the Waikato area, which is a prominent dairy industry region. These commonalities include, fencing, (both fixed and electrical fencing systems), soil analysis, fertilisers, grass seeding, pasture renewal and maintenance, generalised building, water supply and electrical services as well as the veterinary services for livestock including horses.

Fertilizer is a shared input with the dairy industry. The thoroughbred industry represents only a minor share of the fertilizer industry's total business

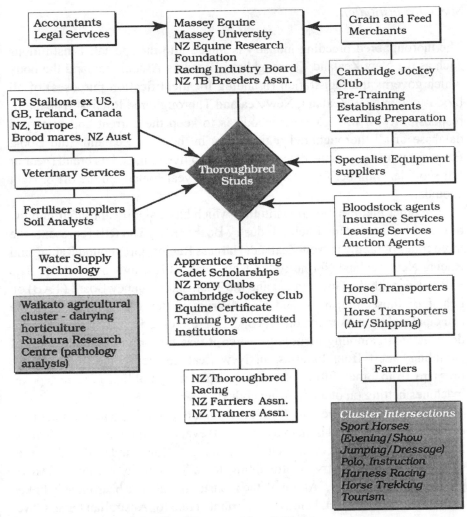

Figure 7.2 The Cambridge Thoroughbred Cluster

in the Waikato and the requirements of each industry are very different. The focus of the dairy industry in New Zealand is in the production of dry matter, which in turn produces milk. In the thoroughbred industry the focus is on animal health and rapid growth of young stock and the health of their mares and stallions. Stud farms look for a fertiliser that is slow releasing providing constant pasture growth throughout the year. For example, Sechura fertilizer is a natural phosphate from Peru that is citric soluble rather than water soluble.

Specialist Institutions

The thoroughbred breeding industry is linked into the specialist institutions such as the New Zealand Thoroughbred Breeders Association and the body which governs the registration (branding for identification purposes) of all bloodstock in New Zealand, New Zealand Thoroughbred Racing. The major responsibility of this governing body is to keep the current and historical database of all thoroughbred registrations in the New Zealand Stud Book. Breeder returns record the date of birth of each live foal, and its brand (near or left shoulder) number foaled and last digit of year foaled, on the off or right shoulder.

The other major national institution which has a significant input into the breeding industry is the Racing Industry Board (RIB) The RIB represents the three codes of racing in New Zealand, Harness Racing, Greyhound Racing and Racing New Zealand (formerly the New Zealand Racing Conference). The RIB liaises with the Government and the Totalisator Agency Board (TAB) on behalf of these industries, and also distributes the TAB grant and is the principal policy maker for the TAB. Horse racing in New Zealand, after decades as a gambling monopoly, when it was the only legitimate form of gambling, apart from lotteries, in New Zealand, has come under severe pressure from other forms of recently legalized gambling (casinos, poker machines betting on other sporting codes).

When racing was the only form of legitimate gambling and the monopoly on betting was (and still is, held by the TAB) every small town in New Zealand had its own racetrack with regular meetings. Now, under the threat of competition the industry is attempting to rationalize its racing outlets by grading the race venues. Although the industry has always been closely linked to the Australian market, being an important venue for Australian buyers, over recent years the Asian markets of Hong Kong, Malaysia, the Philippines and Japan have become attractive outlets for vendors. However, quarantine requirements, a lack of pre training facilities and a lower standard of competitive racing mean that the outlet is more attractive for older, proven racehorses.

Related and Supporting Industries

Sales agents and insurance A specialist supporting industry for thoroughbred breeding is the purpose built auction facility at the Karaka sales complex, conveniently situated between the Waikato area and Auckland airport. This complex opened in 1986 and being located near the main North South Highway route (State Highway One), signaled the beginning of the dominance of the Waikato area over the southern studs when the national yearling sales were moved from their former venue at Trentham in Wellington. The national sales are now run by New Zealand Bloodstock Ltd, formerly Wrightsons, a long-established stock and station agency. Until Wrightsons was bought by New Zealand Bloodstock, it was owned by one of New Zealand's largest firms, Fletcher Challenge. New Zealand Bloodstock also incorporates airfreight services, offering multiple scheduled weekly flights to Australian racing centers (Sydney and Melbourne) and charters to the Northern Hemisphere weekly, and to other destinations on a monthly basis.

Other supporting services are provided by New Zealand Bloodstock services which provide essential services in covering risk, not only related to the purchase and transportation of bloodstock, but also in the breeding side of the business. Bloodstock finance is also provided through purchase and leasing arrangements to owners, which has taxation advantages for owners.

Veterinary services Veterinary services are critical in the equine industry – particularly in the breeding season, where complications in foaling may arise. The local veterinary practice derives 65 percent of its equine work from thoroughbred stud farms, and is also involved with equine nutrition (and associations with the feed suppliers and fertilizer suppliers in joint problem solving). The veterinary practice also uses animal health laboratory services at Ruakura (close to Cambridge) and is the veterinary representative on the New Zealand Thoroughbred Breeders Association in Auckland.

Although the main agricultural research center is located near the University of Waikato at Ruakura it does not specialize in equine research or equine nutrition. This is carried out at the School of Veterinary Science at the University of Massey in Palmerston North. The New Zealand Equine Research Foundation provides funding for the Equine Research Faculty at Massey in Palmerson North, which also receives government funding through the Public Good Science Fund, and is funded in accordance with the priorities set by the members of the thoroughbred industry. It specializes in research into equine nutrition of foals and yearlings, wastage in the thoroughbred horse such as joint, tendon, foot and hoof problems, and bone and cartilage development. It also has facilities for equine surgery (as do some of the local veterinary practices although to a lesser degree) and direct links for specific cases to the local veterinary services.

Feed merchants, specialist equipment There are two specialist feed merchants in the area, covering the feeding requirements of the studs, offering bulk feed (crushed and whole oats, barley, and maize, cut chaff and feed supplements) not only for the thoroughbred industry but also to the complementary dairy industry. In addition to grass pasture, horses have varying requirements for additional feed intake in the form of grains, depending on size, weather conditions, work requirements etc. Hay, or stored grass equivalents (similar to silage) is fed out in winter if the animal is at grass or fed if the animal is stabled. In addition the feed merchants supply proprietary feeds sourced from Australia, New Zealand and the United Kingdom, covering the wide range of nutritional requirements for working and breeding thoroughbred stock. The major studs deal direct with a feed supplier (manufacturer) who supplies to the retail outlets. The company provides a balanced nutrition plan for its thoroughbred customers, through taking herbage samples (from the pasture) and from that work out a diet of balanced nutrition to meet the needs of the respective stud. The relocation to the Waikato area of one of the largest feed merchants in New Zealand suggests that proximity to its major customers is an important consideration.

Cluster Intersections

At the intersections of clusters we find that new insights, skills and technologies from different fields merge as potential entrants and spin-offs occur. A spin-off cluster for the Cambridge thoroughbred cluster has already developed in nearby Matamata. A cluster similar to that of Cambridge has developed, as a result of pressure on the use of the training facilities at the Cambridge Jockey Club, the availability and price of land for studs, and the presence of a similar set of supporting and related industries. The upgrade of the training facilities at Matamata have encouraged new entrants to establish operations at that cluster (including a Trans Tasman operation, where a prominent Australian trainer has established a joint training operation with a New Zealand partner, to train New Zealand bred horses, to campaign in Australia).

The other cluster intersections relate to the development of residual uses for thoroughbred horses. Horses that are not suitable for racing for a variety or reasons (other than soundness) can be trained for show jumping, dressage, eventing or polo or for leisure uses. The New Zealand thoroughbred (and New Zealand riders) campaigning from their bases in England, have, in the last five years dominated the sport of international three day eventing, at the Olympic Games and in the World Championship tables. The New Zealand thoroughbred, with its tough constitution, speed, and competitiveness is well known for its ability in this demanding sport. There is a growing international demand for these horses.

Innovation and Co-operation in the Cluster

A shared vision is important as it has the ability to bring people together for a common purpose (Rosenfeld, 1996). A common purpose gives direction to the activities within a cluster, building the relationships between the determinants of the cluster and creating synergy. For the Cambridge thoroughbred cluster we found evidence that breeders readily share information for the good of the industry and although they compete fiercely, maintain social and business interactions through informal means. Foal share and broodmare leasing arrangements are used to participate in joint production activities. Stud owners and managers also share the cost and risk involved in investing in Northern Hemisphere stallions – which are considered to be of a higher quality than Southern Hemisphere stallions.

The most recent example (1999) is the jointly financed purchase of a United States import – Tale of the Cat[7] estimated to be worth US$10 million. The stallion was brought to New Zealand through a combined deal involving twelve studs and New Zealand bloodstock. This joint purchasing arrangement has a number of advantages, one being that a single stud owner does not bear the financial risk. Despite good conformation, breeding lines and race performance, there is no guarantee that a stallion will be an outstandingly prepotent sire. The other advantage of joint purchasing arrangements is that it enables the industry to have access to new bloodlines that would not be available if breeders had to purchase stallions on their own account. The other form of joint purchasing is through syndication – where a breeder will purchase a stallion and then sell shares in the stallion to other breeders. The shares entitle the owner to a number of stallion nominations that the breeder can use on his own broodmares or sell to another broodmare owner.

Another widely used innovation in recent years has been the use of 'shuttle stallions'. Since Northern Hemisphere and Southern Hemisphere breeding times are opposite to each other, shuttle stallions from the Northern Hemisphere studs have been brought to New Zealand for the Southern Hemisphere covering season. This has introduced bloodlines from the

Northern Hemisphere which otherwise might not be available to breeders in New Zealand. Innovations such as breeding to Northern Hemisphere time have been tried in the 1980s. In the 1990s the innovation of using shuttle mares is being tried – mating to Northern Hemisphere time and being exported *in utero* to the Northern Hemisphere, or foaled in New Zealand to Northern Hemisphere time.

Capital Requirements in the Industry

Capital requirements for the industry start-ups are high, in terms of purchasing of bloodstock, and land. An industry that experiences sporadic cash flows (principally through the annual auction sales of yearlings) is a high risk industry. The gap in time between investment and return on investment in a stud is generally too long for public investors and the venture capital infrastructure is non-existent. During the 1980s when a number of public companies were floated, the industry gained a high profile, although between them these companies controlled a very small proportion (less than ten percent of the registered stallions in New Zealand and less than five percent of the registered broodmares). The collapse of these companies after the share market crash of 1987, was in part due to the conflict between the nature of the industry and the nature of the public company, where the aim is to minimize risk in order to increase shareholder wealth. The high risk nature of the industry is due to the potential risk of injury, death, under-performance of the progeny (relative to the cost of the breeding stock) all uncertainties which may be attributable to a variety of causes, none of which can necessarily be prevented.

Two patterns of stud farm creation are evident. The first is where the stud farm was initially a side industry to the core business of dairy farming. The owner then sold his interest in the dairy farm and invested the realized capital in the stud farm. The second pattern of establishment is hierarchical in character. For a new start-up the potential owner would first need to develop expertise in the thoroughbred industry. In the following sequence the potential stud owner is involved in a series of partnerships, providing the thoroughbred and stud management expertise with capital requirements being provided by the other elements of the partnership. Over time the potential owner may purchase a bigger financial stake in the partnership, with the objective of the third stage being the purchase of property and development of a stud. In the mature stage, the stud owner will have a large band of quality broodmares and a number of stallions from which to breed – or will be involved in syndicated, leasing or shuttle arrangements with other owners.

Public ownership is the third type of firm structure that has been tried and abandoned in the thoroughbred industry. The first publicly listed company was the Ra Ora Stud in 1983, which led to the flotation of a number of companies which, at its peak in 1986 numbered some seven thoroughbred companies and two standardbred companies. The lifetime of these publicly listed companies was short lived, with most of them experiencing losses because of a combination of high holding costs, low profit margins on stud activities and high overheads. Review of operations and winding up of the companies' activities involved the disposal of surplus bloodstock, by culling mares. Unfortunately, being the only realisable assets (along with land and buildings) the value of such bloodstock with the numbers available for disposal exceeded the demand for them. Ironically, DuBourg in 1980, commented that the industry in Australasia, was sacrificing quality in favor of quantity, with increasing numbers of foals being produced, the product of haphazard mating programs. Even then DuBourg recommended culling programs since studmasters were not being recompensed in the commercial yearling ring for the cost of producing the bloodstock. All of the studs in the Cambridge Cluster are either in private ownership or owned by partnerships. This is also the case with the world's largest stud farm operation, the Coolmore stud in Ireland *(The Economist,* 1999).

The Role of Knowledge in the Cluster

Authors such as Marshall (1920) place knowledge or information at the center of the production process. Marshall suggests that information takes two forms: what is occurring within the business, and external conditions of the firm. While the small industrialist may have advantages over the larger firm ('the masters eye is everywhere') the small industrialist is at a disadvantage where information regarding the progress of industries and markets (the external environment). When business networks in a specific district begin to co-operate, this encourages the free communication of ideas, which encourages innovation as successful innovations are taken up by others and improved on. Marshall suggested that size conditions the amplitude of the external conditions a business can develop, so large businesses find themselves in an advantageous position to observe market conditions, through their commercial contacts (Zaratiegu, 1997). Small businesses need to form alliances both to share the cost of the acquisition of this knowledge and to ensure that the knowledge acquired is disseminated to the advantage of the members of the alliance.

More recently, research in business economics has identified the significance of proximity in fostering the interaction between firms in a knowledge creation process characterized as *collective learning*, whereby partly codified and partly tacit knowledge is interchanged and utilized in each of the participating firms. Knowledge creation between firms at the local, regional and national level, through the process of interaction leads to the emergence of specific national and regional systems of knowledge creation (Nelson, 1993). Although individuals find that certain knowledge can be fairly easily learned, it is often difficult to describe or codify that knowledge. Codified knowledge can be communicated and thus has the necessary features to be tradable. The process of codification increases the speed of knowledge-transfer by lowering transaction costs (Zander and Kogut, 1995). Recent developments in global communications, such as information superhighways and on-line databases, mean that information in markets, production technologies and competitive activity is more readily accessible. This would suggest that tacit (non-codified) knowledge would become less important than codified knowledge as it (codified knowledge) becomes globally disseminated. Maskell and Malmberg (1999) suggest the opposite – as codified knowledge becomes more easily accessible, the more crucial does tacit knowledge become for sustaining enhancing the competitive position of the firm. The embedded tacit knowledge and the heterogeneous, localised capabilities for building firm specific competencies become *more* important as the development towards a global economy accelerates.

We would argue that it is the embedded tacit knowledge in the Cambridge thoroughbred cluster that distinguishes it from other horse breeding clusters elsewhere. Thoroughbred horses are reared and trained in a variety of climatic, nutritional and geomorphological conditions. Proponents of certain limestone country, calcium-rich pastures and rainfall are never able to explain this geographical variety. The embedded tacit knowledge, which is at the heart of thoroughbred breeding is knowledge of the science of thoroughbred genetics which suggests that a horse's elementary racecourse ability is determined by its genotype (or genetic makeup). Broadly speaking, the genes control the way in which an animal harnesses its physical and mental resources- such as enzymes, amino acids, bone, muscle, heart and lung capacity and utilizes them as an effective equine athlete. Other vital more abstract qualities such as the fierce competitive spirit, zest for running, and endurance are all the result of the interaction of a horse's inherent genes. Location matters, along with the environmental factors of gestation, rearing, feeding, handling, incidence of disease and injury, changes of climate and terrain, jockeyship, ownership and trainership.

Homozygotes (genes that are alike) and heterozygotes (genes that are unalike) are fundamental concepts in the practice of breeding. Tesio (1958) identified three factors that contributed to the development of the equine athlete:

- inbreeding;
- nicks (or the successful matching of certain bloodlines); and
- the selection of the best quality stock.

The factors that make up conformation (shape) are inherited, as are the nervous, mental and metabolic processes.

Inbreeding refers to the reinforcement of important genes (the homozygous dominant state) through linking of the genes to create male-line dynasties. Lesh and Lesh's (1968) study of winners of classic races throughout Europe and the United States over a ten year period concluded that 72.6 percent of the 241 individual winners were inbred within five generations, many of them with multiple inbreedings. The genotypes of international sires such as Sir Ivor accounts for the exceptional performance of the Cambridge Stud lines of Sir Tristram by Sir Ivor and his grandson – Zabeel (New Zealand Bloodstock, 1999a). Sir Ivor had a remarkable homozygous concentration on both sides of his pedigree.[8]

Outcrossing or 'nicks' refers to the fusion of two vigorous sire lines in which are mutually enhancing process of genetic interaction takes place, a blending and complementing of two distinguished but quite disparate, blood lines. Tesio (1958) believed in tempering a pedigree by trying to balance and mix in due proportion the various genetic qualities inherent in the make up of the parents.

Rough blood or tough, unfashionable outcross genes can play a crucial role in a pedigree. Becker (1936) commenting on the Irish breeding industry noted that the poverty of the Irish breeders was a blessing in disguise, in that they could not afford fashionable bloodlines so they used radical outbreeding of selected stock to improve the industry. A similar approach has been used in New Zealand where financial resources have in the past limited stud owners in the choice of stallions. However, outcrossing with tough, rugged, unfashionable local mares has created horses with tough, resilient constitutions and the critical racing traits of persistence, competitiveness, and powers of acceleration.

Thoroughbred breeding is a combination of using codified knowledge (pedigree information) and tacit embedded knowledge of breeding horses and balancing pedigrees to mix in due proportion the genetic qualities inherent in the make up of the two parents. The objective of breeding specific types is coupled with the tacit knowledge inherent in the activities of the stud farm which include:

- financial skills to arrange the purchase through syndication of valuable stallion stock (and nominations for the stallion's services) the ability to pick performance stallions;
- the skills to manage the covering (service) program for visiting mares; managing the brood mares through the gestation period (eleven months) and the foaling season and the successful raising and weaning of young stock as well as management of the stud farm and staff.

The Internationalization of the New Zealand Thoroughbred Industry

The Decline of Domestic Demand

The thoroughbred industry developed as a response to domestic demand patterns. Thoroughbred racing (gallops) on the flat and jumping (both over hurdles and over fixed fences) were leisure pastimes highly popular in England and Ireland. Since the majority of immigrants to New Zealand were of English and Irish stock, it is not surprising that racing became firmly established in New Zealand. For most of this century, it was the only legalized form of gambling and rigidly controlled by government agency, the Totaliser Agency Board.

Several trends have affected the demand for racing in New Zealand. The first is the increasing urbanization of the population. Population growth has been concentrated in the North Island, making the City of Auckland the most densely populated area in New Zealand. The thoroughbred industry is an expensive industry, and relies on wealth to purchase, keep, race and breed its product. Thoroughbred breeders have moved geographically to keep in touch with their major customers, away from its traditional base in the South Island and the South of the North Island to the Waikato area, close to Auckland.

Originally there were a significant number of mare owners and horse breeders amongst the rural population. Hobby breeders would often breed, train and race horses as an adjunct to their main farm income of dairying or sheep. With the decline in economic strength in the rural sector, studs are increasingly dependent on city owners, who do not have the facilities to maintain thoroughbred horses. About half of the studs' customers are using their facilities for agistment (maintenance of a horse on behalf of the owners).

The domestic demand for thoroughbred horses is steadily declining. There are two reasons for this. First, racing has become only one of a number of leisure activities in which gambling is permitted. The advent of casinos, betting on various sports and lotteries, has affected the racing industry. There is greater demand and competition for leisure activities. The stake money offered by the thoroughbred racing industry has not kept up with the increasing costs of keeping and maintaining a racehorse. New investors are often unaware of the risks involved with breeding animals, and that the costs continue regardless of the on course performance of the animal. Premiums are now offered for selected race series for colts and fillies bought at the National Sales.

The domestic demand conditions suggest that the industry will become more dependent on its ability to internationalize. While there is a strong representation of international buyers at the yearling sales, these are principally from Australia. In terms of the globalization of the industry – and the ability of New Zealand breeders to compete internationally (other than in the Australian and the Asian market) there are a number of factors to consider.

A Globalizing Industry?

Using Porter's (1986) term, the thoroughbred breeding industry is no longer a multi-domestic industry, or even a collection of regional industries. Increasingly, it is becoming a globalized industry.

First, the breeding cycle for the Southern Hemisphere thoroughbred is the opposite to that of the Northern Hemisphere. The majority of foals are born in New Zealand between early September and late November, and all thoroughbred horse are officially one year of age on the first of August, so that they can be classed to race according to age. The cycle in the Northern Hemisphere is that the foals are born in the Northern Hemisphere spring, and their official birthday is therefore the first of January of the following year. If a horse bred to southern time were to race in the Northern Hemisphere it would be on average six months younger than horses bred to Northern Time. Since the majority of horses are raced as two and three year olds this would have an impact on performance.

Breeding to Northern Hemisphere time was attempted in New Zealand in the 1980s. It was subsequently abandoned since the climatic conditions were not considered favourable for autumn rearing. The additional cost of rearing stock indoors would have to be recouped in the price paid for the resultant offspring. Moreover, New Zealand blood lines were not in sufficient demand to make this form of rearing profitable. However, breeding to Northern Hemisphere time looks likely to re-emerge given the current international interest in New Zealand blood lines. Shuttle mares (who are serviced in New Zealand by New Zealand stallions to Northern Hemisphere time) are exported *in utero*, to foal in Northern Hemisphere locations. Alternatively, imported mares can be serviced in New Zealand to Northern Hemisphere time and will produce and rear their progeny in New Zealand.

Second, the respective regulatory authorities in each of the thoroughbred breeding countries, control the quality of the breed through their requirements that only the progeny of registered stock can be entered in a national stud book. To date, despite its use in other spheres, (such as the standard-bred horse, used for harness racing)[9] the regulatory authorities of respective breeding countries do not allow the use of artificial insemination as a breeding technique. There are over fifty different countries with approved thoroughbred stud books, approved meaning that the contents of each stud book is accepted by the other authorities. In the last five to six years the question of artificial insemination has been discussed by the International Stud Book Committee (the international regulatory authority for stud book authorities in member countries), but the current ruling remains unchanged.

Originally, the ruling against artificial insemination was to ensure the paternity of the progeny. However, with blood typing and DNA testing, the paternity issues could be overcome. However, the concern of the industry is allowing artificial insemination would have the effect of reducing further the already limited gene pool. Since the modern thoroughbred horse traces its ancestry back to just three foundation sires, and fifty 'tap root' mares, limiting the gene pool further, by using semen from just a few stallions could affect performance, soundness and conformation to the overall detriment of the breed. It would also have an economic impact, as less fashionable stallions would no longer be in demand, resulting in a loss to the industry of potentially useful blood lines.

Third, even without the use of artificial insemination the innovations in the industry (such as the use of 'shuttle sires' and 'shuttle mares' and exporting foals *in utero*) has ensured that the progeny of prepotent stallions (such as Northern Dancer) are represented in all the major thoroughbred racing locations. Location matters as firms seek to more efficiently deploy their home based assets by maximizing their revenue earning potential. The created assets are the ability of an industry participant to recognize the genetic potential of particular bloodlines and identify locations to deploy these assets. Coolmore Stud in Ireland, one of the most successful stud farms in the world operates five studs in Ireland, one in America and one in Australia (The Economist, 1999). Northern Hemisphere countries also have their localized preferences in racing – the difference between racing on different surfaces and factors such as length of races, all have an impact on the type of horse that is bred for these conditions. However, it is possible to breed horses to take account of these differences.

The task for the future of the New Zealand blood stock industry is to be able to tap into the Northern Hemisphere breeding scene. A comparative analysis of the receipts from the Keenland sales in Kentucky, USA with those of the National Yearling Sales, in Auckland, New Zealand, suggests that New Zealand bloodstock is under valued by international standards.

At Keenland in November, 1998 yearling receipts over the first four days of the annual sales averaged US$197,861 (The Australian, 16 November, 1998). By contrast receipts for the first two days of the premier yearling sales at Karaka in Auckland in February, 1999 averaged US $50,304, about 25 per cent of the sale price for the Kentucky sales (New Zealand Bloodstock Limited 1999b). The highest price paid at the sales for a brood mare was US$7 million – the dam of European classic winners. The record price for a horse at the yearling sales in Karaka was in 1998, for a Zabeel – Eight Carat colt, sold for US $816,000 in 1998 (New Zealand Bloodstock Limited, 1998). Australasia's leading sires are Zabeel (from Cambridge Stud) and Danehill, by Danzig-Northern Dancer, who is a shuttle stallion (Australia, New Zealand, Ireland) from the Coolmore Stud in Ireland. Danehill's progeny, although less highly regarded in the Northern Hemisphere than in this region, have also been successful in Group I and Group II races in Europe (*The Australian*, 1998).

The price differentials reflect the differences in stake money between the Northern Hemisphere and the Southern Hemisphere for the European Classic races. This suggests that the future for the New Zealand thoroughbred industry is in the Northern Hemisphere markets for blood stock. A dearth of good stallions in the Northern Hemisphere, with the Japanese breeding industry having purchased five of the six English Derby winners between 1990 to 1995

(*The Economist*, 1999), suggests that the future potential of the industry is as yet untapped.

Conclusion

The Cambridge thoroughbred breeding industry is an example of a geographically concentrated cluster, which has been stimulated by the presence of stud owners, who saw the potential for the development of a unique industry in the Waikato region. Building on the advantages of a benign climate and suitable free draining soils, they have developed this region into a center internationally known for the production of thoroughbred horses. The supporting and relating industries that have developed around the industry helped build this area of the Waikato into an important breeding center for the local racing industry.

It is also the center of the export of bloodstock to Australia and Asia, and as a spin off, the provision of world class horses for the Olympic sport of three-day eventing. The dairy industry and the thoroughbred breeding industry share some of the same agricultural inputs, but it is the presence of specialist horse breeding knowledge within the industry, which has encouraged the development of this local cluster.

The future international potential of the industry depends on the continuation of the Cambridge thoroughbred cluster. The cluster has developed without government policy interventions (it might also be said in spite of it). Government policy towards the breeding industry and its outputs for the racing industry could best be described as quixotic since racing is classed as gambling. Gambling in all forms can have a potentially negative social impact on an economy. Yet the industry does make an economic contribution, through exports, employment and taxes. The challenge for the thoroughbred industry is to use globalization as a means of compensating for threats to the future of the industry, arising out of changes in the domestic demand patterns, and the potential of technological discontinuities as a result of changes to regulations governing the use of artificial means for breeding purposes.

The Cambridge thoroughbred breeding industry does clearly demonstrate the importance of the socioeconomy of clusters. The competitive advantage of the cluster depends on the flows of information, the willingness to work with and through other organizations and a constant motivation for improvement. The strength of the cluster lies in the network of relationships within the specific geographic location that produces benefits for the particular firms that are part of the cluster.

Acknowledgments

The author gratefully acknowledges the assistance of Christopher Plowright in undertaking the original case studies of the thoroughbred studs in the Greater Waikato area (Cambridge and Matamata). The participation of all the interviewees in the case research from the related and supporting industries, the specialist institutions and the regulatory authorities is also gratefully acknowledged. The usual disclaimers apply.

Notes

1   Defined in the 'Diamond'as an educated workforce, appropriate physical infrastructure, accurate and timely economic information, and ensuring that there are the institutions to provide them (Porter, 1990).

2   The first acknowledged thoroughbred horse to arrive in New Zealand from Australia was Figaro in 1840. (Power and McClelland, 1975). A thoroughbred horse (TB) is defined as one listed in an approved Stud Book. In England it is the General Stud Book, founded in 1791. The New Zealand Stud Book was established in 1878. The US, Australia etc. have their own equivalents. All thoroughbreds descend from three Oriental stallions imported into England between the mid 17th Century and the mid 18th Century. They were: Darley Arabian (the direct male ancestor of upward of 90 per cent of stallions standing at stud today through his great-grandson Eclipse (1764)); Godolphin Barb; and Byerley Turk. A number of mares most of which were dominated by Oriental rather than British blood were used to start the thoroughbred line.

3   Apart from Foxbridge, Otway stood Gay Shield, Nizami, Columcille, Moorcock, Marco Polo II, Khorassan, Pride of Kildare, Alcimedes, Rousseau's Dream, Trictrac, Patron Saint and Old Soldier

4   These were: Hiraji, Foxzami, MacDougal, Polo Prince, Hi-Jinx, Galilee and Silver Knight.

5   The Sir Tristram – Zabeel line can be traced back to Sir Ivor who has been described as having some of the most prepotent blood evolved in world breeding history DuBourg 1980). Sir Ivor (1965, Sir Gaylord –Attica) won the English Derby, the English 2,000 Guineas, the Washington DC International Stakes, the Newmarket Championship stakes and came second to Vaguely Noble in the Longchamp Prix de l'Arc de Triomphe). The Zabeel line is an example of a 'nick' or a specialised and highly focussed application of outcrossing where two vigorous sire lines are crossed to achieve a mutually enhancing genetic interaction (q.v). On

the dam's side Zabeel's grandsire is Northern Dancer, described by duBoug (1980) as being destined (in 1980) to play an epochal role in the Southern Hemisphere. Bred in Canada (1961) the Northern Dancer 'nick' represents a link between two dominant sire lines from North America and England (Sir Ivor).

6　The 1998 Melbourne Cup was an extraordinary triumph for the Cambridge cluster. The first *and* second horses (Jezabeel and Champagne) were both sired by Cambridge Stud's Zabeel. They were both mares, and both bred by Cambridge breeders (Jeanette Broome and Patrick Hogan). They were also both trained near Cambridge, by local trainers.

7　Tale Of the Cat has the type to produce horses for the Golden Slipper (2 year old race) which is one New Zealand bred horses find hard to win – being renowned for its stamina (staying) lines rather than its speed lines.

8　The term prepotency in a sire refers to the ability of a sire to stamp its genotype on its progeny (i.e. consistent performance characteristics).

9　The standard bred horse is a more robust animal, races over longer distances and at slower gaits (pacing or trotting). Artificial insemination therefore is not considered likely to weaken the blood lines.

References

Akoorie, M. (1998), 'The Historical Role of Foreign Investment in the New Zealand Economy', in P. Enderwick (ed), *Foreign Investment: The New Zealand Experience*, The Dunmore Press, Palmerston North.

Akoorie, M. and J. Scott-Kennel (1999), 'The New Zealand Dairy Board: A Case of Group Internalisation or a Monopolistic Anomaly in a Deregulated Free Market Economy?' *Asia Pacific Journal of Management*, vol. 16, no 1, pp. 127-156.

Akoorie, M., and P. Enderwick, (1992), 'The International Operations of New Zealand Companies', *Asia Pacific Journal Of Management*, vol. 9, no.1, pp. 99-117.

Anderson, J. (1998), 'Eventing Horses join Sporting Talent Drain', *National Business Review*, 18 December, p.4.

Antonelli, C. (1990), 'Induced Adoption and Externalities in the Regional Diffusion of Information Technology', *Regional Studies*, vol. 24, no. 1, pp. 31-40.

Antonelli, C. 1994), 'Technology Districts, Localised Spillovers and Productivity Growth: the Italian Evidence on Technological Externalities in Core Regions', *International Review of Applied Economics*, pp. 18-30.

Arthur, W. (1994), *Increasing Returns and Path Dependence in the Economy*, Michigan University Press, Michigan.

Arthur, W. (1996), 'Increasing Returns and the New World of Business', *Harvard Business Review*, July-August, pp.100-109.

The Australian (1998), ' Thoroughbreds: the National and International Guide', 16 November, p.20.

Barro, R. and X. Sala-i-Martin, (1995), *Economic Growth*, McGraw Hill, New York.

Beccatini, G. (1990), 'The Marshallian Industrial District as a Socio-economic Notion', in F. Pyke, G. Beccatini and W. Sengenberger, (eds), *Industrial Districts and Inter-Firm Co-operation*, International Institute for Labour Studies, Geneva.

Becker, F. (1936), *The Breed of the Racehorse*, The British Bloodstock Agency Ltd, London.

Cartwright, W. (1993), 'Multiple Linked Diamonds and the International Competitiveness of Export-Dependent Industries: The New Zealand Experience', *Management International Review*, vol. 33, no. 2, pp. 55-70.

Du Bourg, R. (1980), *The Australian and New Zealand Thoroughbred*, Thomas Nelson, Melbourne.

Dunning, J. (1998), 'Location and the Multinational Enterprise: A Neglected Factor?' *Journal of International Business Studies*, vol. 29, no.1, pp. 45-66.

The Economist (1999), 'Thoroughbred Racing: Licensed to Thrill', 10 April, pp. 84-85.

Enderwick, P. and M. Akoorie (1996), *Fast Forward: New Zealand Business in World Markets*, Longman Paul, Auckland.

Enright, M. (1995), 'Organisation and Co-ordination in Geographically Concentrated Industries', in D. Raff and N. Lamoreaux (eds), *Co-ordination and Information: Historical Perspectives on the Organisation of Enterprise*, University of Chicago Press, Chicago.

Ffowcs Williams, I. (1997), 'Local Clusters and Local Export Growth', *New Zealand Strategic Management Journal*, Summer, pp. 24-30.

Garofoli, G. (1991), 'Local Networks, Innovation and Policy in Italian Industrial Districts', in E. Bergman, G. Maier and F. Todtling (eds), *Regions Reconsidered*, Mansell, London.

Krugman, P. (1991), *Geography and Trade*, MIT Press, Cambridge, MA.

Krugman, P. (1993), 'On the Relationship between Trade Theory and Location Theory', *Review of International Economics*, vol. 1, pp. 110-122.

Krugman, P. (1994a), 'Complex Landscapes in Economic Geography', *American Economic Review*, vol. 84, no.2, pp. 412-416.

Krugman, P. (1994b), 'The Myth of Asia's Miracle', *Foreign Affairs*, vol. 73, no.6, pp 62 – 78.

Krugman, P. (1995), *Development, Geography and Economic Theory*, MIT Press, Cambridge, MA.

Lesh, T., and D. Lesh, (1968), 'Application of Modern Genetics to Thoroughbred Breeding', 'Heterosis' and 'Inbreeding.' September/October/December, vol. 20, nos. 3, 4 and 5.

Marshall, A. (1919), *Industry and Trade*, Macmillan, London

Marshall, A. (1920), *Principles of Economics*, 8th edition, Macmillan, London.

Martin, R. (1999), 'Critical Survey: The New 'Geographical Turn' in Economics: Some Critical reflections', *Cambridge Journal of Economics*, vol. 23, pp. 65-91.

Maskell, P. and A. Malmberg, (1999), 'Localised Learning and Industrial Competitiveness', *Cambridge Journal of Economics*, vol. 23, pp 167-185.

Nelson, R . (1993), *National Innovation Systems- A Comparative Analysis*, Oxford University Press, Oxford.

New Zealand Bloodstock Limited (1999a), *73rd National Yearling Sales Series: Premier Sale*. Catalogue, Karaka, Auckland.

New Zealand Bloodstock Limited (1999b), *National Yearling Sales Results*.

New Zealand Thoroughbred Breeders' Association (1997), *Register of Thoroughbred Stallions of New Zealand, 1997*, vol 24.

New Zealand Thoroughbred Breeders' Association (1998), *Register of Thoroughbred Stallions of New Zealand, 1998*, vol 25.

Porter, M. (1968) *Competition in Global Industries*, Harvard Business School Press, Boston.

Porter, M. (1990), *The Competitive Advantage of Nations*, Macmillan, London.

Porter, M. (1994), 'The Role of Location in Competition', *Journal of the Economics of Business*, vol. 1, no. 1, pp. 35-39.

Porter, M. (1996), 'Competitive Advantage, Agglomeration Economies and Regional Policy', *International Regional Science Review*, vol. 19, nos 1-2, pp. 85-90).

Porter, M. (1998a), *On Competition,* Harvard Business School Press, Boston.

Porter, M. (1998b), 'Clusters and the New Economics of Competition', *Harvard Business Review*, November/December, pp.77-90.

Power, E. and L. McClelland (1975) *The Horse in New Zealand*, Collins, Auckland.

Rosenfield, S. (1996), *Over Achievers – Business Clusters that Work: Prospects for Regional Development*, Regional Strategies Inc. Boston.

Rugman, A. (1992), 'Porter Takes the Wrong Turn', *Business Quarterly*, vol. 56, no. 3, pp. 59-64.

Tesio, F. (1958), *Breeding the Racehorse*, J. A. Allen and Co., London.

Venables, A. (1996a), 'Equilibrium Locations of Vertically Linked Industries', *International Economic Review*, vol. 37, pp. 341-359.

Venables, A. (1996b), ' Localisation of Industry and Trade Performance', *Oxford Economic Policy Review*, vol. 12, no.3, pp. 52-60.

Zander, U. and B. Kogut, (1995), 'Knowledge and the Speed of Transfer and Imitation of Organisational Capabilities', *Organisational Science*, vol. 6, no. 1, pp. 76-92.

Zaratiegui, J. (1997), 'Twin Brothers in Marshallian Thought: Knowledge and Organisation', *Review of Political Economy*, vol. 9, no. 3, pp. 295-312.

8 In The Flagships' Wake: Relations, Motivations and Observations of Strategic Alliance Activity Among IT Sector Flagship Firms and Their Partners

BEN P. CECIL and MILFORD B. GREEN

Introduction

As the western economies continue to evolve towards the next era of capitalist development, a variety of new industrial organizational structures have been espoused to identify this economic transition amidst the forces of globalization at the end of the twentieth century. Conceptualizations of this restructuring have ranged from the second industrial divide (Piore and Sabel, 1984) to post-Fordism (Leborgne and Lipietz, 1988) to the varied systems of flexible specialization/accumulation (Harvey, 1987; Scott, 1988a). While debate continues about the merits and shortcomings of each theory in its applicability to firms of the new economy, a thread of continuity runs throughout: as the economy evolves, so, too, do the spatial expressions of that economy (Lovering, 1990).

It is this common theoretical thread which sets the stage for the current research. A recurring theme of the shift towards the new economy is the application and exploitation of new technologies, especially 'high technology', by both new and traditional industrial sectors alike. Advanced technologies, or 'high tech', have been the focus of much study on the economic restructuring since the mid 1970s (Oakley, 1981; Scott, 1986a; Castells, 1989; Angel, 1990; D'Cruz and Rugman, 1994; Saxenian, 1994). The success of this sector as a propelling force in the shift to the new economy has been linked to its ability to form and manage appropriate partnerships. In the industry's collective effort of 'high tech' development, inter-firm collaboration and alliances have been identified as the means of transcending the bounds of the firm (Cooke, 1988; Wells and Cooke, 1991). In a era of ever increasing globalization, shorter product life-cycles, and flexible production capacities to satisfy rapidly changing market demand, inter-corporate co-operative activity (alliances) provide firms with access to technologies should such resources not exist within the firm itself (Cecil et al., 1996).

Several authors have contributed to our understanding of alliances among high technology firms and industries; of note are Saxenian (1990, 1994), Angel (1990, 1994), Ahern (1991, 1993a, 1993b) and Anderson (1993, 1995) to name but a few. While these authors present detailed accounts of the collaborative nature of 'high tech' at the firm, industry, or regional level, national studies encompassing a broad range of 'high tech' players have been noticeably absent.

It is the purpose of this chapter to present this national context of technology based alliances. The first section of the chapter provides a theoretical overview and critique of existing alliance motivations (such as resource dependency, transaction cost analysis, core competencies and capabilities, network theory, and 'regional worlds') currently *en vogue* in their application to high technology industries. This section serves to develop an eclectic theory of alliance activity, which fills the void present in much existing alliance literature, which has led to only a partial understanding of the alliance phenomenon. The premise is that the existing application of resource and cost theories has been viewed too narrowly and the broader application of factors usually stated as implicit to the system now requires further explicit clarification.

The second section of this chapter provides the empirical support for the eclectic alliance theory. The support outlines the significance of firm size, location, and flagship network membership, and their collective impact, on the spatial pattern of alliance activity under a two-tiered alliance framework. Subsections that follow that discuss the tiers of the alliance model are identified as (Tier 1) or (Tier 2) depending on the portion of the framework being addressed.

Motivations for Cooperation: Towards and Eclectic Alliance Theory

As the economic conditions evolve toward the next capitalist era, a wake of uncertainty about future conditions is inevitable. There is growing consensus, that for firms to hedge such uncertainty, especially amongst other dynamic firms (as in high technology), alliances are a strategic tool to access the 'four cornerstones' of:

- new or extra regional markets;
- production;
- lower operating costs; and
- technical innovations (Cecil et al., 1996).

A question arising from the cornerstones concept is: 'If such motivations can be identified in a dynamic industry/marketplace, why would a firm opt for an alliance structure rather than internalization – especially since internalization offers greater control?'

Transaction Cost Analysis (Tier 1)

Transaction Cost Analysis (TCA) is often cited in the literature to address this very question. The development of TCA is largely attributed to Williamson (1975, 1981, 1985), but his theoretical grounding came from Coase (1937) in his treatise about the nature of the firm. Transaction Cost Analysis is a micro-analytic framework with a strong emphasis on the behavioral, opportunistic, and information asymmetric characteristics of the production system. Williamson's early considerations of organized production focused on a hierarchically ordered, vertically integrated firm-centered system where the driving force was the internalization/externalization decision for the units of production. Applications of the TCA approach have been noted in Buckley and Casson (1976), Rugman (1981), and within the geographic literature by Scott (1986b). The general tenet of TCA theory is the production dichotomy of 'make or buy' or 'in-source or out-source'. The firm will internalize all aspects of production it can perform at a lower cost than the marketplace, and will rely on the market for activities which other firms possess a competitive advantage. In highly competitive, or low cost, markets, firms are expected to internalize production costs in order to minimize the cost of market exchange.

Williamson's work introduced an avenue of discussion into the organization of production; not all of which has been positive. Criticism of Transaction Cost Analysis falls on three fronts. First, the very nature of 'cost analysis' opens the door to a neo-classical economics' 'Pandora's Box'. By using cost as a basis of measuring organizational behavior, it assumes that economic actors are fully aware of all associated cost considerations, that they make economic decisions cognizant of those costs, and have the ability to predict the outcome of each decision. While rationally economic behavior may be one ideal, it assumes a state of equilibrium not often (if ever) found in reality.

Secondly, basing firm behavior on 'costs' eliminates the often overlooked aspect of corporations – the human dynamic. Social networks and satisficing behavior also play roles in organizational behavior not initially considered by

Williamson.   Finally, the rigid dichotomization of markets/hierarchies, combined with the missed behavioral aspect, raises the issue of intermediate degrees of organization between markets and hierarchies which Williamson identified in later works as being important to the Transaction Cost approach.

It is to this third critique that the nature of alliances has been applied. Strategic alliances are mechanisms between markets and hierarchies which afford firms the ability to achieve minimum cost arrangements not possible in a strict organizational dichotomy of firms and markets. By spreading risks and uncertainty of product development between one or more partners, costs associated with such activity are thereby lowered.   From a production perspective, such linkages with other firms create locational costs – the greater the linkage distance, the higher the cost.   Thus, it would be expected that industries with high levels of inter-firm activity will agglomerate to minimize production/transaction/alliance costs (Scott, 1988b). We will return to Scott's inherently spatial logic of transaction costs later.

Resource Dependency Theory (Tier 1)

The Transaction Cost Analysis approach is dominated by its focus on the minimization of the costs of production. Associated with this focus is a need to access the resources of production. Pfeffer and Salancik (1978) characterize the necessity of extracting the resources of production from the physical or business environments as Resource Dependency. Their Resource Dependency Theory holds as its premise that 'firms will act in self interest, trying to gain access to, and ultimately control over, needed resources' (Cecil et al., 1996). As a minimization function, the firm attempts to minimize its dependencies on other firms for the resource(s) of supply/production while simultaneously shifting product/production dependency to other firms by controlling their supply function.

Core Competencies

At this level of application to alliances, the theories (both transaction cost and resource dependency) fall short of their potential. The focus of the theories tends to be based on what Pralahad and Hamel (1990) term as 'Core Competencies.' Competencies, in the firm context, are the abilities to apply technologies to the development of new products at lower costs and to so do more rapidly than the competition. These competencies are product oriented production abilities which allow firms to control resource requirements (resource dependency) and minimize the costs of production (transaction costs). With a minimization function driving a product-oriented focus, the theories fail to recognize the dynamics of changing economic conditions. When a firm develops a production process, and, therefore, end products as the natural outcome of that process, it assumes a market where there is a demand for such a product (hopefully stable enough to recover sunk costs from product/process development (Clark, 1994)) and that new technologies will not supplant the product in the short-run. In dynamic markets with rapidly changing customer demands and ever rising technological ceilings (such as in 'high tech') firms have need to decentralize some of their productive needs in order to remain competitive on a cost basis.

Production Networks

The result of this decentralized cost-oriented action has been the outsourcing of production to a network of firms with lower transaction costs than the firm in question. The literature on network structures and their application to strategic alliances has been extensive: Cooke and Morgan, 1993; Powell, 1990; Amin and Thrift, 1992; and Johanson and Mattsson, 1987; to name just a few. Consistent with the product oriented approach to defining alliance behavior, Johanson and Mattsson define their network structures as exchange relationships which govern a production system where resources are deployed and developed. The result is an industrial system linked across a broad spectrum of product-based cooperative agreements such as sales contracts, production outsourcing, procurement contracts, and service agreements. At this level of network linkage, the basis of cooperation is transaction cost based and resource dependency enhanced. Minimum cost arrangements are sought to enhance product profitability while simultaneously seeking new resources in suppliers or markets in order to maintain cost/price profit ratios. Due to the quite formalized nature of these network linkages whereby firms have quantified production/sales targets, the alliance structure follows a more contractual nature in order to assure target goals and thereby minimum cost arrangements as well.

While the theoretical base for this chain of events in alliance motivations is a natural evolution from the product perspective, it has its limitations. It relies on a state of economic and technological equilibrium such that this week's 'state-of-the-art' technology is not next month's doorstop. Admittedly, the market presence of high technology products does not always follow such a radical path as the one alluded to above, but given market demands, ever shorter product life-cycles, and rapidly changing technological ceilings (especially at the consumer level), product based alliances are fraught with failure (Bleeke and Ernst, 1993). Florida and Kenney (1990) have been particularly critical of alliance research, citing the failure rate of alliances as a fundamental weakness with this form of corporate governance. They cite examples of large firms controlling resources and hoarding specific products in order to control product development; and *if* new products *are* developed in the marketplace, firms still follow an opportunistic cost relationship with potential/existing suppliers. Unlike Saxenian's claims of a collaborative atmosphere among 'high tech' firms, Florida and Kenney's observations characterize the industry as simply a more dynamic economic beast with sharper, more paralyzing fangs – especially for smaller firms.

Florida and Kenney make an interesting point about alliance failure, but their definition of failure does not do the alliance governance structure justice. Alliances, when initiated, may have a certain objective. If the market changes, or technologies develop throughout the course of collaboration, alliance goals may change such that the original agreement no longer meets the needs of either firm. Alliances change direction, focus, and technical outcomes to meet the technical and market needs of both partners, and thus may not remotely resemble the initial agreement. When those needs cannot be met, alliances dissolve with a minimum risk/cost associated with partnership. This should not be seen as a weakness of alliances, but their strong point.

The core competency/product perspective of alliance motivation deals primarily with the lower level of motivations in Figure 8.1. The second tier of the theoretic rationales for cooperative behavior between firms is often alluded to, but very rarely stated in an explicit form. The following retraces each of the above theories in turn to address the nature of the second tier of theories in Figure 8.1.

Transaction Cost Analysis (Tier 2)

Beginning with Transaction Costs once again, the product/competency perspective holds the minimization of costs as paramount. Williamson, in later works, recognized the limitations of a strictly dichotomized production structure of market or hierarchy. In the intermediate organizational forms of corporate governance and production, the minimization of cost is still important to the continuing existence of the firm, but along side such considerations is a parallel maximization function. In the Transaction Cost vein, a firm will internalize all aspects of production it can perform at a lower cost than the market. In so doing, the result is not only a production process, which has a formal outcome in a specific product, but the process itself creates a 'social architecture' as a result of continuing skill development, internal personnel cooperation, and tacit knowledge about products and processes which are firm specific (Mueller, 1996). By maximizing the 'embedded' nature of the social aspect of production (Granovetter, 1985), the firm produces a second set of transaction costs which act as barriers to entry. These costs involve the inability of other firms to readily replicate the internal web of tacit knowledge interwoven into the social structure of the firm not codified or quantified in any specific product, but is the process of product development itself.

One current example of this second tier Transaction Cost perspective can be found in the alliance between Intel and Hewlett-Packard to develop the Itanium (formerly called Merced) chip. The Itanium chip is a next generation PC processor. The development of this new technology while feasible by either partner, becomes viable through their shared investment of resources, spread of risk, and shared cost. Their partnership creates a degree of cross-corporate interaction amongst project team members whereby their daily cooperation on minor project issues becomes part of the larger social and technological embeddedness of the entire project. It is this larger 'interpersonal world' (Storper, 1997) of activity which facilitates the project completion in a shorter time frame and with lower per firm costs than either firm could achieve independently.

The maximization of this form of firm/project specific knowledge poses a major barrier to entry for other firms attempting to develop similar technologies. Sun Microsystems, a close competitor to Intel's and Hewlett-Packard's Itanium technology, has no alliances for such new chip technology. Their development lag time has created a situation should Sun attempt to introduce a like chip to compete directly along side the Itanium chip, they would have to make such a massive investment the chip would not be profitable, especially under shortened product life-cycles. The result?: Sun will have a dependency on Intel/HP for their Itanium resource should they decide to follow a similar market penetration strategy.

Resource Dependency Theory (Tier 2)

At the second tier of Figure 8.1, the resource dependency issue becomes one of not only products, as in the Itanium example, but also one of the conditions which create such products – the tacit knowledge, skills, information, and the intangibles of the 'interpersonal world' become the new resources. The maximizing of these resources, while costly for the firm to initially create and subsequently maintain, also means to replicate this social and informational network is equally (if not more so) costly for competitors whether they follow an internal development or personnel recruitment strategy.

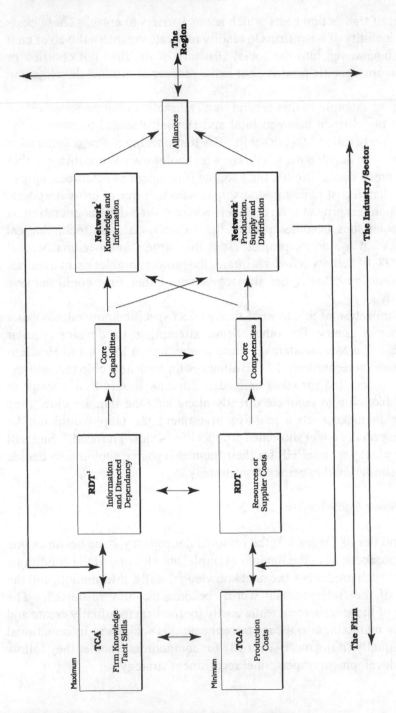

Figure 8.1 Model of Eclectic Alliance Theory

Core Capabilities

At the heart of maintaining this maximization function across the second tier of transaction cost and resource dependency is a focus on the core capabilities of the firm (Stalk et al., 1992). Stalk et al. argue that for firms to remain competitive in dynamic markets, the focus of corporate direction should not be at the product level (as in all tier one cases in Figure 8.1), but at the sources which create information, knowledge, and competitive capability. These capabilities are developed by investing in support infrastructure (capital and personnel), which transcends specific product oriented business units; and this infrastructure gets applied not to product or market development, but to business processes. An example may help to illustrate this point. Casio makes miniature electronic products such as watches and calculators. Rather than refining *ad nauseam* watch technology into more chronograph products, they focused on their capabilities in miniaturization, allowing them to develop laterally into technologies such as LCD televisions and computer screens. The result is the development of their business into emerging markets with radically new technologies based on their technical successes in the stable chronograph market.

Unlike core competencies in products, core capabilities have the added dimension of developing the informational infrastructure of the firm, which allows it to create more, better, and highly differentiated products than what is currently produced by the firm. The natural outcomes of capabilities are product competencies; and those capabilities maximize the transaction cost tier two and resource tier two functions of the firm to further secure and enhance market position.

Information and Knowledge Networks

One of the paramount means in enhancing firm capabilities is to tap into the capabilities of other firms, especially market leaders. A key aspect of core capabilities is the firm's ability to learn and use knowledge. When alliances are struck between firms at the capabilities level they gain access to new forms of knowledge, innovations, and partner specific applications of technology. The two (or more) informationally embedded social networks become intertwined, developing project specific capabilities, which each firm can internalize at project completion. Such networks, as part of the interpersonal world, are characterized by more informal alliances such as standards creation and research and development contracts.

The capabilities which foster this type of informal network structure also recognize the need for, and importance of, tier one network alliances (the production alliances of supply and outsourcing) since products are the outcome of capabilities. Only rarely will a product-oriented focus create a capability network alliance, and when such alliances occur it is usually between a market leader and a very small firm (Bleeke and Ernst, 1993). The small firm looks for research and development and marketing capacity in the large firm, and the large firm seeks the entrepreneurial talent of the small firm. The results most often favor the large firm in the long run, as they tend to acquire the smaller players in the high technology sector (Bleeke and Ernst, 1993).

The second tier of network activity is far more informal in structure than the tier one production network. Innovative capacity has been noted as a major motivation in alliance research (Angel, 1994; Cecil et al., 1996). Innovations stem from the critical mass of information in the network shared among a select group of individuals whose tacit knowledge and complementary skill sets allow them to perceive market opportunities where such innovations have not been applied. The network is knowledge intensive and highly mobile because of its internalized existence in the minds of the network members. The informal nature of this network structure permits for the open exchange of information whereby the cost of information transactions is reduced to a minimum level. The result is a network where trust has become a large untraded commodity (Powell, 1990; Johanson and Mattsson, 1987; Buckley and Casson, 1988) fostered by the successes of independently/jointly created products (the fruits of collaboration).

Second tier network structures have two dimensions – the local and the global. The local dimension is developed by the close-knit groups of individuals sharing information because of common association such as firms or professions. Powell (1990) and Amin and Thrift (1992) note how such interactions breed trust, and proximity favors trust. From that trust comes an 'industrial atmosphere' (Amin and Thrift, 1992) which is bound in place and localized because of the localized action-space of network members. It is this very network structure of untraded, intangible, socially embedded, trust-based capabilities which create the maximization functions for both transaction costs and resource dependencies at the second tier.

When all the information for capabilities-based growth exists within the local network, alliances need not extend beyond the bounds of the local network. In cases where such information is not part of the network skill set, however, alliances will be struck with partners in other areas/regions where their skill set(s) differ from the local network. Tapping into these nodes, or geographical centers, is achieved in two ways. First, if the interpersonal world of the local network has a limited number of extra-regional connections, these linkages facilitate extra-regional information exchange.

The problem, however, is that the distance between nodes generates resistance to information flow, and these lines of communication, because of the limited degree of repeated exchange, have not developed the same degree of trust found in the local network. These lines of communication exist between individuals in each local network, but if no such link exists based on the reputations of individual network members, then the linkages transcend the interpersonal world to consider the reputation of the firm as an alliance criterion. The second form of tier two network structure exists between small (or large) firms, and other large firms (market leaders), or Flagship firms (Rugman and D'Cruz, 1997).

Flagship Firms

Flagship firms, such as IBM, Hewlett-Packard, Microsoft, or NEC among high technology companies, have the reputation and market presence to attract a number of cooperative partnerships between suppliers, customers, government and even other competitors. The Flagship firm, because of its market position, coordinates many of the network functions of its partners (but not the daily operations) since the Flagship becomes the research and development center, the marketing outlet, the key customer/supplier, and application developer for smaller network partners. The Flagship has as part of its network a tier one network of production relationships and a series of localized tier two network connections to develop its productive capacity. By gaining access to the realm of connections developed by the Flagship through partnerships with this market leader, the extra-regional firm expands its network structure (both tier one and tier two) to include aspects of the Flagship's network.

Due to the national or global reputation of Flagship firms, associations with such firms extend a degree of that reputation to partners. The friction of distance associated with linking two regionally based interpersonal worlds is ameliorated by the more structured and formalized links between Flagship firms of different regions. The scale of Flagship operations and global presence these firms possess, give them footholds in a number of interpersonal localized networks. The degree of influence Flagships possess over smaller tier one network partners (production partners) places Flagships in the position to outline industry standards and develop technologies in the interests of Flagship corporate mandates.

A Spatial Logic...

Now, to return to Scott's inherently spatial logic of Transaction Costs. The Flagship firms play a dual role in transaction costs. For other Flagships, the focus on the maximization of capabilities in order to explore new avenues of product development, such that the process itself and the critical mass necessary to achieve product development, become a barrier to entry even for global firms. These inter-Flagship connections, because of the complexity of project scope and the inherently global nature of such firms (from a market perspective) transcend localized networks and connect global nodes of information resources. For smaller firms, the Flagships become coordinators (for their own self-interests) of production oriented activity – tier one actions.

Such networks of producers because of their competency focus will gravitate into nodes of economic activity on the landscape to address the intra-group costs associated with a product/competency focus (Scott, 1988b). The transaction costs of production-style network linkages creates a 'spatial pull whereby firms will tend to agglomerate to shorten the length, and hence the cost, of such external linkages'(Henry, 1992).

The natural extension of this eclectic theory in its application to the pattern of alliance activity is thus:

- Flagship firms play a dominant role within the entire high technology industry because of their centrality as network partners;
- these Flagships, or large firms, exist to develop information and knowledge necessary for innovation development;
- for small firms, Flagships provide the avenues of market access and supply contracts, both with a production focus;
- production oriented alliances should be confined to industrial agglomerations because of the increase in exchange costs associated with distance;
- knowledge-based alliances (tier two networks) should be more informal than production alliances because of the need for free exchange of information. This network is formed among a group in which trust has been fostered through repeated interaction and the success of prior information exchanges. This network is localized due to the contextual nature of the information exchanged (from both a project and personnel reputation perspective);
- when necessary information and skill sets cannot be found in the local network, Flagships are used to overcome the limits of localized information exchange to access the Flagship's global network of information and production connections.

The Database of Alliance Activity

Strategic alliances are relatively difficult to identify as they are not scrutinized nor recorded by a regulatory body as are mergers and acquisitions. As a result, most alliance literature has relied on qualitative interviewing and case study methods, as is evident in the works of Doz (1988) and Ahern (1991, 1993a,1993b). To identify a large number of alliances, the business and trade presses may be consulted over an extended period of time, thus developing a more quantitative rather than qualitative database. Hagadoorn (1990) and Hagadoorn and Schakenraad (1992) employed the trade publication approach to develop their CATI (Cooperative Agreements and Technology Indicators) data set for the information technology sector. Anderson (1992, 1993) employed SCIP (a trade publication) to define over 1700 pharmaceutical alliances, while Hakansson et al. (1993) identified 3584 alliances in the biotechnology sector from BioScan, an industry directory that collects alliance information.

The media/publication approach to identifying alliance activity has its limitations, such as: 'newsworthy' firms may get more press; alliance births may be recorded, but not alliance deaths; and a regional focus/concentration may create a geographic bias.

Despite these problems, the literature counting method is the only way to develop a large-scale database to empirically describe alliance activity within an industrial sector. Some of the disadvantages of this approach can be mitigated by gathering alliance information from a large number of sources, cross-checking between sources, and standardizing the collection and recording process.

Itsunami Inc. of Berkeley, CA markets an electronic database called ITSA (Information Technology Strategic Alliances), similar to CATI, which employs the literature counting approach. ITSA references a broad range of global trade press sources to identify alliance activity, and given the thorough data collection procedures and reporting methods has managed to mitigate may of the shortcomings or the literature counting methodology. The database provides details on alliance partners, industries, type of agreement, date of activity, periodical references, location of alliance action, and a brief description of the alliance agreement. It currently covers over 28,000 alliances which have occurred since 1985. All alliances are recorded only once to eliminate redundancy, unless the alliance structure changes, e.g., if the alliance evolves from a licensing agreement to a joint venture. The ITSA database is the most comprehensive data set available for the IT sector.

The following analysis is based on a sample of 3281 alliances from the ITSA database, spanning ten years from 1985-1994 inclusive. The second section details the rationale used to identify these 3281 alliances, and provides the empirical support for the preceding section.

Analysis

The ITSA database contains a vast number of alliances, many of which have multiple alliance partners. Identifying all the linkages between every member of the data set would produce tens of thousands of connections, and serve little to identify broader trends at a national/global scale, since such a complex pattern can only truly be understood by complete deconstruction of the pattern to observe activity on a case-by-case basis.

In order to avoid handling every alliance among the thousands of firms in the database, the data was subjected to a measure of network centrality to eliminate cases (firms) with few alliances. After successive iterations, the final cut of the centrality measure produces a ranking of the top 122 firms based on their connectivity with other members of the alliance network. The result was a hierarchy of firms with the most connected to other firms heading the list. As a side note, IBM was linked through alliances to 120 of the 122 firms in the list. The centrality measures are based solely on connectivity to other alliance partners. No attempt was made to weight the linkages by importance to the

Table 8.1 Centrality Measures

Firm Name	Centrality Measure [*]
IBM	757.14
AT&T	408.40
Hewlett Packard	381.51
DEC	342.02
Microsoft	249.58
Apple	244.54
Compaq	81.51
Lotus	84.03
Texas Instruments	68.75
Western Digital	10.92

[*] Analysis performed with Borgatti, Everetti, and Freeman, (1992) UCINET IV Version 1.0, Columbia: Analytic Technologies.

Table 8.2 Residual of Population by Employment by Alliance SIC 367 and 737

SMSA	State	Pop1996	HwrEmp	SfwEmp	Alliances	TZResid
New York	New York	19938492	40550	88089	1191	-3.53
Chicago	Illinois	8599774	21900	25000	189	-2.34
Miami	Florida	3514403	3200	7406	12	-1.78
Philadelphia	Pennsylvania	5973463	8950	25696	268	-1.38
Detroit	Michigan	5284171	4250	24756	-	-1.38
Los Angeles	California	15495155	60600	53156	59	-1.29
Cleveland	Ohio	2913430	2900	8506	-	-1.18
Houston	Texas	4253428	4500	18701	4	-1.10
San Diego	California	2655463	14600	12977	-	0.71
Denver	Colorado	2277401	8150	16856	3	0.76
Phoenix	Arizona	2746703	25000	6448	-	1.03
Binghamton	New York	254053	12150	764	-	1.23
Minneapolis	Minnesota	2765116	18800	18909	37	1.66
Austin	Texas	1041330	22900	4555	9	2.06
Dallas Ft Worth	Texas	4574561	22500	36983	189	2.37
Washington	District of Columbia	7164519	4700	94541	56	4.28
Boston	Massachusetts	5563475	42800	49359	677	4.91
San Francisco	California	6605428	115300	60510	1381	12.67

* Abbreviated SMSA titles.

Pop1996 - Population of the SMSA in 1996, HwrEmp -Employment in the Hardware Sector (SIC 367) in the SMSA
SfwEmp - Employment in the Software and Support Sector (SIC 737) in the SMSA, TZResid - Total Z-Score Residual
encompassing both hardware and software employment $y = -1094.928 + 0.00822x$, $r^2 = 0.719$, $p = 0.005$

firm/industry, by sales or revenue impact, nor by cost of collaboration, so that the final centrality measure would identify those firms which act as nodes (of production, marketing, information, and or research) for the industry – the Flagships.

The top six firms of Table 8.1 represent the Flagships for the IT sector. The four other firms of Table 8.1 are representative of the quantitative difference between Flagship network connectivity and all other firms.

Once the top firms were identified by their centrality, two questions naturally arose from the data: To what extent does this firm pattern of Table 8.1 simply reflect the urban hierarchy? If it does, the pattern of strategic alliances is exactly as expected according to the distribution of population, but if it is not, what spatial patterns are at work in the IT sector?

A simple regression analysis was performed to answer the first of these two questions. Comparing populations in the urban centers to their alliance activity and to the employment in SIC codes 367 and 737 (hardware and software respectively) it was determined, as noted in Table 8.2, the New York's metropolitan area (MA) was over predicted in its alliance activity while the San Francisco (MA) (Silicon Valley) was greatly under-predicted. While the observations may be intuitive if one understands the nature of the IT sector, their explicit quantification has been unrecognized to date.

Table 8.2 establishes that the alliance pattern does not exactly reflect the urban hierarchical pattern, but the alliance phenomenon is urban in nature given its concentration in urban areas.

Given that the pattern of alliance activity is not solely representative of the urban hierarchy (especially evident in Silicon Valley) what other phenomenon is at work? Revisiting the model of Figure 8.1 may provide some answers. Those centers with especially high rates of under prediction such as Silicon Valley, Route 128, and the Texas Complexes, (Washington is an anomaly because of its high degree of government related activity with respect to software support) are also those areas known for tier two types of activity – research and development, joint ventures, and standards development. It is in these industrial concentrations where the 'interpersonal worlds' of contacts and associations permit for industrial development through the repeated exchange of information and knowledge in an informal setting (Storper, 1997; Saxenian, 1990, 1994). It is these 'knowledge networks' which become vital to firm strategy and growth. The nature of these networks has been the focus of much study, especially by Saxenian. Noting the more than 12 standard deviations from the mean for Silicon Valley, its dominant position in the study of high technology is justified, especially when its nearest regional/urban rival (Route 128) is over 2.5 times less likely to originate IT activity, even though it has more than half the Valley's employment level (see Table 8.2).

It is interesting to note that the centers at the upper and lower bounds of Table 8.2 are also the locations of most of the Flagship firms identified from Table 8.1. New York holds the dominant position in the urban hierarchy and is thus a large information node (key to success in tier two alliance activity) and the high tech centers of Silicon Valley and Route 128 use their dominant positions in the 'IT hierarchy' to retain Flagships because of their capacity for information and knowledge exchange among the personnel of these centers.

While such conclusions follow the general tenor of past research, the purpose of this chapter is to make explicit some of those past generalizations as above. To this end, the relationships mentioned above were tested with multiple classification analysis (MCA), a variant of analysis of variance, to establish the effect distance has on Flagship network membership and on tier effects. Table 8.3 presents the results.

First the analysis shows that Flagships dominate the alliance scene with 60.4% of alliance activity, and that there are differences between Flagships and smaller firms in their spatial reach. Flagship firms, on average, look 115.56 miles closer for partners than do small firms, who must search 176.55 miles further on average for partners, on average. Flagship firms have greater information so they are more likely to identify nearer candidates. In addition, the Flagships can be more flexible in selection of firms, particularly in cases where there are multiple partners. It is the mix of the partners' advantages that is important not the partners themselves. Smaller firms, without such resources and who cannot offer the same extent of business services as the larger firms much reach further.

Secondly, the analysis presents the tier effects of the model. Tier two, knowledge and information networks, operate in a tighter sphere than do production networks (-86.28 miles versus 112.66 miles from the mean distance). While Scott and Henry have identified in theory the need for

Table 8.3 Multiple Classification Analysis: Flagship Membership Effects

		N	Unadjusted Distance	Adjusted for Factors	Unadjusted Distance from overall mean	Adjusted for Factors Distance from overall mean
Flagship	Small	1298	2315.47	2310.10	181.92	176.55
	Flagship	1983	2014.47	2017.99	-119.08	-115.56
Small	Tier 1	1423	2253.40	2246.21	119.85	112.66
	Tier 2	1858	2041.76	2047.27	-91.79	-86.28

production to agglomerate to overcome the friction of transporting the goods of production, it is evident that the industry deems the friction of 'information decay' as more sensitive than production frictions. If this is indeed the case, the smaller firms in the IT sector (the productive firms of tier one who handle the outsourcing from the larger IT players) should show a steady but sharp distance decay function with a long tail indicating its further spatial function than tier two alliances. The Flagships, however, should therefore have a shorter spatial extent, with a large number of local alliances, but also a concentration of bi-coastal alliances to access the local knowledge networks of

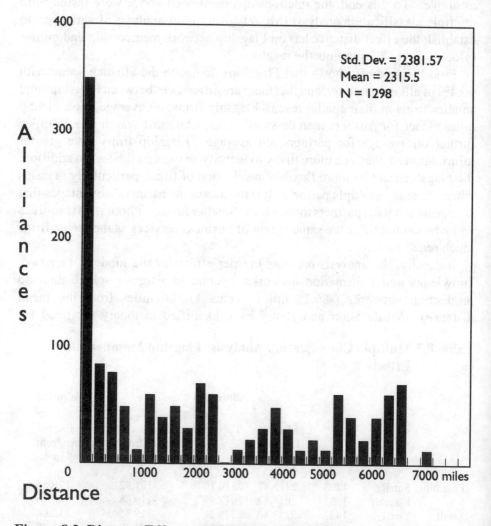

Std. Dev. = 2381.57
Mean = 2315.5
N = 1298

Figure 8.2 Distance Effects on Small Firm Alliances

the two largest outliers of Table 8.2 – Route 128 and Silicon Valley. The histograms below serve to illustrate the above points for smaller firms (Figure 8.2) and for Flagships (Figure 8.3).

Conclusions

The argument in the first section of the paper is that the traditional cost-based approach to alliance study has been overly narrow. This is not to deny the importance of such works, for the development of the eclectic alliance theory of this paper is based upon those efforts. The eclectic alliance theory offers a

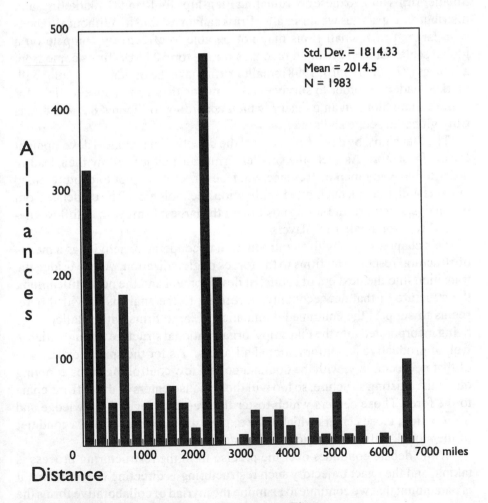

Figure 8.3 Distance Effects on Dominant Firms

new level of integration of knowledge, information, and social networks into the cost-based approach heretofore typically considered as the sole, or at least dominant, motivation for cooperative activity within this industrial system.

Employing an atypical quantified approach, rather than traditional case-study methods, has identified that Flagship firms – those firms that dominate the industry due to their varied relationships with other network firms – are key to the new industrial organizational structures of the new economy. Such firms act as coordinating nodes, centralizing network activities from production to research with a reach that is global in scale. These Flagships and their actions represent the majority of IT cooperative activity, concentrating information and knowledge resources closer to the firms' site than productive requirements. Smaller firms look to these coordinating Flagships for R and D, marketing, and distributive capacities which smaller firms cannot establish. Without alliances with larger firms, small firms may not be able to effectively compete on a global scale. Since 18% of all revenues for the top 1000 US firms come from alliances (*The Economist*, 1998) smaller firms have the option of aligning with market leaders in order to survive and grow, or they can choose to fight for market share alone in an industry, which according to Figures 8.2 and 8.3, is truly global in scope and scale.

The Flagships, by definition, control the direction of technical development for the IT sector. As such, the smaller firms must either follow their lead in order to have any market presence whatsoever, else attempt to capture niche markets with radical, but limited application, technologies. The evidence from the analysis supports the strong position of the largest firms with a 'follow-the-leader' role for smaller IT players.

This chapter began with an introduction to cooperative activity as a means of structural response by firms to the forces of globalization. As we bridge the transition into the next era of capitalist development and the new millennium, the structure of that new economy, according to the analysis provided here, seems to support the continued dominance of large firms with smaller firms being incorporated into the Flagships' organizational structure through a dense web of productive and informational alliances. As for the spatial expression of that new economy, with the dominance of a few controlling firms evolving out of the existing structure, so too will the regions/centers of those firms come to the fore. Those centers which foster the free exchange of knowledge and information, those centers which fully exploit the resources of the second tier of the model, will grow in global economic importance.

While debate continues over the precise form the restructuring process is taking, and the exact trajectory such restructuring is directing the economy, it is paramount that we continue to examine the myriad of collaborative forms the restructuring process demands of the existing economic actors. In this chapter we have provided one small step forward in the understanding of the organizational response of firms by looking at the national pattern of cooperative activities of actors in the IT sector. By understanding the process affecting one industrial sector, and the economic and/or spatial outcomes of that process, we may come to better understand the process of economic restructuring itself.

Acknowledgments

The authors wish to thank Jim Sharp of Itsunami Inc. for his continued assistance throughout the endeavors of this work. A special thanks is extended to Rod McNaughton for allowing access to the data. Dr. McNaughton acquired the database through a SSHRC grant while at the University of Lethbridge. As always, any errors or omissions are the sole responsibility of the authors.

References

Ahern R.D. (1991), *International Strategic Alliances: The Use of Cooperation by Canadian Firms*. U.M.I., Ann Arbor.

Ahern R.D. (1993a), 'The Role of Strategic Alliances in the International Organization of Industry', *Environment and Planning A*, vol. 25, pp. 1229-1246.

Ahern R.D. (1993b), Implications of Strategic Alliances for small R and D intensive firms, *Environment and Planning A,* vol. 25, pp. 1511-1528.

Amin A. and Thrift N. (1992), 'Neo-Marshallian nodes in Global Networks', *International Journal of Urban and Regional Research*, vol. 16, no. 4, pp. 571-587.

Angel D. (1990), 'New firm formation in the semiconductor industry: elements of a flexible manufacturing system', *Regional Studies,* vol. 24, pp. 211-221.

Angel D. (1994), 'Tighter Bonds? Customer-Supplier Linkages in Semiconductors', *Regional Studies*, vol. 28, no. 2, pp. 187-200.

Anderson M.J. (1992), *The Collaborative Edge: The Role of Collaborative Integration in the Organization and Locational Structure of Industry*, unpublished Ph.D. dissertation, Department of Geography, Queen's University, Kingston, Ontario.

Anderson M.J. (1993), 'Collaborative integration in the Canadian pharmaceutical industry', *Environment and Planning A*, vol. 25, pp. 1815-1838.

Anderson M.J. (1995), 'The role of Collaborative Integration in Industrial Organization: Observations from the Canadian Aerospace Industry', *Economic Geography*, vol. 71, pp. 55-78.

Bleeke J. and Ernst D. (1993), 'The Way to Win in Cross Border Alliances', in J.Bleeke and D. Ernst (eds.) *Collaborating to Compete: Using Strategic Alliances and Acquisition in the Global Marketplace.* Wiley, New York, pp. 17-34.

Buckley P. and Casson M. (1976), *The Future of the Multinational Enterprise.* Macmillan, London.

Buckley P. and Casson M. (1988), 'A Theory of Cooperation in International Business', in F. J. Contractor and P. Lorange (eds) *Cooperative Strategies in International Business.* Lexington Books, Lexington MA.

Castells M. (1989), *The informational city: information technology, economic restructuring and the urban regional process*. Basil Blackwell, Cambridge MA.

Cecil B., Green M., and McNaughton R. (1996), 'Patterns of Strategic Alliances among Information Technology firms in the United States', *Geografiska Annaler*, vol. 78B, no. 3, pp. 129-146.

Clark G. (1994), 'Strategy and Structure: Corporate Restructuring and the Scope and Characteristics of Sunk Costs', *Environment and Planning A*, vol. 26, pp. 9-32.

Coase R. (1937), 'The Nature of the Firm', *Economica* vol. 4, pp. 386-405.

Cooke P. (1988), Flexible Interaction, Scope Economies, and Strategic Alliances: Social and Spatial Mediations, *Environment and Planning D: Society and Space*, vol. 6, pp. 281-300.

Cooke P. and Morgan K. (1993), The Network Paradigm: New Departures in Corporate and Regional Development, *Environment and Planning D: Society and Space*, vol. 11, pp. 543-564.

D'Cruz J.R. and Rugman A.M. (1994), 'Business Network Theory and the Canadian Telecommunications Industry', *International Business Review*, vol. 3, no. 3, pp. 275-288.

Doz Y. (1988), 'Technology Partnerships Between Large and Smaller Firms: Some critical issues,' in F.J. Contractor and P. Lorrange (eds) *Cooperative Strategies in International Business*, Lexington Books, Lexington, MA.

Economist, The (1998), 'The Science of Alliance', April 4, 1998, pp. 69-70.

Florida R. and Kenney M. (1990), 'Silicon Valley and Route 128 Won't Save Us', *California Management Review*, vol. 33, no. 1, pp. 68-88.

Granovetter M. (1985), 'Economic Action and Social Structure: the problem of Embeddedness', *American Journal of Sociology*, vol. 91, pp. 481-510.

Hagedoorn J. (1990), 'Organizational Modes of Inter-firm Cooperation and Technology Transfer', *Technovation* , vol. 1.

Hagedoorn J. and Schakenraad J. (1992), 'Leading Companies and Networks of Strategic Alliances in Information Technology', *Research Policy*, vol. 21, no. 2, pp. 163-190.

Hakansson P. Kjelberg H. and Lundgren A. (1993), 'Strategic Alliances in Global Biotechnology - A Network Approach', *International Business Review*, vol. 2, no. 1, pp. 65-82.

Harvey, D. (1987), 'Flexible accumulation through urbanization: reflections on post modernism in the American city', *Antipode*, vol. 19, pp. 260-286.

Henry N. (1992), 'The New Industrial Spaces: Locational logic of a new production era', *International Journal of Urban and Regional Research*, vol.16, no. 3, pp. 375-396.

ITSA (1994), Information Technology Strategic Alliances database, Itsunami Incorporated, Berkeley California.

Johanson J. and Mattsson L.G. (1987), 'Interorganizational Relations in Industrial Systems: A Network Approach Compared with the Transaction-Cost Approach', *International Studies of Management and Organization*, , vol. 17, no. 1, pp. 34-48.

Leborgne D. and Lipietz A. (1988), 'New technologies, new modes of regulation: some spatial implications', *Environment and Planning D: Society and Space*, vol. 6, no. 3, pp. 263-286.

Lovering J. (1990), 'Fordism's unknown successor: a comment on Scott's theory of flexible accumulation and the re-emergence of regional economies', *International Journal of Urban and Regional Research*, vol.14, no.1, pp. 159-174.

Mueller F. (1996), 'Human Resources as Strategic Assets: an evolutionary resource-based approach', *Journal of Management Studies*, vol. 33, no. 6, pp. 757-785.

Oakey R. (1981), *High Technology Industry and Industrial Location*, Gower, Aldershot.

Pfeffer J. and Salancik G.R. (1978), *The external control of organizations: a resource dependence perspective*. Harper and Row, New York.

Piore M. and Sabel C. (1984), *The Second Industrial Divide*. Basic Books, New York.

Powell W. (1990), 'Neither Market nor Hierarchy: Network forms of organization', *Research in Organizational Behavior*, vol. 12, pp. 293-336.

Pralahad C. and Hamel G. (1990), 'The Core Competence of the Corporation', *Harvard Business Review* May/June, pp. 79-91.

Rugman A.M. (1981), *Inside the Multinationals*. Croom Helm, London.

Rugman A.M. and D'Cruz J.R. (1997), 'Strategies of Multinational Enterprises and Governments: the theory of the Flagship Firm', in G. Boyd and A. Rugman (eds) *Euro-Pacific Investment and Trade*, Elgar, Brookfield, pp. 37-68..

Saxenian A. (1990), 'Regional Networks and the Resurgence of Silicon Valley', *California Management Review*, vol. 33, pp. 89-112.

Saxenian A. (1994), *Regional Advantage: Culture and competition in Silicon Valley and Route 128*. Harvard University Press, Cambridge MA.

Scott A. (1986a), 'Industrial Organization and Location: Division of Labor, the Firm and Spatial Process', *Economic Geography*, vol. 62, pp. 215-231.

Scott A. (1986b), 'High technology industry and territorial development: the rise of the Orange County complex, 1955-1984', *Urban Geography*, vol. 7, no. 1, pp. 3-45.

Scott A. (1988a), 'Flexible production systems and regional development: the rise of new industrial spaces in North America and Europe', *International Journal of Urban and Regional Research*, vol.12, no. 2, pp. 171-185.

Scott A. (1988b), *New Industrial Spaces*. Pion, London.

Stalk G., Evans P., and Schulman E. (1992), 'Competing on Capabilities: The new rules for corporate strategy', *Harvard Business Review* March/April, pp. 57-69.

Storper M. (1997), *The Regional World: Territorial development in a global economy*. Guilford, New York.

Wells P. and Cooke P. (1991), 'The Geography of International Strategic Alliances in the Telecommunications Industry', *Environment and Planning A*, vol. 23, pp. 87-106.

Williamson O. (1975), *Markets and Hierarchies: Analysis and Antitrust Implications*. Free Press, New York.

Williamson O. (1981), 'The Economics of Organization: The Transaction Cost Approach', *American Journal of Sociology*, vol. 87, no. 3, pp. 548-577.

Williamson O. (1985), *The Economic Institutions of Capitalism*. Free Press, New York.

9 The Role of External Technological Services in the Innovation Performance of Small and Medium-Sized Manufacturing Firms

ALAN D. MacPHERSON

Introduction

There is now a considerable body of empirical work on the role of geographical location in the business performance of manufacturing firms (e.g., Acs and Audretsch, 1990; Bennett and Robson., 1999; Britton, 1996; Feldman, 1994; Gertler, 1995). An important theme in this literature is that some regions are more likely to contain innovative and/or fast-growing industrial establishments than others, not least because of spatial variations in the depth and quality of local technological resources (Feldman and Florida, 1994). These resources include first-tier universities (Anselin et al., 1996), corporate research and development facilities (Malecki, 1994), government research units (Lawton-Smith, 1996), and a diverse range of specialists in the producer services (Harrington, 1995). The latter include consultants with technical expertise in fields such as industrial design (O'Connor, 1996), contract research and development (Haour, 1992), production engineering (Bessant and Rush, 1995), management consulting (Chandra, 1992), and laboratory testing (Feldman, 1994). It is increasingly recognized that these types of external resources are spatially concentrated in major metropolitan areas, leaving some regions with only weak local supplies of technological inputs (O'Connor, 1996). Despite the growing transportability of specialized know-how via telecommunications, several scholars have argued that close physical proximity between suppliers and users can play a key role in the innovation efforts of firms (Gertler, 1995; Illeris, 1994; Malecki, 1994).

Much of this proximity advantage reflects the fact that successful linkages between technical specialists and users typically involve complex and frequent face-to-face meetings (Coffey and Bailey, 1993; O'hUallachain, 1991). A further factor is that technologically important interactions often take place on the basis of informal connections between members of localized business networks (Malecki and Tootle, 1996). As Scott (1986) and several others have maintained, the potential for useful interaction is generally stronger in locations that contain dense clusters of specialists (see also Goe et al., 1999). This implies a geography of innovation that mirrors the regional distribution of technological resources, in line with the US findings reported by Feldman and Florida (1994).

A second theme that has emerged in the recent literature on innovation is that small and medium-sized firms (SMFs) often exhibit higher levels of research and development productivity than their larger counterparts (Audretsch and Feldman, 1996; Ceh, 1996; Koeller, 1995; Rothwell, 1992). Part of this contrast would seem to flow from the fact that SMFs have become increasingly adept at tapping knowledge spillovers from the external environment (Liesch and Knight, 1999; Link and Rees, 1990). This said, regional disparities in innovation rates have persisted across most of the advanced market economies (Malecki, 1994), and this holds true for all size-classes of firms (Acs and Audretsch, 1990).

Keeping these themes in mind, the goal of this chapter is to explore the role of location in the innovation performance of SMFs in New York State's scientific instruments sector. Particular attention is given to the use of specialized technological services by these firms, notably for product development purposes. Although SMFs typically rely upon a wide range of external inputs to support innovation, it is argued in this chapter that five specific classes of outside help are of special importance. These classes include contract research and development, industrial design, laboratory testing, production engineering, and management consulting.

Data for the inquiry come from a sample of eighty-one companies that responded to a postal survey in 1994. Additional data come from a number of follow-up efforts, including personal interviews (on-site), telephone interviews, and a second postal survey (using an abbreviated version of the original instrument). The discussion which follows revolves around two key questions. First, why do some regions perform better than others in terms of the innovation/external-sourcing relationship? Second, to what extent do external services support the innovation efforts of SMFs? Before looking at the survey results, however, it is first necessary to supply a research context for the analysis, as well as a brief overview of the study region and its main characteristics.

Regional Context

New York State (NYS) can be described as a subnational region that consists of three distinct territories as far as economic activity is concerned (see Figure 9.1 for a delineation of these regions). The downstate region, which centers around the New York City (NYC) metropolitan area, contains the world's dominant concentration of advanced producer services (Mitchelson and Wheeler, 1994), as well as a dense and diverse cluster of post-secondary educational institutions (MacPherson, 1997a). Although downstate manufacturing employment has been falling at close to the national average for some time, SMF growth within this region has been higher than the New York State (NYS) average for many years. The Western New York (WNY) region, in contrast, belongs to a declining segment of the US Rustbelt that has been experiencing net factor out-migration for at least the last ten years. Aside from Kodak and Xerox, both of which are prominent in Rochester, WNY can be characterized as an almost archetypal sunset region that has failed to participate in the national growth thrust of the 1990s. Situated between the Downstate and WNY, the Upstate Central (UC) region can be described as a resource-based economy that relies primarily upon tourism, logging, farming, and outdoor recreation (alongside public administration in Albany, the NYS capital). Ranked on the basis of technological infrastructure, it is no surprise that NYC occupies first place, distantly followed by WNY (which itself is distantly followed by UC).

For the purposes of this chapter, however, it is interesting to note that all three regions contain comparable proportions of industrial employment in the scientific instruments sector (expressed as a percentage of total manufacturing employment at the regional level). This small but technologically advanced sector is dominated by SMFs, most of which spend close to ten percent of their annual sales on applied research and development.

In terms of producer service employment, the three regions are very different. On the basis of standard definitions of producer services (i.e., business services plus FIRE), NYC leads the pack (if not the world) with a score of 29 percent (i.e., almost a third of all NYC jobs are in the producer services). In contrast, WNY (13 percent) and UC (nine percent) rank much lower (Mackun and MacPherson, 1997). With regard to employment in the industrial design field, for example, approximately 90 percent of New York

State's independent design specialists are located within the NYC region. While this is not very surprising, it is important to indicate from the outset that virtually all of the producer service categories examined in this project are overwhelmingly concentrated in the NYC area.

On this note, two empirical themes from the literature serve as a backdrop for the analysis which follows. First, evidence from Jaffe (1989), Acs et al. (1994), Feldman (1994) and Rothwell (1992) reveal that successful innovation among SMFs in knowledge-based industries is strongly influenced by the extent to which such firms can obtain external scientific and technical assistance. Although in-house research and development is often a critical predictor of SMF innovation, external expertise has been shown to play an important role in promoting and/or accelerating the innovation process (Deb, 1996). Second, regional variations in the mix and quality of local technological resources can affect the innovation performance of particular places (Acs et al., 1994; Feldman and Florida, 1994; Jaffe et al, 1994). Although these two themes have been empirically confirmed for several NYS industrial sectors (see MacPherson, 1997a), the scientific instruments sector is of special interest for at least two reasons. First, manufacturers of precision

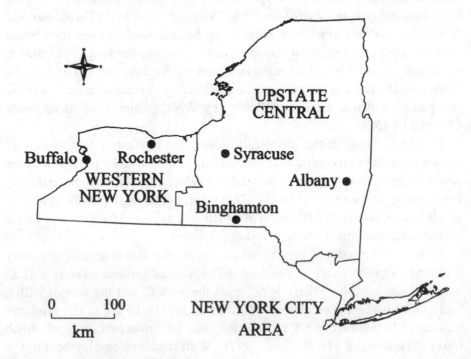

Figure 9.1 Study Areas

Table 9.1 The Use of Technology-based Services Among the Survey Firms

Region		NYC	UC	WNY	State	
	a) sample size	38	15	28	81	
	b) no. of users	30	4	16	50	*
	c) % of sample	78.9	26.7	57.1	61.7	
	d) mean outlays	41.4	9.1	14.2	35.3	**
	e) local supply	68.8	31.2	48.1	49.4	**

Where:

a) total number of respondents per region;
b) number of firms with mean annual expenditures on external technological services of > US$5000 over the study period;
c) percent of firms with significant external expenditures;
d) mean annual outlays on external services over the study period (US$000s);
e) percent of service expenditures within the same region.

* χ^2 for region by service use = 12.8 (p = 0.0016)
** All 3 regions differ at p = < 0.05 (t-tests).

instruments have been shown to rely upon external technical inputs by a wide variety of scholars (e.g., Berman, 1995; Chandra, 1992; Rothwell, 1992). Second, this is a highly competitive sector, in that market concentration is low (i.e., the industry consists mainly of SMFs). To an extent, then, the scientific instruments sector provides a good test case as far as the two empirical themes noted above are concerned.

While there is now a wide body of spatially informed theory that pertains to the innovation and/or business performance of SMFs (see Ettlinger and Tufford, 1996), this chapter looks only at the five classes of external inputs noted earlier. While these inputs are insufficient on their own to fully explain regional differences in the innovation patterns of SMFs, a selective picture is offered here as a starting point for broader discussion of the factors that promote new product and/or process development among small firms. In short, this chapter takes an 'other things being equal' approach toward the question of regional variations in SMF behavior.

Research Method and Main Results

In a preliminary effort to probe some of the issues outlined above, self-administered surveys were mailed to a total of 234 scientific instruments firms in 1994. A total of eighty-one valid returns were obtained after two follow-ups, giving a response rate of thirty-four percent. The survey method was based upon a systematic sampling of approximately half of the total population of New York State SMFs in this sector. All of the respondents were single-plant firms with fewer than 500 employees. Several tests for nonresponse bias were conducted for the three regional samples. These tests included difference of means comparisons between respondents versus nonrespondents across several variables, including company size (fulltime employment), age and product focus (using published data from industrial directories). No significant differences were uncovered between the two groups.

On this note, Table 9.1 compares the three regions in terms of the use of technology-based services. The term 'technology-based' in this instance refers to a package of external inputs that have been shown on previous occasions to support industrial innovation. As mentioned earlier, the package presented in this analysis includes industrial design, laboratory testing, management consulting, production engineering and contract research and development. For simplicity, Tables 9.1 and 9.3 present these external contacts in an aggregated form. In Table 9.1 for instance, the thirty NYC users of external services enjoy 'user' status as a result of average annual expenditures of US$5,000 or more on the combined package of services over the study period (1989-1993).

Several features of Table 9.1 are noteworthy. First, firms in the NYC region stand out as having significantly higher expenditures on external services than their WNY and UC counterparts. NYC firms spent an annual average of more than US$40,000 per annum on outside technological support over the 5-year study period, compared to only US$9,000 among firms in the UC region (the average for WNY was US$14,200). These spending patterns are significantly different across all regional combinations at $p = 0.05$ or less (t-tests). At the same time, however, t-tests failed to uncover significant regional differences in the types of demographic and/or market-related variables that might be expected to influence these patterns (e.g. company size, number of years in business, and product mix). In short, we have groups of firms across the three regions that look quite similar in terms of size, age, and product focus (important differences shall be discussed later).

Table 9.1 also shows that NYC firms exhibit a higher propensity to exploit external technological support than their counterparts in the other two regions (the 3 x 2 χ^2 is 12.82 at p = 0.0016). For example, almost 80 percent of the NYC firms exploit external consultants, compared to only 27 percent among UC firms (WNY = 57 percent). At the county level, it should be noted that there is a positive correlation between producer service employment (a rough proxy for technological resources) and county level spending on the five service classes (r = 0.465, p = 0.03). An implication here is that total spending on external services is influenced by local supply.

Keeping these relationships in mind, a cross tabulation of innovation by region is shown in Table 9.2. Innovation was defined as the successful introduction of at least one new or radically improved product over the study period (excluding items that failed to succeed in the marketplace). The data suggest an innovation advantage for NYC firms relative to their more northerly counterparts. For example, 73 percent of the NYC firms introduced product innovations over the study period, compared to 54 percent of the WNY firms and only 33 percent of the UC firms (χ^2 = 7.82; p = 0.02). A different way of picturing the data is to consider the odds of innovation across the three regions. For example, odds ratio analyses revealed that NYC firms were 2.42 times

Table 9.2 Regional Variations in Innovation Performance

Region		NYC	UC	WNY	State
Successful	No	10	10	13	33
Innovation		(30.3)	(30.3)	(39.4)	[40.7]
		[26.3]	[66.7]	[46.4]	
	Yes	28	5	15	48
		(58.3)	(10.4)	(31.3)	[59.3]
		[73.7]	[33.3]	[53.6]	
	Total	38	15	28	81

n = count
( ) = percentage row
[ ] = percentage column

more likely to be innovators than WNY firms (the odds ratio for NYC versus UC was 5.60). Comparing WNY with UC, it would appear that WNY producers are 3.46 times more likely to be innovators than their UC counterparts. No matter how the data are treated, NYC emerges as the best location as far as innovation propensity is concerned (for additional tests, including tests that address modifiable areal unit problems, see Curtis and MacPherson, 1996).

For the sample as a whole, Table 9.3 collates two measures of innovation against the incidence of links to external consultants. The first measure (product innovation) has already been defined (see Table 9.2). The second

Table 9.3 External Support and Innovation (Product and Process)

Technical Support		Yes	No	Total
Product Innovation	No	14 (42.4) [28.0]	19 (57.6) [61.3]	33 [40.7]
	Yes	36 (75.0) [72.0]	12 (25.0) [38.7]	48 [59.3]
Process Innovation	No	17 (26.7) [38.7]	19 (52.8) [61.3]	36 [44.4]
	Yes	33 (73.3) [66.0]	12 (26.7) [38.7]	45 [55.6]
	Total	50	31	81

n = count
( ) = percentage row
[ ] = percentage column

χ^2 for product innovation = 8.78 p = 0.003
process innovation = 5.77 p = 0.016

measure (process innovation) refers to the introduction of new or significantly improved manufacturing procedures via capital spending (1989-1993).

Interestingly, both measures of innovation are positively associated with external technical support at $p = < 0.05$. In terms of odds ratios, successful product innovation is 4.07 times more likely to occur among firms that exploit outside consultants (the comparable ratio for process innovation is 3.06). For both of the innovation measures, then, it would appear that outside consultants can make an important contribution. Although the n-sizes for a regionally disaggregated version of Table 9.3 are too low to permit reliable significance testing, data presented elsewhere (based upon an expanded version of this survey) indicate that the relationships shown in Table 9.3 are noticeably stronger within the NYC region (MacPherson, 1997b).

An additional perspective is shown in Table 9.4, which presents a summary of the main barriers to innovation identified by the survey firms. These data come from a mix of sources, including the original survey instrument, an expanded survey based upon an abbreviated version of the same instrument (which brought the n-size for NYS as a whole to 204), follow-up telephone inquiries, and on-site interviews (for methodological details, see MacPherson, 1997a). The data are presented as average scores across 5-point scales (ranging from 1 = no importance whatsoever to the innovation process, to 5 = critically important factor). For NYS as a whole, the availability of skilled labour turned out to be the chief obstacle to innovation (3.4), followed by government regulatory barriers (3.0), the local availability of technical services (2.9), the

Table 9.4 Barriers to Innovation*

Region	NYC	UC	WNY	State **
1 lack of skilled people	1.9	4.1	4.3	3.4
2 regulatory barriers	2.9	3.0	3.1	3.0
3 local service availability	1.6	3.5	3.7	2.9
4 university resources	1.9	3.2	3.4	2.8
5 access to capital	1.7	2.9	3.2	2.6

* This Table comes from a mix of sources (see text).
** In every case except two, the two upstate regions differ from the New York City metropolitan area at $p = < 0.05$ (t-tests).

quality of local university resources (2.8) and access to capital (2.6). While we are not concerned with all of these obstacles in this chapter, it should be noted that almost every barrier listed in Table 9.4 has a significantly stronger score for the two upstate regions. Interestingly, the data hint at the existence of a local service supply problem for WNY and UC, but not for NYC. Significantly, evidence presented elsewhere suggests that upstate SMFs that import at least some of their technical needs from nonlocal vendors outperform non-importers across a variety of metrics, including process innovation, new product development, export intensity, and sales growth (see MacPherson, 1997a).

Although the original survey generated a good deal more data than have been shown here, Tables 9.1-9.4 provide an empirical backdrop for discussing a number of key themes that have recently become prominent in the literature on SMFs, innovation, regional economic conditions, and technological change. The following section fleshes out some of these themes with regard to the statistical snapshots shown earlier. Particular attention is given to the following considerations. First, policymakers have become increasingly interested in the construction of regional advantage. More specifically, public efforts to support local innovation and/or job growth have proliferated in recent years. Second, strategies to compensate for local supply-side weaknesses have also become popular, not least because few regions contain all of the technological and/or institutional resources necessary for the creation of an innovative milieu (Camagni, 1995). Third, special attention has focused in recent years upon the role of formal and/or informal business networks in the promotion of regional advantage. These three themes are interlinked in a number of ways. The section which follows explores some of the main interconnections between these themes.

Discussion

The results sketched above were drawn from a broader inquiry that included a wider range of external inputs to the innovation process (e.g., distributors, suppliers, large manufacturing firms, customers, universities, formal/informal business services, government agencies, and other producer service [e.g., specialists in areas such as advertising, computer software, accounting, and marketing]). I have not documented these alternative sources of advice in this chapter for two reasons. First, the five classes of external support analyzed earlier typically represent non-substitutable inputs. For instance, a firm that requires contract research and development services is unlikely to find a suitable supplier within the university community or within an informal business network (though these sources might help identify and/or evaluate a potential supplier). Second, the five classes explored earlier (albeit in aggregate form) appear to contribute to specific aspects of the innovation process. For example, contract research and development can assist in the identification of technical possibilities; industrial design services can help with the improvement of prototypes; production engineering advice can support the creation of efficient manufacturing procedures for particular products (or product families); laboratory testing services can provide product evaluations and technical feedback (as well as advice on certification issues); while management consulting services can assist in the development of product strategies (e.g., specialization versus diversification).

Notwithstanding the fact that many other external and internal inputs support SMF innovation (both product and process), the existence of major regional variations in the local availability of the five 'key' classes would appear to have ramifications for local innovation potential. The question thus arises: what strategies might firms and/or policy agencies in disadvantaged regions pursue in an effort to compensate for supply-side deficiencies at the local scale? At least three options spring to mind. The first and most obvious option is to import expertise from other regions. After all, high-order scientific and technical skills can be traded across regions by moving people, data, or both. A second option would be to create local business information networks and/or collaborative inter-firm relationships to support innovation via collective efforts (both private and public). A third option would be to invest heavily in upgrading in-house human capital via worker training, possibly in conjunction with increased in-house research and development. By now, of course, these are fairly standard prescriptions. At a practical level, however, each of these options is problematic. To illustrate this point, the remainder of this chapter explores only the first of these options (imports).

A logical response to local supply deficiency is to buy appropriate inputs from nonlocal vendors. From a regional balance of payments perspective, there is no major difference (at first blush) between imports of raw materials or semi-manufactures and imports of specialized services. After all, the latter can be moved just as quickly as the former (if not more so). For instance, technical specifications can be moved from an industrial design specialist in NYC to a customer in WNY over the internet, while other service-based transactions can be conducted face-to-face by hopping on a plane, train, or automobile. Still other transactions can be completed by e-mail, telephone, fax, or surface mail.

Despite the rising importance of interregional/international trade in advanced services, the import option is not as easy as it might appear. In rank order, SMFs from the WNY and UC regions identified the following problems regarding the import option:

- difficulties associated with the identification and evaluation of nonlocal specialists;
- the perception that nonlocal vendors would not pay enough attention to nonlocal clients (especially small ones); and
- a lack of confidence in the ability of nonlocal consultants to deliver good inputs at reasonable cost.

By applying a mix of quantitative and qualitative approaches to these responses, common denominators included terms like 'trust', 'confidence', 'respect', 'dedication', and 'quality'. More bluntly, it would seem that nonlocal vendors are simply not trusted by local customers (both extant and potential).

With regard to the first item in the list, it should be noted that roughly half of all the external technical services consumed by WNY firms come from vendors located outside the WNY area (mainly Toronto), whereas 65 percent of the services purchased by UC firms come from suppliers in the New York City metropolitan area. On balance, then, service consumers in the Upstate regions are import-oriented. In contrast, fully 88 percent of the services consumed by NYC firms come from within the NYC region itself. Follow-up interviews with importers from the Upstate regions revealed a common set of irritants regarding supplier search, evaluation, contract negotiation, and service delivery.

A key problem is that rather few service importers have been buying external inputs from nonlocal vendors for very long (i.e., the 'typical' importer had less than five years of import experience at the time of the survey). Many of the firms in this category stated that it is hard to find external specialists, not least because many of the latter do not advertise nonlocally (fewer still have websites). Moreover, specialists with expertise in areas such as industrial design are often employed within larger units that advertise engineering or graphic design services -- but not industrial design services. As a further example, many of the technical specialists that can advise on matters such as capital equipment selection are employed within multinational public accounting firms. The initial problem facing most importers (especially first-time importers) is to search multiple databases to find potential suppliers. In doing so, most firms rely upon local business networks to provide advice (i.e., who are the 'best' suppliers?). This is not an easy process, if only because most firms seek external help in fields that are task-specific within any given area of expertise. For an importer in WNY or UC, then, the process of import initiation is not as straightforward as one might suspect. And, in the absence of local demonstration models (examples of firms that have successfully obtained nonlocal expertise), the import option becomes more difficult still.

A second problem is that nonlocal vendors are generally perceived as having only a 'peripheral' interest in SMFs that are themselves geographically 'peripheral'. For example, many of the larger contract research and development establishments in the NYC area are accustomed to multi-million dollar contracts with corporate clients, as opposed to small jobs for SMFs. Without naming names, it would appear that few of the larger engineering consulting units in the NYC area are terribly interested in the technical needs of small firms (especially very small ones). This problem (real or perceived) compounds a third problem, in that many SMFs from outside the NYC area feel that nonlocal consultants do not deliver appropriate solutions at reasonable prices, mainly because such consultants earn more money from larger firms.

This said, many SMFs from Upstate New York do import services successfully. Innovative firms that contain good managers can counter all of the usual problems associated with nonlocal sourcing. In many respects, these firms can be considered 'extroverts', in line with Malecki and Poehling's (1999) personality-based model of firms' use of outside information sources. Following from this model, 'introverts' are less ambitious in their search for external help, as well as less inclined to view innovation or growth as strategic priorities. The point, however, is that the import option is not an easy one for the SMF population as a whole. In WNY, for example, almost half of the sample consists of firms that refuse to explore the import option because of the reasons cited above. Moreover, most of the active importers cited diluted versions of these obstacles as reasons for 'cautious' import activity. The upshot of all this is that there are many SMFs in service-poor regions that opt for either:

- greater in-house provision (stretching internal resources to the limit);
- recourse to local inputs (a second-best external option); or
- operate without the desired input altogether.

Possible Solutions

There is little doubt that business executives listen to other business executives more readily than they listen to academics, policymakers, or public officials. After all, the former can provide practical advice of potentially immediate importance, whereas the latter typically know comparatively little about the specific needs of any given company or sector. A useful direction for future research might be to fuse the interests of both groups, perhaps with a view to constructing more efficient ways of linking private and public ventures for economic development purposes. In this regard, at least three sets of initiatives might be worth considering.

As a starting point for promoting stronger service-to-manufacturing linkages, it would be useful to assemble a detailed inventory of the types of technological resources (both private and public) that are available within specific regions or cities. An internet-based information system could be designed with a view to accelerating the process of supplier search and initial evaluation. At present, for example, there is no single directory or database that lists and/or describes the NYS population of consulting firms with expertise in contract research and development. The task of finding such firms is often completed on the basis of referrals from business associates or public agencies, searching the Yellow Pages, or more random processes (e.g., stumbling upon potential suppliers rather than systematically seeking them out). This said, a consolidated electronic database would need to supply more than the standard fare that one normally finds in business directories (e.g., names, addresses, contact numbers, etc). Users ought ideally be able to scan layers of information on individual entries, so that detailed profiles can be constructed. For example, does the listed firm have a track record of serving SMFs? Is there a threshold contract size that defines the minimum requirements of the supplier? Does the service supplier insist that users forfeit their legal rights regarding potential product liability claims in the future? Although a multi-layered electronic inventory could include a wide variety of indicators, the key point is that a one-stop shopping approach to the initial round of supplier search and evaluation might be worth considering. New York State already has an information system of this type that lists public sources of technical assistance. Perhaps a logical second step would be to expand this inventory to cover the private sector.

Another option worth considering concerns the 'demonstration' approach that has been used in a wide variety of advocacy applications by urban planners. In WNY, for example, the commercial benefits of a university-industry program for technology transfer have been advertized to the local business community in the form of 'success stories'. These demonstration models are designed to illustrate precisely how a particular relationship can generate benefits to program participants. If the demonstration model consists of information and/or data supplied by a company that has successfully exploited a particular initiative, then the credibility of the model is enhanced.

As mentioned earlier, business people listen to other business people. In the present context, it would do little harm for local development agencies to advertise the potential benefits of looking afar for technical support (imports) by using case examples to illustrate the advantages of nonlocal sourcing. One problem with this approach, of course, is that political factors might discourage such an option. After all, development agencies in places like UC or WNY may not want to create the impression that their home regions are sparsely endowed with technological resources.

A third option, though hardly a new one, would be to establish contact subsidies to encourage experimentation with external consultants. These subsidies, especially if granted at close to 100 percent for first-time users, might change the attitudes of SMFs that refuse to import services on the grounds that prices are too high relative to potential benefits. A once-only subsidy would go a long way to testing the accuracy of these perceptions. Britton (1993) has argued in support of this type of initiative in a Canadian context for several years, reflecting, in part, the respectable performance of the UK's Enterprise Initiative and Business Link (see Bennett and Robson, 1999).

It should be emphasized that the three options outlined above were identified on the basis of personal and/or telephone interviews with the CEOs of thirty scientific instruments producers in New York State. Almost all of these CEOs indicated a need for better search procedures for supplier identification, 76 percent (n=23) stated that they would investigate the implications of demonstration models if such models were presented to them, and 86 percent (n=26) indicated that they would explore new types of service-based outsourcing if contact subsidies were to be made available. In short, it would appear that the business community sees a positive role for some sort of public/private partnership for information brokerage and/or subsidized experimentation with consultants. Variants of the three options outlined above have appeared in several outcrops of contemporary literature on SMF performance, including recent contributions by Bennett and Robson (1999), Britton (1993), Maillat (1998), Mackun and MacPherson (1997), and Malecki (1994). In a US context, the task remains to convince public officials that

Table 9.5 Temporal Trends in External Sourcing: Results from a Twenty Firm Tracking Study (Spending as a Percentage of Total Sales)

	1993	1994	1995	1996	1997	1998
Top 10 in 1993	4.6	4.1	3.2	0.6	2.1	3.8
Bottom 10 in 1993	0.7	1.9	4.2	1.5	1.3	4.9
Mean	2.6	3.0	3.7	1.0	3.4	4.3

Innovation impact *

	1993	1994	1995	1996	1997	1998
Top 10 in 1993	3.7	2.9	2.3	1.9	3.6	3.2
Bottom 10 in 1993	1.8	2.7	4.0	2.0	2.3	4.1
Mean	2.7	2.8	2.9	2.0	2.9	3.6

Main category: **

	1993	1994	1995	1996	1997	1998
Top 10 in 1993	CR and D	IDES	PENG	MGMC	IDES	MGMC
Bottom 10 in 1993	LABT	MGMC	IDES	LABT	PENG	CR&D

*   Importance of aggregate external spending to the product development process (where 1 = no importance whatsoever, to 5 = critically important).

** single largest external spending category

Where:

CR&D = contract research and development services
IDES   = industrial design services
PENG = production engineering services
MGMC = management consulting services
LABT = laboratory testing services

programs to support SMF innovation may need to include more active information brokerage and/or information subsidy components.

As an aside, however, it is important to note that service-based outsourcing among the NYS survey firms appears to be cyclical (unpredictable) rather than constant. Ongoing tracking studies by the author suggest that expenditures on external technical services vary quite dramatically over time. These tracking studies began in 1994, and continue today (consisting of ten major spenders in 1993, and 10 minor spenders in 1993). Over the period 1994-1998, the rank orders for external spending turned out to be conspicuously unstable, such that, in several cases, major spenders in 1993 were found to be negligible spenders in 1998 (and vice versa). Although the twenty firm subsample is unlikely to be representative of the population as a whole (the exercise was designed as an easy-to-execute monitoring experiment), the results imply that cross-sectional and/or limited time-series analyses may not give an accurate picture of the service-to-manufacturing relationship (Table 9.5). Nevertheless, for this particular subsample of twenty firms, the general trend as far as external spending is concerned is modestly upward (i.e., scaled as a proportion of total sales, as well as in absolute dollar terms). Perhaps a more interesting finding is that patterns of service-specific outsourcing vary even more dramatically than aggregate expenditures. For instance, several of the firms that spent a good deal of money on contract research and development over the 1989-1993 period spent very little money on the same type of service over the 1994-1998 period, whereas several of the firms that spent nothing on design services over the initial study period turned out to be 'bigger spenders' over the tracking period. Brief telephone interviews over the five years of post-survey work suggest that these patterns have little to do with service satisfaction ratings. Rather, the results confirm that specific types of services are purchased as the need arises. These needs are unpredictable. Over the six year period for which tracking data are available, however, a notable finding is that radically different mixes of inputs are purchased at different times. The author intends to continue with the twenty firm tracking study for as long as the cohort remains reasonably intact (provided that the panel remains receptive to annual reviews).

Conclusions

There is good reason to suspect that the geography of SMF innovation among NYS producers of scientific instruments differs little from the broader geography of innovation among US manufacturers as a whole, in that the NYS findings are consistent with the national results reported by Feldman and Florida (1994). Specifically, innovation propensity varies directly with the local and/or regional availability of technological resources. These results also converge with the findings of other scholars that have employed different methodologies (e.g. Acs et al., 1990; Jaffe, 1989). In peripheral or declining regions, policy efforts to compensate for the local absence of appropriate external inputs may be required. Although it is not possible to build an innovative milieux around every region, it is possible to minimise the negative effects of peripheral location by tapping the positive attributes of neighbouring places. Rather than attempt to create a local technological infrastructure as part of an import substitution strategy, a cheaper and more realistic option would be to encourage imports.

There is, of course, much more to the innovation/location relationship than the availability of external expertise. Important factors that were not dealt with in this chapter include the role of local/regional demand conditions (e.g. the presence of technologically sophisticated customers), the existence of related or supporting industries (complementary firms), local rivalry conditions (degree of competition), and factor endowments (e.g. the supply of skilled labor). While these factors are part of Porter's (1990) diamond paradigm, many other factors could also be considered. For instance, recent research suggests a close relationship between successful innovation and the presence of technological alliances between complementary firms (Freeman, 1991; Hall, 1999; Rothwell, 1992). There is also a good deal of accumulated evidence on the importance of user-producer interaction in both product and process innovation (Gertler, 1995; Von Hippel, 1988). In short, this chapter has presented a rather unidimensional perspective on the innovation process.

On this note, a more integrative style would seem warranted as far as future research is concerned. New research might also benefit from a longitudinal approach that involves firm-specific monitoring, if only because the importance of specific types of innovation support would appear to vary over time. In this regard, it might be useful to employ the tracking approach as a standard feature of survey-based research on industrial innovation (or anything else for that matter). Given that most regional scientists now recognize the importance of dynamic relationships (see Maillat, 1998), future studies that lack a temporal perspective will hopefully become less common.

References

Acs, Z.J. and Audretsch, D. B. (1990), *Innovation and Small Firms*, MIT Press, Cambridge, MA.

Acs, Z.J., Audretsch, D. B. and Feldman, M. P. (1994), 'R&D spillovers and innovative activity' *Managerial and Decision Economics*, vol. 15, pp. 131-138.

Anselin, L., Varga, A. and Acs, Z. (1996), 'Local geographic spillovers between university research and high technology innovations', Paper presented at the Forty-Third North American Meeting of the Regional Science Association International, Washington DC, November.

Audretsch, D.B. and Feldman, M. P. (1996), 'R&D spillovers and the geography of innovation and production', *American Economic Review*, vol. 86, pp. 630-640.

Beesant, J. and Rush, H. (1995), 'Building bridges for innovation: the role of consultants in technology transfer.' *Research Policy*, vol. 24, pp. 97-114.

Bennett, R. J. and Robson, J. (1999), 'The use of external business advice in Britain', *Entrepreneurship and Regional Development*, vol. 11, pp. 155-180.

Berman, D. (1995), *The internationalization and external knowledge acquisition processes of small manufacturing firms: evidence from metropolitan Toronto*, Ph.D. dissertation, Department of Geography, State University of New York at Buffalo, Buffalo NY.

Britton, J. N. H. (1993), 'A regional perspective on Canada under free trade', *International Journal of Urban and Regional Research*, vol. 17, pp. 559-577.

Britton, J. N. H. (1996), 'Specialization versus diversity in Canadian technological development', *Small Business Economics*, vol. 8, pp. 121-138.

Camagni, R. P. (1995), 'The concept of innovative milieu and its relevance for public policies in European lagging regions', *Papers in Regional Science*, vol. 74, pp. 317-340.

Ceh, S. L. B. (1996), 'Temporal and spatial variability of Canadian inventive companies and their inventions: an issue of ownership', *Canadian Geographer*, vol. 40, pp. 319-337.

Chandra, B. (1992), *High-Technology Manufacturing in Western New York: An Assessment of the Internationalization Processes of Innovative Firms*, Ph.D Dissertation, Department of Geography, University at Buffalo, Buffalo NY.

Coffey, W. J. and Bailly, A. S. (1993), 'Producer services and systems of flexible production', *Urban Studies*, vol. 29, pp. 857-868.

Curtis, A. and MacPherson, A. (1996), 'The zone definition problem in survey research: an empirical example from New York State', *Professional Geographer*, vol. 48, pp. 310-320.

Deb, C. (1996), 'Accessing external sources of technology', *Research-Technology Management*, vol. 39, pp. 48-56.

Ettlinger, N. and Tufford, M. (1996), 'Evaluating small firm performance in local context: a case study of manufacturers in Columbus, Ohio', *Small Business Economics*, vol. 8, pp. 409-430.

Feldman, M. P. (1994), *The Geography of Innovation*, Kluwer Academic Press, Boston.

Feldman, M. P. and Florida, R. (1994), 'The geographical sources of innovation: technological infrastructure and product innovation in the United States', *Annals of the Association of American Geographers*, vol. 84, no. 2, pp. 210-229.

Freeman, C. (1991), 'Networks of innovators: a synthesis of research issues', *Research Policy*, vol. 20, pp. 499-514.

Gertler, M.S. (1995), 'Being there: proximity, organization and culture in the development and adoption of advanced manufacturing technologies', *Economic Geography*, vol. 71, pp. 1-26.

Goe, R., Lentnek, B., MacPherson, A. and Phillips, D. (1999), 'Towards a contact-based theory of producer service location', forthcoming in *Environment and Planning (A)*.

Hall, L. (1999), 'Innovation and collaboration in the biotechnology sector: evidence from Canada and the United States', forthcoming as an *Occasional Paper, Canada-United States Trade Centre*, State University of New York at Buffalo, Buffalo NY.

Haour, G. (1992), 'Stretching the knowledge base of the enterprise through contract research', *R&D Management*, vol. 22, pp. 177-182.

Harrington, J. W. (1995), 'Producer service research in US regional studies', *Professional Geographer*, vol. 47, pp. 66-69.

Illeris, S. (1994), 'Proximity between service producers and users', *Tijdschrift voorEconomische en Sociale Geografie*, vol. 85, pp. 185-196.

Jaffe, A. (1989), 'Real effects of academic research', *American Economic Review*, 79, pp. 957-970.

Jaffe, A., Trajtenberg, M. and Henderson, R. (1994), 'Geographic localization of knowledge spillovers as evidenced by patent citations', *The Quarterly Journal of Economics*, August, pp. 577-598.

Koeller, C.T. (1995), 'Innovation, market structure and firm size: a simultaneous equations model', *Managerial and Decision Economics*, vol. 11, pp. 259-269.

Lawton-Smith, H. (1996), 'Externalization of research and development in Europe', *European Planning Studies*, vol. 1, pp. 465-482.

Liesch, P.W. and Knight, G.A. (1999), 'Information internalization and hurdle rates in small and medium enterprise internationalization', *Journal of International Business Studies*, vol. 30, pp. 383-396.

Link, A.N. and Rees, J. (1990), 'Firm size, university based research, and the returns to R&D'. *Small Business Economics*, vol. 2, pp. 25-32.

Mackun, P. and MacPherson, A. (1997), 'Externally-assisted product innovation in the manufacturing sector: the role of location, in-house R&D and outside technical support', *Regional Studies*, vol. 31, pp. 659-668.

MacPherson, A. (1997a), 'The role of producer service outsourcing in the innovation performance of New York State manufacturing firms', *Annals of the Association of American Geographers*, vol. 87, pp. 52-71.

MacPherson, A. (1997b), 'A comparison of within-firm and external sources of product innovation', *Growth and Change*, vol. 28, pp. 289-308.

Maillat, D. (1998), 'Innovative milieux and new generations of regional policies', *Entrepreneurship and Regional Development*, 10, pp. 1-16.

Malecki, E. J. (1994), 'Entrepreneurship in regional and local development', *International Regional Science Review*, vol. 16, pp. 119-154.

Malecki, E. J. and Poehling, R.M. (1999), 'Extroverts and introverts: small manufacturers and their information sources', forthcoming, *Entrepreneurship and Regional Development*.

Malecki, E. J. and Tootle, D.M. (1996), 'The role of networks in small firm competitiveness', *International Journal of Technology Management*, vol. 11, pp. 43-57.

Mitchelson, R. L. and Wheeler, J. O. (1994), 'The flow of information in a global economy: the role of the American urban system in 1990', *Annals of the Association of American Geographers*, vol. 84, pp. 87-107.

O'Connor, K. (1996), 'Industrial design as a producer service: a framework for analysis in regional science', *Papers in Regional Science*, 75, pp. 237-252.

Ó hUallacháin, B. (1991), 'Industrial geography', *Progress in Human Geography*, vol. 15, pp. 73-80.

Porter, M.E. (1990), *The Competitive Advantage of Nations*, Free Press, New York.

Rothwell, R. (1992), 'Successful industrial innovation: critical factors for the 1990s', *R&D Management*, vol. 22, pp. 221-239.

Scott, A. J. (1986), 'Industrial organization and urbanization: a geographical agenda', *Annals of the Association of American Geographers*, vol. 76, pp. 25-37.

Von Hippel, E. (1988), *The sources of innovation*, Oxford University Press, New York.

10 Interfirm Linkage Patterns and the Intrametropolitan Location of Producer Services Firms

PAUL SABOURIN

Introduction

The producer service sector has constituted one of the fastest growing sectors in the American economy since the 1960s, and has consequently attracted a great deal of attention from geographers and other regional scientists in recent years. There has been a substantial amount of documentation and analysis regarding the rapid growth of these activities, their distribution among different metropolitan areas, and their significance for regional economic development. Yet, thus far the locational patterns of firms in this rapidly expanding sector *within* metropolitan areas have received rather less attention, even though this particular group of activities is characterized by an exceptional locational pattern. Although the importance of suburban locations for producer services functions has been growing, the producer services as a group have been conspicuous in the degree to which they have remained highly concentrated in downtown locations, counter to the widespread general trend of employment suburbanization that has dominated the post-war era.

This chapter reports on one aspect of a study of the employment of flexible production techniques by producer service firms, namely, the relationship between the intrametropolitan location of advertising agencies in the Twin Cities area and their backward linkage patterns. The topic of flexible production has received a great deal of attention in economic geography over the past 20 years (Piore and Sabel, 1984; Scott, 1988a, 1988b, 1993; Storper and Christopherson, 1987; Storper and Walker, 1989; Walker, 1988), but to date, most research dealing with producer services has been biased toward the manufacturing sector (Gertler, 1992). Work involving flexible production and producer services has tended to deal with the linkages between manufacturers and producer service providers, or with the role of producer services in regional development (e.g., Goe, 1990; Marshall, 1989, Wood, 1991). Yet, although only a few studies have examined in any detail the level of vertical

211

disintegration of production within producer services industries themselves, there are indications that the pattern of intrasectoral linkages between producer service firms is often even more highly developed than the linkages between producer service firms and manufacturers (Coffey and Bailly, 1991; Michelak and Fairbairn, 1993). This chapter reports on the results of an investigation that documents the utilization of flexible production techniques in the advertising industry in the Twin Cities, and identifies differences in the linkage characteristics of advertising agencies located in different parts of the metropolitan area.

Flexible Production and Producer Services

Scott has defined flexible production as a form of production that is '...(in contrast to mass production)...oriented to the production of small batches of output for specialized market niches, and where competitive strategy typically entails constant product differentiation and/or significant levels of customization' (Scott, 1996, p. 307). Firms engaged in this type of production maintain intensive linkage networks with other firms, and these interrelated firms are commonly located in close proximity to one another in distinct spatial agglomerations which help to minimize the transactions costs associated with maintaining external material and information linkages between firms. Flexible production allows for rapid adaptation to changing market conditions, including for example, those arising from rapid technological developments, increasing global competition, and the saturation of mass consumer markets (Coffey and Bailly, 1991; Sayer and Walker, 1992). The primary characteristic of flexible production, however, is *vertical disintegration*, whereby production of a good or service is accomplished though the combined contributions of a network of specialized, and most commonly small, firms. Flexible coalitions are formed from within a network of specialized firms on the basis of the particular requirements of individual projects, and dissolved upon completion of each project. The coalitions are co-ordinated by lead firms that are ultimately responsibility for design and production, with these lead firms making widespread use of outsourcing to independent firms for specialized inputs. The mix of firms engaged by the lead firm can be readily varied from project to project, depending on the particular requirements of each different project. In effect, 'the organization of firms' becomes more central than 'the firm as organization' (Scott, 1988b). As a production complex grows, it evolves towards increasing levels of externalization, and as the increasing size of the complex further increases the potential for external economies, new establishments are attracted to the complex. As the number and variety of specialized firms increases, so does the intricacy of the network of inter firm linkages (Scott, 1993).

Scott's analysis of the development of flexible production complexes is grounded in transactional analysis. Based especially on work by Coase (1937) and Williamson (1979, 1985, 1986), transactional analysis examines production activities as a system of transactions that arise from the division of labor both within firms (the technical division of labor) and between firms (the social division of labor). Production is conceptualized as a series of labor processes linked by transactions, with firms seeking to minimize the costs of these transactions. Firms determine whether it is less expensive to produce a commodity (or element of the production process) internally or to obtain it via an external transaction, and behave accordingly. Firms have the greatest level of control over production when it is done within the firm, as the internal hierarchy of the firm allows for co-ordination of the various transactions involved in production by managerial fiat. External transactions with other firms are market transactions, and are governed especially by price signals, although they are also embedded in a more complex network of social relations.

Linkages, Transaction Costs, and Location

Externalized transactions occur over geographic space, and so incur linkage costs related the movement of physical goods as well as to the amount of direct personal contact and information exchange required to complete particular transactions. By locating in close proximity to one another, the firms that make up a flexible production complex minimize distance-dependent transportation and communication costs, and maximize their accessibility to one another (Scott, 1988a, 1993). However, in addition to these benefits, spatial agglomeration may also impose additional costs on firms, including for example, higher rents and wages (Storper and Walker, 1989). Thus, the mere existence of linkage networks, even extensive ones, does not necessarily imply the existence of compact spatial agglomerations in a particular industry. Rather, the spatial form actually taken by flexible production complexes depends on the nature of the linkage patterns involved, and especially on the costs associated with maintaining these external linkages compared to the value of the goods or services obtained through these transactions.

According to Scott, compact agglomerations are most closely associated with systems of inter-firm linkages characterized by high distance-dependent costs per unit of flow. This cost structure characterizes small scale, unstandardized, and unstable linkages, as well as linkages that require a large degree of personal intermediation. Conversely, linkages that are large scale, standardized, and stable over time typically have lower distance-dependent transactions costs per unit of flow, and allow for a greater degree of freedom in the location of linkage partners. Large establishments with large production runs, routinized patterns of production, and relatively predictable patterns have a large degree of locational freedom vis-à-vis their transactional partners, whereas smaller, flexibly organized plants with much less routine input-output relations will have much more to gain by locating in close proximity to their linkage partners (Scott, 1988a, p. 51).

The Role of Flexible Production Arrangements in Producer Service Industries

Many producer services are characterized by a number of attributes that suggest a high propensity to make use of flexible production techniques. For example, the exchange of information, often in an intangible form, is typically quite important in the provision of producer services. In one sense this lowers the significance of transportation costs, especially as improvements in telecommunications technology have made the cost of transmission for some types of information nearly independent of distance. On the other hand, some services involve the provision of intangibles that are difficult to deliver by means other than in through direct face-to-face contact. By their nature, there tends to be little standardization of such services, and these services must be produced and consumed in the same location. Thus, large production runs and inventories are rare in service provision. Instead, they commonly must be produced where and when demanded, incurring high transactions costs. Storper and Walker (1989) in discussing the nature of 'office-based industries' emphasized the highly unstandardized nature of the much of the knowledge and labor processes involved in these information-handling industries. Multiple meetings of mid- and high-level managers are frequently involved in arranging for and receipt of some intangible producer services (Scott, 1988a, p. 51), and frequently individuals from several different service providers may need to be present at the same time for a service to be produced and delivered[1]. When these attributes are present, the cost of these external transactions is high. Perry (1990) noted that issues of management control, efficiency of production, and the costs of fragmented markets are particularly relevant to the outsourcing of producer services. In particular, Perry asserted that quality control is an issue, because service-buyers have a greater degree of difficulty observing actions of service providers, providing incentives to encourage outside service providers to exert the desired level of effort. In addition, when the quality of an intangible service is found wanting, it is less easily returned for improvement than would be a physical commodity.

Scott (1988b, p. 11) identified the expansion of services as one of the three main characteristics of contemporary capitalism (along with the revival of high-quality crafts and the increasing importance of 'high-technology') associated with the rise of flexible production, and used a review of office location research to document the centralization of office functions in CBD locations as one of his introductory illustrations of how certain industrial processes take on distinct geographic forms at the intrametropolitan scale. According to Scott, 'the office sector is much given to vertical disintegration and to market intermediation of interoffice transactions.' Within office complexes, '... innumerable, small, varied and changeable transactions are carried out by individual sub-elements of the system so that each can operate most efficiently as an independent economic agent rather than as part of a single, large, and unwieldy bureaucracy' (1988a, p. 85). He concluded, after reviewing the work of Gad (1979), Goddard (1973), and others, that the clustering of offices in central locations is associated with the importance of access to a wide range of transactional partners, and to the importance of accessibility to the metropolitan labor force. He accepted the general assumption that the functions performed by suburban offices involve more routine functions, and require less contact with external firms, and attributed the locational pattern of these suburban offices to other factors, for example the availability of an abundant supply of relatively compliant and inexpensive labor (see Nelson, 1986).

More recently, Scott (1996) has investigated the role of flexible production in what he has termed the 'cultural-products industries' in Los Angeles. He included in this group both goods-producing sectors such as apparel, furniture and jewelry, as well as service sectors including advertising, architectural firms, and entertainment production. These industries are all subject to rapid changes in styles and fashion ('hyper-innovation') in the markets for their products. This susceptibility to rapid changes in markets means that firms in these sectors face an especially high degree of uncertainty, which discourages large-scale capital investments and encourages more flexible and labor-intensive production processes. As with the garment and printed circuit industries, the various cultural-products industries were found to form distinct geographic clusters of specialized firms, linked by an intensive network of transactions. Beyond simply the flexible structure of relations between firms in these industries, however, Scott also emphasized other benefits of agglomeration for the different cultural-products industries, including the development of a labor force with 'agglomeration-specific skills, sensitivities, and tacit knowledge' unavailable elsewhere, access to knowledge of potential opportunities for interaction, and, finally, the motivation to innovate and to excel associated with the high degree of competition between firms in each of these agglomerations.

In a study of producer service firms in Edmonton, Michelak and Fairbairn (1993a) documented the backward and forward linkages of producer service firms, and found that producer service firms had their most numerous and intensive linkages with other producer service firms, rather than with firms in the primary or secondary sectors. Based on these findings, the authors suggest that producer service firms, in addition to enabling the use of flexible production in other sectors, also make extensive use of flexible production techniques themselves. The authors concluded that the operating patterns of certain producer service sectors in fact puts them at the forefront of the different sectors utilizing flexible production techniques, and noted that the very efficiency and rapid adoption of new techniques made possible by flexible production arrangements within producer services helps in turn to make the utilization of external sources of producer services attractive to firms in other sectors. The importance of linkages among producer service providers was also documented by Beyers and Lindahl (1994), who found that the use of outsourcing in the production of producer services was indeed quite common: 83 percent of legal firms, 76 percent of accounting firms, and 77 percent of engineering firms in their study collaborated with other producer service firms in the course of their work.

Ó hUallacháin and others conducted a series of studies regarding the inter- and intrametropolitan location of producer services firms (e.g., Ó hUallacháin, 1989; Ó hUallacháin and Reid, 1991 and 1992; Ó hUallacháin and Satterthwaite, 1992) which, while not directly measuring the level of interfirm linkages for firms in highly centralized producer service sectors, were highly suggestive of the importance of central locations for firms in certain producer services sectors. Ó hUallacháin and Reid (1992), for example, noted that producer services with very similar intermediate markets were often characterized by quite different levels of intrametropolitan employment decentralization. They attributed sectoral differences in the centralization of producer services to the traditional explanation -- the need for face-to-face contact. The concentration in central cities of employment in sectors such as legal services, accounting, and advertising was attributed to the need by firms in these sectors for intrasectoral, interfirm communication via face-to-face contact. Firms in less centralized sectors, such as computer and data processing services, were presumed to be less dependent on interfirm collaborations, and more influenced by rent levels, proximity to workers and clients, and other factors favoring suburban locations.

The Twin Cities Research Area

The Twin Cities metropolitan area is one of the most important centers of corporate headquarters and business service activity in the US (Borchert, 1978, Noyelle and Stanback, 1984, Wheeler and Mitchelson, 1989). With a total population of 2.46 million people, the area was the sixteenth largest metropolitan area in the US as of 1990. The Twin Cities area has enjoyed a relatively prosperous economy over the past thirty years, with total employment more than doubling between 1960 and 1990. As would be expected given the growth of producer services nationally over this period and the Twin Cities' role in the national urban system (Noyelle and Stanback, 1984; O' hUallacháin and Reid, 1991), business and professional service employment grew at an even faster rate than total employment over this period. Employment in business services (SIC 73, the largest component of producer services) in the Twin Cities underwent a nine-fold expansion, growing from ten thousand in 1960 to more than ninety thousand by 1990. As a result, business services increased from 1.4 percent of the area's total employment in 1960 to approximately six percent by 1990 (US Bureau of the Census, *County Business Patterns*, various years).

In terms of its general layout and pattern of development in the post-World War II period, the Twin Cities shares most of the 'typical' features of American metropolitan areas[2], and the postwar combination of growth and a transition to auto-based mobility has produced a sprawling, low-density, multinucleated metropolis. The population of the metro area is overwhelmingly suburban, with the combined populations of the central cities of Minneapolis and St. Paul now accounting for less than a third of the metro area's total population. Although suburban employment lagged somewhat behind residential suburbanization, for some time suburban locations have accounted for the vast majority of new jobs created in the region, and by the early 1990s, employment in suburban locations accounted for 63 percent of the area's total employment (Adams and VanDrasek, 1993). With increasing mobility, the relative importance of downtown Minneapolis has diminished greatly for nearly all types of commercial activity. While downtown Minneapolis remains highly accessible and centrally located in the metropolitan area, it is now only first among a number of highly developed commercial centers in the Twin Cities.

As a group, the producer services have been no exception to general pattern of suburban dominance in the region's job growth since the 1960s. As is depicted in Figure 10.1, in the Minneapolis-St. Paul metropolitan area total employment in business services (SIC 73), the largest single component of producer services, grew from 8,216 in 1958 to 94,151 in 1992 an increase of nearly 86,000 jobs. Although the city of Minneapolis added nearly 16,000 jobs in business services over this period, it nevertheless saw its share of the metro area's business service employment decline from 63 percent in 1958 to only 22 percent in 1992.

Of course, not all of the wide range of activities that fall under the 'producer services' umbrella have undergone the same degree of suburbanization in American metropolitan areas. Ó hUallacháin and Reid documented wide variation in the extent of suburbanization in different service sectors in their 1992 study of service employment in large metropolitan areas, and a similar pattern is found in the Twin Cities. Computer Programming Services (SIC 737), for example, tends to be a highly decentralized subset of business

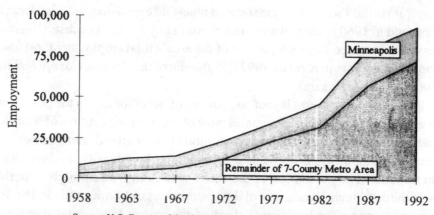

Source: U.S. Bureau of the Census, Census of Business and Census of
Service Industries, various years

Figure 10.1 Change in Business Service (SIC 73) Employment in the Minneapolis-St. Paul Study Area and in the City of Minneapolis

services, and the city of Minneapolis accounts for less than a quarter of the region's employment in this sector. Other business services, including the advertising industry, have remained highly centralized. In Ó hUallacháin and Reid's investigation, advertising trailed only the legal services in its high degree of employment centralization in central cities. Figure 10.2 illustrates the degree to which advertising agency employment in the Twin Cities area has remained highly concentrated in the city of Minneapolis over the same period of time that business services as a group were seen to have undergone widespread suburbanization. As of 1992, Minneapolis still accounted for seventy-two percent of the metropolitan area's advertising agency (SIC 7311) employment, in stark contrast to its 22 percent share of business services (SIC 73). Employment in a number of other sectors closely allied to advertising, such as professional photography, has likewise remained highly centralized through the recent era of employment suburbanization.

The advertising industry is prominent among the producer service sectors that are well represented in the Twin Cities area. Nationally, the Minneapolis - St. Paul metropolitan area ranked eighth in the country in terms of advertising agency receipts in 1992, although it was only the sixteenth largest metropolitan area in the country based on its population. The approximately US$350 million in advertising agency receipts for the Twin Cities placed it ahead of a number of metropolitan areas that are significantly larger[3]. For example, reported receipts for Minneapolis-St. Paul were US$74 million (27 percent)

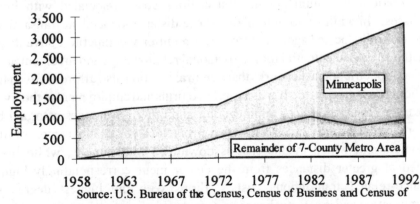

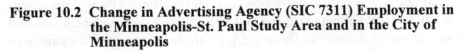

Source: U.S. Bureau of the Census, Census of Business and Census of Service Industries, various years.

Figure 10.2 Change in Advertising Agency (SIC 7311) Employment in the Minneapolis-St. Paul Study Area and in the City of Minneapolis

greater than those of the Philadelphia CMSA, a metropolitan area with a population more than twice that of the Minneapolis-St. Paul MSA. The Seattle-Tacoma CMSA had a total population that was slightly greater than that of the Twin Cities in 1990, yet advertising agency receipts in the Twin Cities amounted to nearly three times the receipts of Seattle area agencies. The significance of the advertising complex in the Twin Cities was also apparent in a factor analysis of employment proportions in various service sectors in done by Ó hUallacháin and Reid (1993). The Twin Cities had the second highest factor score (only Chicago was higher) on the factor that grouped advertising, mailing, reproduction, commercial art, and personnel supply, a grouping the authors attributed to the mutual attraction of firms in these interrelated sectors.

As was discussed earlier, a number of researchers have suggested that the persistent geographic concentration of employment in information intensive producer service sectors reflects the development of a particular type of flexibly specialized industrial district. Flexible production arrangements are well suited to the production of services which are highly unstandardized, and for which demand levels are highly variable. The general absence of standardization in the inputs purchased by advertising agencies means that contacts between agencies and their vendors are non-routine in nature, and require high levels of personal intermediation, resulting in high distance-related transactions costs per unit of input purchased. Under these conditions, spatial proximity between agencies and vendors can become an important consideration in minimizing the transactions costs associated with input purchases. In addition to minimizing these distance-dependent transactions costs, centrally located agencies also derive additional competitive advantages from the increased potential for interpersonal relationships and involvement in industry-specific social networks that a central location also affords. Given the locational distribution of advertising-related firms and employment in the Twin Cities, the transaction cost minimization and other advantages afforded by agglomeration would be greatest for firms located at the center of the agglomeration, which in this case is downtown Minneapolis, while firms located at greater distances from the center incur correspondingly higher distance-related transactions costs. Firms with the highest degree of diversification and greatest reliance on outside suppliers will benefit most from the minimization of these transaction costs that is afforded by agglomeration, and will be most willing to pay the higher costs associated with being located in downtown Minneapolis. Therefore, it would be expected that the pattern of transactional activity between agencies and vendors would vary according to the location of advertising agencies within the Twin Cities area. Because they face lower distance-related transactions costs, agencies located in downtown Minneapolis would be expected to make more widespread use of input outsourcing than would comparably sized agencies located farther from the center.

Survey Method

In order to establish a broad-based set of data regarding advertising agency activity, in particular the extent of vertical disintegration in the industry and the attributes of the linkages between advertising agencies and other firms, a mail survey of advertising agencies in the Twin Cities was conducted in 1995. The questionnaire used for this survey dealt with three main topical areas: basic agency characteristics, such as revenues, employment, and location; the use and purchase of a range of different creative goods and services by agencies; and the sales of creative goods and services by agencies. Special attention was devoted to the location of suppliers and customers and to the means of contact between agencies and their suppliers and customers.

The mail survey was administered to a total of 277 advertising agencies in the Twin Cities area. The primary source for identifying agencies was *The Gold Book*, a locally published directory of firms engaged in advertising, graphic arts, print communications, broadcast communications, and other 'creative service industries' in the Twin Cities. The initial mailing list was supplemented by the addition of advertising agencies listed in the Minneapolis and St. Paul editions of the *US West Yellow Pages* that were not included in The *Gold Book*. A total of 127 usable responses were received, giving a response rate 45.8 percent. Comparison of the agencies responding to the survey with benchmark data showed that the respondent group closely resembled the region's population of advertising agencies in terms of both geographic location and agency size.

Results

Vertical Disintegration in the Twin Cities Advertising Industry

The survey results documented a high degree of vertical disintegration in the production of advertising in the Twin Cities. The majority of advertising agencies were found to have relied on outside vendors to satisfy virtually their entire requirements for such specialized inputs as animation, film and television production and editing, and sound recording and editing. While agencies were more self-sufficient in the production of other inputs such as art direction and copywriting that are core functions central to the planning and conceptualization of advertising, outside vendors were still found to contribute a significant, if smaller, share of total agency requirements for many of these inputs as well. Agencies responding to the survey also indicated that they attributed a great deal of significance to face-to-face contact with vendors, in particular with the vendors that provided the most widely outsourced specialized inputs. In addition, comparison of the forward and backward linkage patterns of agencies showed that backward linkages between agencies and their various suppliers were much more locally oriented than was the case for the forward linkages between agencies and their clients. Clients outside the study area provided an average of 29 percent of the revenues of agencies, while suppliers located outside of the Twin Cities accounted for an average of only seven percent of agency input purchases. The survey also identified large variations in agency attributes related to the size of advertising agencies, including, not surprisingly, the propensity of large agencies to engage in a wider range of activities and to outsource a greater variety of inputs than was the case for smaller agencies.[4] Because the average level of employment of an agency in downtown Minneapolis was nearly four times that of the average for agencies in the remainder of the study area, the following comparisons involving linkage patterns of downtown Minneapolis agencies and agencies in other parts of the metropolitan area will take the size as well as the location of advertising agencies into account.

Location and Linkages

The widespread use of outsourcing, and other findings summarized above indicated that the Twin Cities advertising industry did indeed function as a vertically disintegrated, transactions-intensive flexible production complex. The remainder of this chapter is devoted to comparing the patterns of input usage and outsourcing of downtown Minneapolis advertising agencies with those of agencies located elsewhere in the study area, in order to determine whether these patterns provide evidence that distance-related transactions costs affect the extent to which agencies in different parts of the metropolitan area take advantage of the opportunities for external economies presented by the area's supply of vendors providing a wide array of goods and services used in the production of advertising.

The use of individual inputs Survey respondents were presented with a list of sixteen different inputs used in the production of advertising, and asked to indicate which of them their agency had made use of in the past year. The respondents were also asked to indicate, for each input that they had used, the proportion that was supplied by outside vendors. Figure 10.3 depicts usage rates for each of these inputs agencies with gross incomes under US$1 million. Usage rates for some inputs, in particular for the core inputs including art direction, copywriting, graphic arts, imaging, and photography, are quite similar for agencies throughout the Twin Cities. There was somewhat greater variation in usage rates of the less widely used specialized inputs corresponding to agency location, with downtown agencies normally exhibiting higher usage rates for these types of inputs than agencies in other locations.

The use of individual inputs by the largest agencies, i.e., those with gross incomes of over US$1 million, is also depicted in Figure 10.3. The greater propensity of larger agencies to make use of the more specialized inputs, especially those used in the production of radio and television advertisements is apparent in this figure. In terms of locational differences, the pattern found here is similar to what was seen for the smaller agencies. That is, when

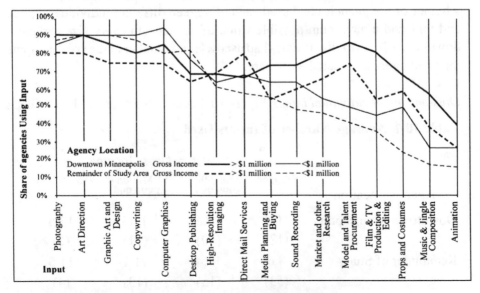

Figure 10.3 Use of Individual Inputs: Agencies with Gross Income Less Than and Greater Than US$1 Million

differences in usage rates exist, downtown agencies typically had higher usage rates than agencies in other locations. The pattern of usage of film and television production and editing services illustrates these traits. Larger agencies as a group were noticeably more likely to have used this particular input than were smaller ones, with 73 percent of agencies with gross incomes over US$1 million having used film and television production and editing services, compared to only 38 percent of agencies with incomes under US$1 million. However, there was a noticeable difference in the usage levels of this input by agencies in different locations. 88 percent of the downtown agencies in the over US$1 million gross income category had made use of film and television production and editing, compared to 59 percent of agencies in the same size group in the remainder of the study area. In fact, the proportion of large non-downtown agencies that made use of film and television production and editing was closer in percentage point terms to the usage rate of downtown agencies with incomes under US$1 million (45 percent) than it was to the usage rate of downtown agencies in its own size category.

Total number of inputs used Table 10.1 shows the average number of the sixteen different inputs identified on the questionnaire used by agencies in downtown Minneapolis and in the remainder of the study area in the year prior to the survey. The total number of inputs used was based on responses to whether or not agencies had used each of sixteen different individual inputs, and thus had a maximum possible value of sixteen. In every size category, downtown Minneapolis agencies had used a larger number of the sixteen inputs than had agencies located elsewhere.

Outsourcing of individual inputs Figure 10.4 depicts the average share of each

Table 10.1 Average Number of Inputs Used

	Agency Gross Income			
Agency Location	≤$499,999	$500,000-$999,999	$1 Million -$4,999,999	≥$5 Million
Downtown Minneapolis	10.3	10.6	12.6	12.6
	(12)	(10)	(11)	(5)
Remainder of Study	8.6	10.4	11.1	11.5
	(53)	(15)	(13)	(4)

Figures in parentheses are base Ns for adjacent averages.

of the sixteen different inputs identified on the questionnaire that had been provided by outsourcing. Agencies in the under US$1 million size group showed large differences in the rate of outsourcing by downtown and other agencies for several inputs, in particular for such specialized inputs as animation and music and jingle composition. Whereas downtown agencies in this size category relied on outside suppliers for the vast majority of these inputs, the non-downtown agencies in this size group showed a strong tendency to produce these inputs for themselves rather than obtain them from vendors.

A closer look at where these agencies obtained animation services illustrates this contrast between downtown and other agencies. The downtown agencies in the under US$1 million income group obtained an average of 83 percent of their animation needs from vendors, a figure that is comparable to the degree to which downtown and other agencies with incomes over US$1 million relied on animation vendors. The non-downtown agencies in the under US$1 million income category stand in sharp contrast to these other groups. These agencies were much more self-sufficient in supplying their need for animation, and relied on outside vendors for an average of only 41 percent of their requirement of this input. Only eleven of the sixty-eight non-downtown agencies with gross incomes under US$1 million reported having made use of animation in the past year, and of these eleven agencies, six reported that they had produced all of their own animation. Of the remaining five agencies, one reported having

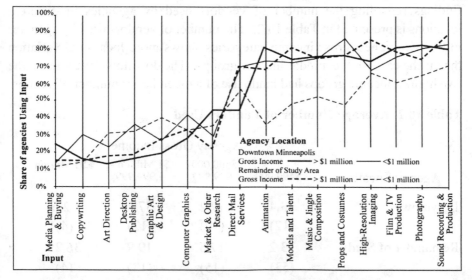

**Figure 10.4 Share of Individual Inputs Supplied by Outsourcing –
Agencies with Gross Incomes Less Than and Greater
Than US$1 Million**

outsourced half of its animation needs, and four had outsourced their entire need for animation. Similar behavior accounts for most of the large differences between the outsourcing rates of downtown and other agencies with gross incomes under US$1 million for inputs such as photography, film and TV production, and music and jingle composition.

The rate at which the largest agencies, i.e., those with gross incomes over US$1 million, outsourced their requirements for individual inputs is also depicted in Figure 10.4. In contrast to the pattern seen for smaller agencies, the extent to which different inputs were supplied by outside vendors was quite similar for agencies in both locational groups in this higher income group. For these large agencies, differences in the mean share of each individual input provided by outsourcing tended to be rather small. The differences that did exist do not follow a consistent pattern. For some inputs, the downtown agencies outsourced a larger share of their total requirements than did comparably sized agencies elsewhere in the study area, but for other inputs, the downtown agencies outsourced a smaller share of their total requirements than did large agencies located elsewhere.

Number of vendors used The number of different vendors with whom agencies did business in the past year provides another measure of the level of transactional activity of advertising agencies. The tabulation of the survey findings regarding the number of vendors used by agencies in different locations is presented in Table 10.2. The number of vendors used by agencies in the two highest gross income categories shows more locational variation than is the case for the middle-income groups. The downtown agencies in the two highest income groups had made use of a much larger number of vendors

Table 10.2 Average Number of Vendors Used

Agency Location	Agency Gross Income			
	≤$499,999	$500,000-999,999	$1 Million - 4,999,999	≥$5 Million
Downtown	23.4	17.2	37.8	92.5
	(12)	(10)	(12)	(4)
Remainder of Study	13.2	17.5	19.9	36.25
	(53)	(15)	(13)	(4)

Figures in parentheses are base Ns for adjacent averages.

than had agencies of comparable size but in other locations. For the highest income category (i.e., agencies with annual gross incomes exceeding US$5 million), this reflects in part the presence in downtown Minneapolis of the largest agencies in the study area, and the fact that the number of vendors used measure had no fixed maximum value, making this measure unlike the preceding measures of input usage and outsourcing. However, it is unlikely that the difference in the number of vendors used by downtown and other agencies is entirely due to this effect, since the effect does not come into play for agencies with gross incomes between US$1 million and US$5 million, and within this group the average number of vendors utilized by downtown Minneapolis agencies was still almost twice as large as the average number used by agencies elsewhere in the study area.

Expenditures on vendors The final aggregate measure of the outsourcing behavior of agencies to be considered here is the total expenditures of agencies on inputs purchased from vendors in the year prior to the survey. Table 10.3 is a cross-tabulation of agency location, income, and expenditures on vendors. Part I of this table pertains to expenditures by agencies in downtown Minneapolis, and Part II to agencies in the remainder of the study area. Downtown agencies in all size categories had higher levels of expenditures on vendors than did comparably sized firms in other parts of the study area. For agencies with gross incomes under US$1 million, expenditures by downtown agencies on inputs purchased from outside vendors exceed those of agencies in other locations to a degree that was not apparent in the number of different inputs used by these agencies. For instance, while the number of vendors used by downtown Minneapolis and other agencies in the US$500,000 to US$999,999 income category were approximately equal, the patterns of vendor expenditures by these same agencies varied noticeably, with seventy percent of the downtown agencies having spent more than US$100,000 on vendors, a level of spending reached by only 53 percent of the comparably sized agencies in the remainder of the study area. Expenditures on vendors by downtown agencies with incomes of between US$1 million and US$5 million outpaced the spending levels of their counterparts in the remainder of the study area by a wide margin, with 45 percent of the downtown agencies in this size group spending at least US$1 million on inputs, a level of spending that was reached by only 25 percent of the non-downtown agencies. Some 80 percent of the downtown agencies with gross incomes greater than US$5 million spent at least US$1 million on inputs purchased from outside vendors. Only a quarter of the non-downtown agencies in this size category matched this spending

Table 10.3 Total Expenditures on Vendors

I. Agencies in Downtown Minneapolis

	Agency Gross Income			
Expenditures	≤$499,999	$500,000-999,999	$1Million - 4,999,999	≥$5Million
≤US$49,999	50%	30%	18%	0%
US$50,000-99,999	18	0	9	0
US$100,000-499,999	33	60	18	20
US$500,000-999,999	0	0	9	0
>US$1 Million	0	10	45	80
N	(12)	(10)	(12)	(5)

II. Agencies in Remainder of Study Area

	Agency Gross Income			
Expenditures	≤$499,999	$500,000-999,999	$1Million - 4,999,999	≥$5Million
≤US$49,999	83%	27%	50%	0%
US$50,000-99,999	6	20	8	0
US$100,000-499,999	9	40	8	50
US$500,000-999,999	2	13	8	25
>US$1 Million	0	0	25	25
N	(53)	(15)	(12)	(4)

level. As was the case with the total number of vendors used, the data regarding expenditures on vendors clearly indicates the very high levels of outsourcing activity by downtown agencies in the highest income category, and reflects the presence in downtown Minneapolis of the largest advertising agencies in the study area. These data suggest a higher level of expenditures per-vendor by the downtown Minneapolis agencies compared to agencies located elsewhere, with the most likely cause of this pattern being the greater usage by the downtown agencies of relatively costly inputs such as those used in the production of broadcast advertisements.

Discussion

The survey findings show that the patterns of input usage and outsourcing by advertising agencies differ according to the location of agencies within the Twin Cities study area. While agencies in all parts of the metropolitan area made use of input outsourcing, the pattern of input use and outsourcing by advertising agencies located in downtown Minneapolis differed from the pattern of inputs use and outsourcing by agencies located elsewhere in the study area, even after controlling for the larger average size of agencies in downtown Minneapolis. Downtown agencies used a larger number of inputs than did agencies in other locations, and they also outsourced a larger number of inputs, made use of a larger number of vendors, and had higher levels of expenditures on vendors than was the case for agencies in the remainder of the study area. Most likely because of the greater scope and potential for outsourcing of specialized inputs that characterizes larger agencies, the influence of location on input usage and outsourcing was most pronounced for agencies with annual gross incomes of more than US$1 million. Downtown agencies in these size categories were found to have made use of a larger number of different inputs, to have made use of a larger number of vendors, and to have made much greater expenditures on vendors than was the case for comparably sized agencies in the remainder of the study area. Since these large agencies accounted for the vast majority of total advertising agency employment and revenues in the Twin Cities, these findings can be considered to be significant regarding the advertising industry in the study area as a whole.

The geographic differences in the overall levels of outsourcing were not a product of downtown agencies acquiring a larger share of any given input from outside vendors than was the case for non-downtown agencies. For large advertising agencies, the location of the agency had little bearing on the proportion of a given input that was supplied by outside vendors, as large agencies throughout the study area were quite similar in the share of any given input that was provided by outside vendors. Rather, the contrast between downtown and other agencies in the overall level of outsourcing was a product of differences in the rate at which certain inputs, in particular specialized inputs such as animation, film and television production and editing, and sound recording and production, were used by agencies in different locations. All of these inputs were primarily supplied by outside vendors, and these are the same inputs that were rated highest in terms of the importance of face-to-face contact between agencies and in a separate component of this study. For large agencies, the location of the agency had little bearing on the share of these inputs that was outsourced, but agencies located outside of downtown Minneapolis were noticeably less likely than agencies located in downtown Minneapolis to have made use of inputs such as film and television production in the first place.

This finding can be interpreted as reflecting the impact of distance related transactions costs on the ability of advertising agencies in different locations to take advantage of the potential external economies afforded by the advertising agglomeration. The advertising production complex is geographically centered on downtown Minneapolis, making downtown Minneapolis the optimal location in the study area for the minimizing the distance related transactions costs that accompany outsourcing by advertising agencies. The significance of downtown locations goes beyond simply minimizing the cost of maintaining contact with individual vendors, since the nature of advertising production may require that the services of several different vendors be delivered simultaneously, for example, in the recording of a broadcast television advertisement. This joint consumption of inputs reinforces the importance of centrality in minimizing distance dependent transactions costs. According to the results of this study, advertising agencies located outside of downtown Minneapolis do not typically compensate for the higher distance related transactions costs they face by substituting internal provision for outsourcing, and producing a greater share of their specialized input requirements internally. Rather, agencies outside of the main advertising cluster in downtown Minneapolis are simply less likely to make use these inputs.

An additional aspect of this study that is noteworthy has to do with the size of the Twin Cities metropolitan area. Most earlier studies of intrametropolitan variations in linkage patterns have been situated in metropolitan areas much larger than the Twin Cities, with Los Angeles, the second-largest metropolitan area in the United States, having been the locale for a large number of the most commonly cited studies. The difference in scale between the Twin Cities study area and Los Angeles is apparent in a comment made by Allen Scott in his analysis of the animated film industry in Los Angeles. In discussing his findings, Scott described the residences of animated film workers in Los Angeles as being 'confined to a remarkably narrow area' (Scott 1988a, p.145). The area he was discussing, which contained the residences of ninety-five percent of animated film workers, was a rectangular area extending some fifty-five kilometers east to west, and forty kilometers north to south. In the context of metropolitan Los Angeles, this may qualify as a 'remarkably narrow area,' but a rectangle of the same size would encompass virtually the entire urbanized portion of the Twin Cities metropolitan area. This study has demonstrated that distinctive geographic differences in intrametropolitan linkage patterns are not limited to places as populous and expansive as the Los Angeles area.

Conclusion

Rather surprisingly, given the rate of growth of producer services and their importance the economies of central cities, the intrametropolitan location of producer services has been an under-studied research topic. Earlier studies of the intrametropolitan location of these activities have commonly emphasized the role of client location and forward linkages in explaining the intrametropolitan location of producer services firms (Illeris, 1991; Lentnek et al., 1992), but this study emphasized the role played by backward linkages in accounting for the location of firms in a vertically disintegrated producer service production complex. This was accomplished through an examination of the use of flexible production arrangements in the advertising industry in the Twin Cities, with a particular focus on the patterns of input usage and outsourcing by advertising agencies in different parts of the metropolitan area. The central finding of the investigation summarized here is that the advertising industry in the Twin Cities is a vertically disintegrated production complex that makes widespread use of flexible production techniques, and within this production complex there are distinct differences between the backward linkage patterns of advertising agencies located in downtown Minneapolis and those of agencies located elsewhere in the metropolitan area that reflect the transaction cost minimization afforded by a central location. The findings of this study demonstrate the feasibility and merit of applying the flexible production framework to the producer services by providing empirical evidence in support of some often stated but seldom tested claims regarding the employment of flexible production techniques by producer services firms, but it remains a cross sectional investigation of a single industry in a single location. The utility of this study would be enhanced by further research at the intrametropolitan scale investigating the relationship between location and the processes by which producer services are themselves produced.

Notes

1 This characteristic was termed 'joint demand' by Robbins and Terleckyj (1960) in their study of New York City's financial services complex.

2 A somewhat unusual feature of the area is the presence of a second, if significantly smaller, CBD in St. Paul, a reminder that the present metropolitan area developed from the coalescence of two distinct cities and their respective suburbs. Throughout this chapter, the term 'study area' is used to refer to the seven counties that account for the vast majority of the population and economic activity in the region. These are: Anoka, Carver, Dakota, Hennepin, Ramsey, Scott, and Washington counties, all in Minnesota.

3 The Twin Cities ranked as the sixth largest advertising center in the country in a more recent *Advertising Age* 'Agency Report.' This ranking was based on a survey that was restricted to the country's largest advertising agencies (*Advertising Age* 1995).

4 For a more detailed discussion of these aspects of the study, see Sabourin, 1998.

References

Adams, J. S., and VanDrasek, B. J. (1993), *Minneapolis-St. Paul: People, Place, and Public Life*, University of Minnesota Press, Minneapolis.

Advertising Age (1995), 'Advertising age agency report, 1995', special section in *Advertising Age*. April 10, p. 15.

Beyers, W. B. and Lindahl, D. P. (1994), 'Competitive advantage and information technologies in the producer services', paper presented at the annual meeting of the Association of American Geographers, San Francisco, CA.

Borchert, J.R. (1978), 'Major control points in American economic geography', *Annals of the Association of American Geographers*, vol. 68, pp. 214-232.

Coase, R. H. (1937), 'The nature of the firm', *Economica,* vol. 4, pp. 386-405.

Coffey, W. J. and Bailly, A. S. (1991), 'Producer services and flexible production: an exploratory analysis', *Growth and Change*, vol. 22, pp. 95-117.

Gad, G. (1979), 'Fact-to-face linkages and office decentralization potentials: a study of Toronto', In P. W. Daniels (ed) *Spatial Patterns of Office Growth and Location*, John Wiley & Sons, Chichester, pp. 277-323.

Gertler, M. (1992), 'Flexibility revisited: districts, nation-states, and the forces of production', *Transactions of the Institute of British Geographers*, vol. N.S. 17, pp. 259-278.

Goddard, J. B. (1973), *Offices, Linkages and Location: A Study of Communications and Spatial Patterns in Central London,* Pergamon, Oxford.

Goe, W. R. (1990), 'Producer services, trade, and the social division of labor', *Regional Studies* vol. 24, pp. 327-42.

Gold Book, The: Minneapolis and St. Paul (1993), Prime Publications Inc, Minneapolis.

Illeris, S. (1991), 'The location of services in a service society,' In P.W. Daniels and F. Moualaert (eds) *The Changing Geography of Advanced Producer Services*, Belhaven Press, London, pp. 93-107.

Lentnek, B., MacPherson, A., and Phillips, D. (1992), 'Optimum producer service location', *Environment and Planning A*, vol. 24, pp. 467-479.

Marshall, J. N. (1989), 'Corporate reorganization and the geography of services: evidence from the motor vehicle aftermarket in the West Midlands of the UK', *Regional Studies*, vol. 23, pp. 139-150.

Michalak, W. Z. and Fairbairn, K. J. (1993), 'The producer service complex of Edmonton: the role and organization of producer service firms in a peripheral city', *Environment and Planning A*, vol. 25, no. 6, pp. 761-77.

Nelson, K. (1986), 'Labor demand, labor supply and the suburbanization of low-wage office work', In A. J. Scott and M. Storper (eds) *Production, Work, Territory: The Geographical Anatomy of Industrial Capitalism*, Allen and Unwin, Boston, pp. 149-71.

Noyelle, T.J. and Stanback, T.M. (1984), *The Economic Transformation of American Cities*, Rowman and Allanheld, Totowa, NJ.

Ó hUallacháin, B. (1989), 'Agglomeration of services in American metropolitan areas', *Growth and Change*, vol. 20, no. 3, pp. 34-49.

Ó hUallacháin, B. and Reid, N. (1991), 'The location and growth of business and professional services in American metropolitan areas, 1976-1986', *Annals of the Association of American Geographers*, vol. 81, pp. 254-70.

Ó hUallacháin, B. and Reid, N. (1992), 'The intrametropolitan location of services in the United States', *Urban Geography*, vol. 13, no. 4, pp. 334-354.

Ó hUallacháin, B. and Reid, N. (1993) 'The location of services in the urban hierarchy and the regions of the United States', *Geographical Analysis*, vol. 25, pp. 252-67.

Ó hUallacháin, B. and Satterthwaite, M.A. (1992), 'Sectoral growth patterns at the metropolitan level: An evaluation of economic development incentives', *Journal of Urban Economics*, vol. 31, pp. 25-58.

Piore, M. and Sabel, C. (1984), *The Second Industrial Divide: Possibilities for Prosperity*, Basic Books, New York.

Robbins, S. M. and Terleckyj, N. E. (1960), *Money Metropolis, Cambridge*, Harvard University Press, Cambridge, MA.

Sabourin, P. (1998), *The Intra-Metropolitan location of Producer Services -- A Case Study of the Advertising Industry in the Twin Cities (Minneapolis - St. Paul, Minnesota)*, unpublished Ph.D. dissertation, University of Minnesota, Minneapolis.

Sayer, A. and Walker, R (1992), *The New Social Economy: Reworking the Division of Labor*, Basil Blackwell, Cambridge, MA.

Scott, A. J. (1988a), *Metropolis*, University of California Press, Berkeley.

Scott, A. J. (1988b), *New Industrial Spaces*, Pion, London.

Scott, A. J. (1993), *Technopolis: High-Technology Industry and Regional Development in Southern California*, University of California Press, Berkeley.

Scott, A. J. (1996), 'The craft, fashion, and cultural-products industries of Los Angeles: competitive dynamics and policy dilemmas in a multisectoral image-producing complex', *Annals of the Association of American Geographers*, vol. 86, no. 2, pp. 306-23

Storper, M. and Christopherson, S. (1987), 'Flexible specialization and regional industrial agglomerations: The case of the U.S. motion picture industry', *Annals of the Association of American Geographers*, vol. 77, no. 1, pp. 104-117.

Storper, M. and Walker, R. (1989), *The Capitalist Imperative: Territory, Technology, and Industrial Growth*, Blackwell, Oxford.

US Bureau of the Census (various years), *County Business Patterns – Minnesota*, US Government Printing Office, Washington, DC.

Walker, R. (1988), 'The geographical organization of production systems', *Environment and Planning D*, vol. 6, pp. 377-408.

Wheeler, J. O. and Mitchelson, R. L (1989), 'Information flows among major metropolitan areas in the United States', *Annals of the Association of American Geographers*, vol. 79, no. 1, pp. 523-543.

Williamson, O. E. (1979), 'Transaction cost economics: the governance of contractual relations', *Journal of Law and Economics*, vol. 22, no. 2, pp. 233-261.

Williamson, O. E. (1985), *The Economic Institutions of Capitalism*, Free Press, New York.

Williamson, O. E. (1986), 'Vertical integration and transaction costs', in J. E. Stiglitz and G. F. Mathewson (eds), *New Developments in the Analysis of Market Structure*, Macmillan, London.

Wood, P.A. (1991), 'Flexible accumulation and the rise of business services', *Transactions of the Institute of British Geographers*, vol. N.S.16, pp. 160-72.

Yellow Pages, The: Minneapolis and Surrounding Communities July 1994/1995 (1994), US West Direct, Englewood, CO.

Yellow Pages, The: St. Paul and Surrounding Communities July 1994/1995 (1994), US West Direct, Englewood, CO.